9 Good Habits
FOR ALL READERS

Authors

Leslie W. Crawford, Ed.D.
Dean of the John H. Lounsbury
  School of Education
Georgia College & State University

Charles E. Martin, Ph.D.
Associate Professor of Early Childhood
  and Middle Grades Education
Georgia College & State University

Margaret M. Philbin, Ed.D.
Associate Professor of Early Childhood
  and Middle Grades Education
Georgia College & State University

Zaner-Bloser

Special thanks to these educators who participated in the development of these materials.

Bonnie Lynn Fahning (Bloomington Lutheran School, Bloomington, Minnesota)
David Kreiss (Thomas Creighton Elementary School, Philadelphia City School District, Philadelphia, Pennsylvania)
Connie Longville (Schumacher School, Akron City School District, Akron, Ohio)
Dawn Pittman (Davis Elementary School, Camden City School District, Camden, New Jersey)
Kristin Scherman (Thomas Lake Elementary School, Eagan, Minnesota)
Carol Toussant (West Elementary School, Minerva School District, East Rochester, Ohio)
Geraldine Weems (Williams Elementary School, Austin Independent School District, Austin, Texas)

Story Credits

Excerpts from *Pedro's Journal* by Pam Conrad. Text copyright © 1991 by Pam Conrad. Published by Boyds Mills Press. Reprinted with permission. "The Sound of Drums and Gongs" from *Red Scarf Girl* by Ji Li Jiang. Copyright © 1997 by Ji Li Jiang. Foreword copyright © 1997 by HarperCollins Publishers. Excerpts from *Zlata's Diary* by Zlata Filipović. Copyright © 1994 Editions Robert Laffont/Fixot. Used by permission of Viking Penguin, a division of Penguin Putnam Inc. "Rainbow Snake" reprinted with the permission of Margaret K. McElderry Books, an imprint of Simon & Schuster Children's Publishing Division from *The Golden Hoard* by Geraldine McCaughrean. Text copyright © 1995 Geraldine McCaughrean. "First Job" from *Local News*, copyright © 1993 by Gary Soto, reprinted by permission of Harcourt, Inc. "Family Resemblance" reprinted with permission of Holly Gems Timberline, originally appeared in *Cricket* magazine © 1998. "Thank You, M'am" from *Short Stories* by Langston Hughes. Copyright © 1996 by Ronald Bass and Arnold Rampersad. Reprinted by permission of Hill and Wang, a division of Farrar, Straus, and Giroux, LLC. Excerpts from *Mrs. Frisby and the Rats of NIMH* by Robert C. O'Brien. Reprinted with the permission of Atheneum Books for Young Readers, an imprint of Simon & Schuster Children's Publishing Division. Copyright © 1971 Robert C. O'Brien. Excerpts from *The Mermaid Summer* copyright © 1998 Maureen Mollie Hunter McIlwraith. Excerpts from *Stinker From Space* by Pamela F. Service. Reprinted with the permission of Atheneum Books for Young Readers, an imprint of Simon & Schuster Children's Publishing Division. Copyright © 1988 Pamela F. Service.

Editorial Development, Photo Research, and Art Buying: Brown Publishing Network

Photo Credits

Cover photography, title page: George C. Anderson; Models: Nancy Sheehan
p7, Norris Blake, Visuals Unlimited, Inc.; p9 (top), Corbis; (middle), Glen Oliver, Visuals Unlimited, Inc.; p11, David M. Phillips, Visuals Unlimited, Inc.; pp12, 15, Courtesy of Living Technologies; p13, Terry Hazen, Visuals Unlimited, Inc.; p14, Natalie Stultz, Courtesy of Living Technologies; p16, Alan Jakubek; p19 (top), John Gerlach, Dembinsky Photo Assocs, Inc.; (bottom), Corbis; p21, John Eastcott, Photo Researchers, Inc.; p22 (top), Stan Osolinski, Dembinsky Photo Assocs, Inc.; (bottom), Mark Thomas, Dembinsky Photo Assocs, Inc.; p23, Corbis; p24 (top), Joe Prater, Visuals Unlimited, Inc.; (bottom), Mark J. Thomas, Dembinsky Photo Assocs, Inc.; p25, Tony Freeman, Photo Edit; p26, Photo Researchers, Inc.; pp29, 32, Corbis; p30, Simon Fraser, Photo Researchers, Inc.; p31 (top), Visuals Unlimited, Inc.; (bottom), Jacques Jangoux, Photo Researchers, Inc.; p33 (top), Bachmann, The Image Works, Inc.; (bottom), Photo Researchers, Inc.; p34, Ray Pfortner, Peter Arnold, Inc; p35, David Lassman, The Image Works, Inc.; p37, T. Stewart & R. Baxter, Tony Stone Images; pp39, 43, 45, North Wind Picture Archives; pp46, 49 (top), 53, 56, 57, Corbis; pp49 (bottom), 54, 55, AP/Wide World Photos; p52, Richard Harrington, Hulton Getty Picture Library; pp61, 67, 68, The Image Works, Inc.; p62, Bill Bachman; pp63, 66, 70, Archive Photos; p64, M. Corvetto, The Image Works, Inc.; p73, Lester Lefkowitz, The Stock Market; pp75, 78, Hulton-Deutsch Collection/Corbis; pp77, 79, DPA/MKG/The Image Works, Inc.; pp80, 81, Archive Photos; p82, Popperfoto/Archive Photos; pp85, 89, 91, Corbis-Bettmann; p87, Underwood & Underwood/Corbis; p88, Hulton-Deutsch Collection/Corbis; p90, New York Times Co./Archive Photos; p92, American Stock/Archive Photos; p95 (top), Shirley Briggs, North Wind Picture Archives; (bottom), Jack K. Clark, The Image Works, Inc.; pp96, 99 (top), 102, Rachel Carson History Project; p97 (top), Underwood & Underwood/Corbis; (bottom), Mary Frye, Rachel Carson History Project; pp98, 103, Shirley Briggs, Rachel Carson History Project; p99 (bottom), Rex Gary Schmidt, Rachel Carson History Project; p100, Archive Photos; p101, Corbis-Bettmann; p105, "Cadmus and the Dragon," Zuccarelli, Rafael Valls Gallery, London, The Bridgeman Art Library; p133, Wolfgang Kaehler; pp135 (top), 138, Gianni Dagli Orti, Corbis; pp135 (bottom), 137 (right), The Granger Collection, New York; p137 (left), Hulton-Deutsch Collection/Corbis; p139 (top), Bachmann, The Image Works, Inc.; p140 (top), Vanni Archive/Corbis; (bottom), Gail Mooney, Corbis; p141, Dr. E.R. Degginger, Color-Pic; pp142, 145, 147 (bottom), The Granger Collection, New York; p147 (top), Nada Pecnic, Visuals Unlimited, Inc.; p148 (top), Wolfgang Kaehler, Wolfgang Kaehler Photography; pp149, 150, Wolfgang Kaehler, Corbis; p151, Archive Photos; p152, Wolfgang Kaehler Provia, Wolfgang Kaehler Photography; pp155 (top), 156 (left), The Granger Collection, New York; p155 (bottom), Corbis; pp156 (right), 157, 159, 160, 161, North Wind Picture Archives; p158, Archive Photos; p162, Ed Eckstein, Corbis; p163, Richard T. Nowitz, Corbis; p165, Nova Online/Gamma Liaison; p167 (bottom), The Granger Collection; pp167 (top), 169 (top), 170, 172, Culver Pictures Inc.; pp171, 173, The Granger Collection, New York; pp177, 180, 181, 185, Culver Pictures Inc.; p182, Peter Arnold, Inc; p184, Roland Seitre, Peter Arnold, Inc; p186, Design and Patents Act; p188, Scott Polar Research Institute; p189 (top), AP/Wide World Photos, (bottom), Hulton-Deutsch Collection/Corbis; p191, Bachmann, The Image Works, Inc.; p192, Express Newspapers/Archive Photos; p193, Archive Photos; p197, M. Lee Fatherree, "Encounter" by David Park, collection of the Oakland Museum of California, gift of the Women's Board of the Oakland Museum Assocn; p223, Stanley Martucci, Stock Illustration Source; p255, Peskin, FPG Intl; p257, AP/Wide World Photos; pp259, 263, Corbis; p261, FPG Intl; p262, AP/Wide World Photos; p264, Andrew Wagner; p267, AP/Wide World Photos; p269, FPG Intl; pp271, 273, AP/Wide World Photos; p274, Archive Photos; p277, Hulton-Deutsch, Allsport Photography (USA), Inc.; p278, FPG Intl; pp279, 280, 281, AP/Wide World Photos; pp282, 283, Liaison Agency, Inc.

Art Credits

pp41, 82, 107 (top), 115 (top), 125 (top), 257 (map), Susan Dahl; pp42, 51 (map), 65, John Sanderson; p101, Rose Zgodzinski; pp107 (bottom), 109–112, Francisco X. Mora; pp115 (bottom), 117–122, Alexander Farquharson; pp125 (bottom), 126–131, Kathy Mitchell; pp139 (map), 148 (map), 169 (map), 183 (map), 190 (map), John Sanderson; pp199, 201–206, Susan Guevara; pp209, 211–214, Chi Chung; pp217–221, Ruben DeAnda; pp225, 227–232, Kristina Rodanas; pp235, 237–242, Scott Cameron; pp245-253, K.D. Maxx.

ISBN 0-7367-0836-7

Zaner-Bloser, Inc., P.O. Box 16764, Columbus, Ohio 43216-6764 (1-800-421-3018)

Table of Contents

Getting to Know the 9 Good Habits
FOR ALL READERS

A habit is something you do over and over until it becomes automatic. In this book, you will learn nine good habits to use when you read. Read the habits below.

Before I Read

1. Check it out!
2. Think about what I know about the subject.
3. Decide what I need to know.

While I Read

4. Stop and ask, "How does it connect to what I know?"
5. Stop and ask, "Does it make sense?"
6. Stop and ask, "If it doesn't make sense, what can I do?"

After I Read

7. React to what I've read.
8. Check to see what I remember.
9. Use what I've read.

Unit 1
Saving the World Around Us
Theme: Nature

In this unit, you will develop these 3 habits for all readers.

Before I Read Habit:
Check it out!

While I Read Habit:
Stop and ask, "Does it make sense?"

After I Read Habit:
Use what I've read.

Learn 3 of the 9 Habits

In this unit, you will develop three habits—one for before you read, one for while you are reading, and one for after you finish reading. Start with **Before I Read**. Read the habit and strategy. Then read my notes below.

Before I Read

Which **HABIT** will I learn?
Check it out!
If I develop this habit, I can find out something about what I am going to read so that I know what to expect.

Which **STRATEGY** will I use to learn this habit?
Identify features to preview the selection and decide which are the most useful.

My Notes

- Strategy says to identify features to preview the selection. I can use the headlines, photos, vocabulary words, and captions.

- The title is a good place to start. I wonder what a "living machine" is. I'll look at the vocabulary words. I see "pollution" and "oceanographer." The article must be about a machine for cleaning up polluted water.

- Now I'll look at the photos. What do they tell me?

John Todd's LIVING MACHINE

Picture a very large plastic tank. Snails cling to the tank walls. Three kinds of colorful fish glide back and forth. Healthy green plants wave in the clear water. Would you ever think that this peaceful environment could be used to clean up water **pollution**? An **oceanographer** named John Todd thought so. He developed a system to purify water. It was called the *Living Machine*.

pollution
(puh·**loo**·shuhn)—
poisons in water, air, soil, etc.

oceanographer
(oh·shuh·**nah**·gruh·fur)—
scientist who studies oceans

John Todd (left) discussing his Living Machine

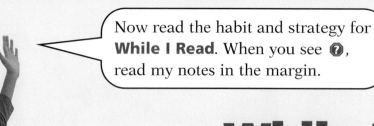

Now read the habit and strategy for **While I Read**. When you see ❷, read my notes in the margin.

While I Read

Which **HABIT** will I learn?

Stop and ask, "Does it make sense?"

If I develop this habit, I will stop now and then to make sure I understand what I'm reading.

Which **STRATEGY** will I use to learn this habit?

Decide how the examples help explain a main point.

carbon dioxide
(**kahr**·buhn die·**oks**·ied)—
a gas that is breathed out by animals and used by plants

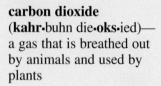

Stop and Ask ❷

Does it make sense? Decide how the examples help explain a main point.

The examples of the plants and the fish show how things are linked in nature. That makes sense.

Nature's Web

Todd knew that plants and animals are all linked together in nature. The waste of one life-form can be a source of food or energy for another. Photosynthesis [foe·toe·**sin**·thi·sis] is a good example of this idea. Green plants use sunlight to change water and **carbon dioxide** into oxygen. Then, animals and people breathe in the oxygen. When they breathe out, they breathe out carbon dioxide. Then the cycle begins again. The food chain is another example that shows how creatures are linked. A big fish eats a small fish that ate a smaller fish. The smallest fish ate tiny creatures or plants. In nature, everything is used. Todd believed that what people saw as waste—sewage—could be used by other living things. ❷ *Strategy Alert!*

Down the Drain

Water pours out of the faucet into your kitchen sink. Then it swirls around the drain and disappears. With it go bits of food from the dinner dishes. Dish-washing detergent also goes down the drain. All the water that is thrown away after it is used is called wastewater. Think about all the wastewater that flows out of the sinks, tubs, and toilets in your home. Then multiply that by all the houses, schools, stores, and hospitals in your town. A lot of dirty water is going down the drain—nearly 100 gallons for every person in the United States every day! Where does all that dirty water go?

The water flows into the sewer system where it gets cleaned up, or treated. If it were left dirty, sewage would flow freely into rivers and harbors. The pollution caused by this sewage would be a terrible health hazard. It would also be awful to look at and to smell! To keep this from happening, the sewage is treated. First, the wastewater goes through screens. Any solid objects in the wastewater are removed. The second treatment relies on nature's smallest and most powerful life-form—microbes. Microbes are tiny plants and animals. They are so small that they can only be seen with a microscope. (That's why they are *microscopic*.) Bacteria are one kind of microbe.

Bacteria: Good and Bad

Bacteria can be harmful and helpful. You probably know about the harmful things that bacteria can do. For example, they can give a person an earache or an infected finger. But if there were no bacteria, all the dead plants and animals that ever lived would still be here, covering Earth! Fortunately for us, bacteria use these substances as food.

For instance, in a natural environment, like a forest, bacteria also eat animal waste and help it **decompose**. They change the chemical elements in this waste into a chemical that is food for plants. The plants use this chemical to grow leaves and roots. Then, an animal eats the plant. The elements from the waste have been rearranged to build the body of the animal. And bacteria got it all started! *Strategy Alert!*

decompose
(dee·kuhm·**pohz**)—
to rot or decay

Decomposing bacteria magnified 12,000 times

Stop and Ask ❓

Does it make sense? Decide how the examples help explain a main point.

• • • • • • • • • •

The main point is that bacteria are good and bad. The examples of the earache and how bacteria eat waste help that idea make sense.

Living Machines

Todd thought that a link was missing from most sewage treatment systems. The new material made by the bacteria—the material plants would normally use—was not being used. He wanted to find a way to use that material to **purify** water. In 1984, he began to develop his ideas. He built a series of tanks. The tanks were filled with wastewater, living plants, and living creatures. He called these tanks Living Machines. As bacteria in the tanks broke down waste, they made food for the plants. The bacteria, plants, and fish all **thrived** together, and the wastewater became clean. Todd's work was so successful that in 1989 he won an award from the U.S. government. In 1992 he faced a new challenge.

Water purification system at work at a chocolate factory

Chattanooga Creek

Pollution is not only ugly, it can kill. For example, the Chattanooga [**chat**·uhn·oo·guh] Creek had become so polluted that people living near it were getting sick and even dying. For more than 150 years, factories had poured chemical wastes into the creek. Now there were at least 33 different poisons in the water. Some were **pesticides;** others were cleaning fluids and coal tar. *Strategy Alert!*

purify (**pyoor**·uh·fie)— to make pure or clean

thrived (thrievd)—grew strong and healthy

pesticides (**pes**·ti·siedz)— poisons used to kill weeds or insects

Stop and Ask ?

Does it make sense? Decide how the examples help explain a main point.

• • • • • • • • • • • •

The main point is that pollution is dangerous. The example of the sick people in Chattanooga shows that. That makes sense.

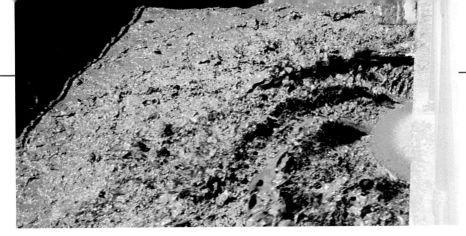

Activated sludge sewage treatment

The problem in Chattanooga, Tennessee, was very serious since more than the water was polluted. The poisons were buried deep in the bottom of the creek bed, in thick, black **sludge**. It would take thousands of years for bacteria to break down these poisons. For all that time, more people would be getting sick. If the sludge from the creek bottom were dug up and burned, the smoke and ashes might still be full of poisons. Then these would become part of the air people breathed. Burying the sludge would only move the poisons to another place.

The people of Chattanooga asked Todd for help. So far, Todd's Living Machines had been used only to clean up sewage water. Todd did not know whether his Living Machines would be able to clean up the sludge. But he made a plan.

Two Different Tanks

Todd's plan was to have two different tanks. One tank would be a large aquarium. The second, smaller tank would hold **toxic** sludge. Todd had an unusual "recipe" for this smaller tank. He started with 16 **liters** of fresh water (not salt water). He added pieces of rotten wood from old railroad ties. Then he stirred in moldy leaves from a forest floor. He included marsh mud that smelled like rotten eggs. Todd also put in bacteria he had bought from a bacteria supply company. He combined all this with three liters of Chattanooga Creek sludge.

Everything in nature is connected. Todd used this big idea to make his strange mixture. He wanted as many kinds of bacteria as he could have. For example, the marsh mud held a type of bacteria that can live without oxygen. These bacteria would work on some of the worst toxins. The rotten wood held bacteria that could break down the coal tar in the sludge.
 Strategy Alert!

Todd wanted his bacteria to be very healthy! So he designed the Living Machine to give his bacteria super living conditions. Bacteria grow well in a warm climate. So, the small sludge tank was always heated. Most microbes need oxygen to live. So, Todd made sure air was always bubbling through the tank. Finally he knew the fresh water would **dilute** the poisons in the sludge. Without it, the toxins would kill the valuable bacteria.

sludge (sluj)—heavy, slimy waste

toxic (**tok**·sik)—poisonous

liter (**lee**·tuhr)—a measure equal to a little more than a quart

dilute (die·**loot**)—to thin out or weaken by mixing with water

Stop and Ask

Does it make sense? Decide how the examples help explain a main point.

Everything in nature is connected. The examples of the different kinds of bacteria in the tank show that. That makes sense! Todd knew that it made sense, too!

Bacteria will break down almost anything, but they do their work very slowly. To make the microbes work faster, Todd thought they should be well-fed. He gave them plenty of acetate, a type of food. The small tank was now a perfect place for microbes, and they multiplied very quickly. The mixture was stirred three times a day. This gave the microbes the best chance of working together to break down the toxins.

The second tank was a very large aquarium. This tank held three kinds of fish, snails, **algae,** and other green plants. It also was home to a crayfish (which looks like a small lobster). Bacteria lived here, too. The tank was always lighted, so the plants could make oxygen around the clock. This aquarium was called the *bioassay tank*. *Bio* means "living" and *assay* means "test." The idea behind this "living test" was simple. Todd needed a way to know whether the microbes in the first tank were breaking down the toxins in the sludge. The living things in this tank would be the test. He would add water from the sludge tank to the bioassay tank to test the water's purity.

A Living Machine cleaning water inside a greenhouse

Students visit a Living Machine in Vermont.

The First Test

After eight days, Todd was ready for the first test. The small sludge tank had been making foam for three days. The foam was made of millions of bubbles. These bubbles were produced by gas that is formed when microbes are eating and breaking down chemicals. This was a good sign.

Todd took a very small amount of water from the bioassay tank and put it in the sludge tank. Then, he took the same amount of water from the top of the sludge tank and put it in the bioassay tank. The next day, four fish in the bioassay tank were dead. This showed that the toxins were still powerful. Todd was discouraged. He wondered whether he should continue. He decided to make another water exchange. The next day, all the fish were dead. There was still enough poison in just a tiny bit of sludge water to kill the fish.

But there were signs that the water was getting cleaner. The crayfish was still alive. Also, the oxygen-producing plants still seemed healthy. So, Todd continued to exchange water between the tanks every day. As the microbes kept working together to break down the toxins, he exchanged greater amounts of water.

Animals' **reproductive patterns** can show whether their environment is healthy. Todd noticed, for example, that he could watch the snails to know how healthy the water was. If the snails stopped laying eggs, he knew he was adding too much poison to the bioassay tank. He would stop adding sludge water until the snails were laying eggs again. By the end of the first month, he was exchanging two quarts of water a day. The creatures in the bioassay tank stayed alive and healthy. *Strategy Alert!*

reproductive patterns
(ree·pruh·**duk**·tiv
pat·uhrnz)—typical ways
that organisms produce
offspring

Stop and Ask (?)

Does it make sense? Decide how the examples help explain a main point.

The example of the snails in the bioassay tank show how a dirty environment can stop an animal from having a baby. Animals have more babies when they are healthy. That makes sense!

The Results Are Reported

It was time for a scientific test. Todd sent two quarts of water from the bioassay tank to a government lab. The results were **remarkable**. The water was nearly pure! But what about the sludge? Had the Living Machine been able to clean that, too? Todd took the whole system apart. He sent samples of the plants and animals to the lab. Most important, he sent the entire contents of the sludge tank.

The results were amazing. More than half of the sludge that Todd had placed in the tank was gone! It had been eaten by microbes. Twenty-one of the 33 poisons were almost gone. The microbes had broken down those toxic chemicals in only two months! This was wonderful news. It showed the power of the Living Machine.

There were other results, though, that were not as good. The amounts of three of the poisons did not change. Even worse, the lab found that nine of the toxins had increased. The microbes must have rearranged some elements to help these toxins grow. Todd was puzzled. He wished he could continue observing the two tanks, but the test was over. The results had given him a lot of important information, though. He knew that his idea was a good one.

Using Nature's Example

Todd had shown that his Living Machines could reduce toxic waste. That made the machines popular in different kinds of places. Today, Living Machines are used in 13 states and 7 countries. For example, in Vermont, a Living Machine treats the wastewater at a tourist information center. In Australia, the system cleans the waste from a food-processing plant. The cleaned water that comes out of these Living Machines can be used to water farm crops. *Strategy Alert!*

One of Todd's goals is to teach people about the environment. His systems are models of our natural world. He hopes that Living Machines will remind people that nature works in balance. The machines combine light, heat, water, and living things. The living things provide food for each other. They work together to clean up their environment. Todd hopes that if Living Machines can do that, so can we.

John Todd

Congratulations! You finished reading. Now read the habit and strategy for **After I Read**. Then read my notes below.

After I Read

Which **HABIT** will I learn?
Use what I've read.
If I develop this habit, I will think about how I can apply what I just read to my schoolwork and my life. This makes reading really useful.

Which **STRATEGY** will I use to learn this habit?
Recap the main points (or big ideas) in the selection.

My Notes

- Strategy says to identify the major points in the selection.

- One point is that sewage is bad for people, but bacteria love it! The living machine used the bacteria to clean up water that had sewage in it.

- Todd showed how the balance of nature can clean up pollution.

Practice 3 of the 9 Habits

Now it's time to practice the three habits and strategies you learned when you read "John Todd's Living Machine." Start with **Before I Read.** Look at the box below. It should look familiar! Reread the habit you will practice. Reread the strategy you will use—then do it!

Before I Read

Which **HABIT** will I practice?
Check it out!
If I develop this habit, I can find out something about what I am going to read so that I know what to expect.

Which **STRATEGY** will I use to practice this habit?
Identify features to preview the selection and decide which are the most useful.

 Use the **Before I Read Strategy Sheet** for "Are We Wasting Our Wetlands?" (page 6 in your *Strategy Practice Book*) to find out something about what you're going to read.

Are We Wasting Our WETLANDS?

Tuttle's Marsh, Michigan

The shallow waters of a swamp shine in the sun. Ferns spread their soft leaves where soil shows through the water. Grasses stand tall. A long-legged heron strides through the water. Is he hunting frogs? Ripples spread in a long, smooth line. A water snake weaves its way through moss and other plants. The wetland is quiet.

Then a rumble breaks the stillness. A bulldozer plows through the reeds. Dump trucks follow. Soon, the swamp is filled with layers of gravel. Later, a new mall sits where the heron once nested. Where has that heron gone? A hard, black parking lot has spread across the ground. What has happened to the soft, green moss? Where are the ferns and cattails? Another wetland has disappeared.

Highway construction in Sweetwater Marsh National Wildlife Refuge

Reread the habit and strategy below. Look for the *Strategy Alerts!* as you continue to read.

While I Read

Which **HABIT** will I practice?

Stop and ask, "Does it make sense?"

If I develop this habit, I will stop now and then to make sure I understand what I'm reading.

Which **STRATEGY** will I use to practice this habit?

Decide how the examples help explain a main point.

 Use the **While I Read Strategy Sheet** for "Are We Wasting Our Wetlands?" (page 7 in your *Strategy Practice Book*) as you read.

acre (**ay**·kuhr)— a measure of land

Is the Problem Serious?

The U.S. Fish and Wildlife Service keeps track of wetlands. The agency reports that more than 117 million **acres** of wetlands in the United States have disappeared in the last 200 years. That area is larger than the state of California! As time goes on, wetlands are disappearing faster and faster. Should we be worried? The answer lies in the nature of wetlands themselves.

What Is a Wetland?

Wetlands are low places where water and land come together. They can have fresh water or salt water. You can find freshwater wetlands at the edges of lakes, ponds, streams, and rivers. Saltwater wetlands get their water from ocean tides. They are found near coasts in areas that are protected from waves. Wetlands are found every place on Earth except Antarctica. Some are in the hot tropics; others are in cold places.

There are many different types of wetlands. Each type has its own kind of water, soil, plant life, and animal life. For example, marshes, swamps, and peat lands are all wetlands.

Marshes are flooded by either fresh water or salt water. Some marshes are always flooded. Others are flooded from time to time. Only a few types of plants can grow in marshes. They include cattails and some kinds of grasses. These plants are able to live in water or very wet soil. The type of water in the marsh depends on where the water comes from. The water in saltwater marshes comes from ocean tides. In freshwater marshes, it comes from groundwater, streams, and rain.

Swamps are another type of wetland. Like marshes, swamps may be flooded all year or just a small part of the year. Swamps can be seen at the flood plains of rivers, in shallow parts of lakes, and along coasts. Most plants in swamps are trees and shrubs.

Peat **bogs** are the third type of wetland. In peat bogs, plants such as moss and grass grow very fast. They grow faster than they rot. The rotted plant material builds up. This material is called *peat*. ❓ *Strategy Alert!*

bogs—small swamps or marshes

Stop and Ask ❓

Does it make sense? Decide how the examples help explain a main point.

Sierra Club members paddle canoes through layers of water hyacinth in the Atchafalaya Swamp in Louisiana.

Alligator and turtle sunning in the Florida Everglades

Are Wetlands Wastelands?

Wetlands have been on Earth for thousands and thousands of years. In the past, people did not think wetlands were important. People used wetlands as dumping grounds for all kinds of junk. Many wetlands were drained or filled in. Then the land was used for houses, malls, farms, and highways.

Many wetlands smell like rotten eggs! People thought that building things on this smelly, useless land meant progress. They were proud to be reclaiming the land for human use. If humans were "reclaiming" the land, who or what had claimed it before?

A water moccasin

A Home for Wildlife

Wetlands are important for the well-being of many animals and plants. Millions of birds and other animals make their homes in wetlands. Amphibians [am·**fib**·ee·uhnz] such as turtles, snakes, and alligators are commonly found there. Frogs, salamanders, and toads live in wetlands for at least part of their lives. Many kinds of fish depend on wetlands for food and safety. Many birds visit wetlands to find food, to rest, and to make their nests. Raccoons, beavers, **muskrats,** and other animals also make their homes here in wetlands.

Many amphibians, fish, birds, and plants that live in wetlands are endangered species. Plants and animals that are endangered are in danger of disappearing completely from the earth. **(?)** *Strategy Alert!*

The fish and shellfish that live in wetlands are important sources of food for humans. Shellfish beds and fishing areas depend on good water quality. Without healthy wetlands, these food sources can be lost. Wetlands are important for many other reasons as well.

muskrats (**musk**·rats)— large, rat-like animals that live in water

Stop and Ask **(?)**

Does it make sense? Decide how the examples help explain a main point.

A Help for Humans

Wetlands are valuable to people, too. For example, low wetland areas act as sponges during storms. They help control floods by storing water and letting go of it slowly. In this way, they prevent flood damage to nearby roads and buildings. Along the coast, wetlands keep ocean waves from washing away beaches. If it were not for wetlands, people would need to build expensive systems and sea walls to prevent floods and **erosion**.

Another way wetlands help people is by supplying and purifying water. In freshwater wetlands, surface water seeps into the ground. This adds to the water that is already there. Wells for homes and communities tap this water for many uses. Wetlands also serve as natural filters. Their soil and plants trap toxic materials. In some cases, they can break down these materials and make them **nontoxic**. This filtering improves water quality.

Wetlands are also special places for recreation. People enjoy bird watching, fishing, hiking, and canoeing in these peaceful, lovely areas.

Wetlands can be used as "labs" for scientists and other interested people, too. They hold much information about science and history. In a peat bog in England, scientists found the body of a man who lived about 300 B.C. Because of the soil in the bog, the body was very well preserved. Scientists have been able to learn a great deal about this man. For example, they could tell what he had eaten at his last meal. They found out what his blood type was. They even learned that he had had a haircut! Thousands of bodies have been found in bogs throughout Europe. These discoveries have helped scientists learn more about the times in which these people lived. *Strategy Alert!*

erosion (i·**roh**·zhuhn)— a wearing away

nontoxic (non·**tok**·sik)— not harmful

Stop and Ask

Does it make sense? Decide how the examples help explain a main point.

Boardwalks let people enjoy wetlands without harming them.

Great blue heron in Florida's Everglades National Park

Saving the Wetlands

As you can see, wetlands affect almost everyone. Luckily, people realized how important wetlands are before time ran out. In the early 1980s, wetland science became a separate field of study. Better information about the importance of wetlands became available. People's attitudes began to change. Scientists thought about ways to return destroyed wetlands to their natural states. Across the country, laws were passed to protect and preserve wetland areas. However, laws can help only if they have community support. It is important to stay informed. You know why wetlands need to be saved. Now you need to know what to do—and what not to do—to protect this valuable resource.

Ways to Learn More

The more you know about wetlands, the more you can help. There are many different ways you can learn about wetlands.

- Visit one of the almost 400 National Wildlife Refuges in the United States. There you can often find programs for the public.
- Along the coast, National Estuarine Reserve Research Areas have visitor centers. They may have tours, educational programs, and workshops.
- Local conservation groups are active in many areas. They can help you learn more about local issues and laws. They can teach you about what is being done to clean up wetlands in your area.
- Most city and town councils hold regular open meetings. Often, these councils hear from builders who want to develop property. They hear from people who want to open new businesses. Such groups think about the fate of wetland areas when they make decisions about these issues. Ask your parents to attend meetings, and go with them.
- The Environmental Protection Agency is another source of information on wetland protection.
- Many nonprofit organizations work to protect wetlands and other endangered areas. For information on their work, contact groups such as the National Audubon Society and the Nature Conservancy.

What You Can Do

Even one person can make a difference. Here are some examples of things you can do.

- Create a display explaining why wetlands are important and need to be saved. Arrange to exhibit the display in your school, public library, or city hall.
- Join or start a group to clean up a local wetland or river.
- Find out whether weed killers and other toxins are used in local parks and along roadsides. Write a letter asking local officials to cut back on their use. When it rains, these chemicals pollute groundwater, lakes, and rivers. This pollution destroys plants and endangers fish, birds, and animals.
- If you live in an area with cold, snowy winters, ask officials to use less salt, or to use sand instead of salt, on the roads. Saltwater runoff kills freshwater plants and animals.
- If you live near a waterway, do a survey. Find out what is being dumped into the water and who is doing the dumping. Farms often use great amounts of **pesticides** and **fertilizers**. Factories may dump toxic wastes into storm sewers. This is against the law. If you see illegal dumping, tell someone.
- If you live in a rural area and see a situation that harms a wetland, report it to the U.S. Department of Agriculture. You can find the toll-free phone number in the telephone directory.
- When issues about wetlands come before the U.S. Congress, let your voice be heard. Write to your representative and senator. You can get their names and addresses at the library.
- Express your opinions and ideas to state legislators. Introduce yourself in a letter or on the phone. Tell why you are for or against the issue. Be specific about what you want done. (?) *Strategy Alert!*

pesticides
(**pes**·ti·sieds)—
poisons used to kill
insects and weeds

fertilizers
(**fur**·tl·ie·zuhrz)—
chemicals put in soil
to feed plants

Stop and Ask

Does it make sense? Decide how the examples help explain a main point.

What You Should Not Do

One person's harmful actions can add to the problem. Here are some examples of things you should not do.

- Don't use weed killers, pesticides, and other harmful chemicals inside or outside your home. Through runoff, they end up in our water supply.
- Never pour motor oil, paint, or cleaning fluids down the drain. Never pour these things onto the ground or down a storm sewer. Again, these will enter the water supply and pollute groundwater.
- Try not to let a dog or other pet leave its waste in or near a stream. Animal waste can pollute the water.
- Do not waste water. Did you know that you could save ten gallons of water a day by shutting off the water when you brush your teeth? Replacing older toilets with new low-flow toilets can save lots of water. Placing a brick in the tank of older toilets can also save water.
- Do not waste electricity. The production of electricity pollutes our waterways and wetlands. ⑦ *Strategy Alert!*

Stop and Ask ⑦

Does it make sense? Decide how the examples help explain a main point.

Disposing of hazardous materials properly protects our water supply.

One Last Thing

More than half of this country's original wetland area has been lost to farming and urban growth. Time is running out for our wetlands. We must act now to save what is left before wetlands are gone forever.

Now that you've finished reading, review the **After I Read** habit and strategy below. Think about what you read in "Are We Wasting Our Wetlands?" as you practice the strategy.

After I Read

Which **HABIT** will I practice?

Use what I've read.

If I develop this habit, I will think about how I can apply what I just read to my schoolwork and my life. This makes reading really useful.

Which **STRATEGY** will I use to practice this habit?

Recap the main points (or big ideas) in the selection.

Use the **After I Read Strategy Sheet** for "Are We Wasting Our Wetlands?" (page 8 in your *Strategy Practice Book*) to use what you've read.

Apply

Now read "Taking Care of Our Mother, the Earth" and apply these three habits and strategies.

Before I Read

Which **HABIT** will I apply?
Check it out!

Which **STRATEGY** will I use to apply this habit?
Identify features to preview the selection and decide which are the most useful.

While I Read

Which **HABIT** will I apply?
Stop and ask, "Does it make sense?"

Which **STRATEGY** will I use to apply this habit?
Decide how the examples help explain a main point.

After I Read

Which **HABIT** will I apply?
Use what I've read.

Which **STRATEGY** will I use to apply this habit?
Recap the main points (or big ideas) in the selection.

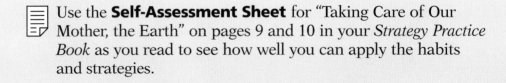

Use the **Self-Assessment Sheet** for "Taking Care of Our Mother, the Earth" on pages 9 and 10 in your *Strategy Practice Book* as you read to see how well you can apply the habits and strategies.

TAKING CARE OF OUR MOTHER, THE EARTH

O our Mother the Earth, O our Father the Sky,
Your children are we, and with tired backs
We bring you gifts.
—*Song of the Sky Loom (Tewa)*

The Earth Is Our Home

Like many Native Americans, the Tewa people honored and protected the land. They thought of the earth as their mother. R. Buckminster Fuller—an **architect** and engineer—looked at the earth in another way. In 1964, he wrote, "I am a passenger on the spaceship Earth." Fuller saw the earth as a ship carrying us on a journey through space. As passengers on this spaceship, we are responsible for its care. A scientist named James Lovelock proposed that the planet is alive. To him, it is a living thing that keeps the environment suitable for life. Mother, spaceship, or living planet, Earth is our home. It is clear that its system is finely balanced and complex. When any part of the system is changed, it is hard to know what the results will be.

architect (ahr·ki·tekt)—
a designer of buildings

Steelworks producing smog near the city of Aviles, Spain

Human Mistakes

Long before people lived on Earth, the planet existed. Forests grew, rivers flowed, and clean rain fell—all undisturbed by humans. Today, more than six billion people live and work on Earth. For years, many of us gave little thought to what our planet needed. If it didn't meet our needs, we changed it. Because most people didn't know any better, we harmed our planet in many ways. We cut down forests and dumped poisons into rivers. We polluted our air and wasted resources. We now know that what we do to one part of Earth affects the whole planet. It also affects every living thing on it.

We must try to repair past mistakes and keep from making new ones. To do that, we must learn about Earth's system and how what we do affects it.

Disappearing Forests, Disappearing Species

Everything we do affects Earth's system. Every time we eat, drink, or breathe, we use the environment. In itself, this is not bad. All living things use the environment. The harm comes when we take too much, waste resources, or destroy them.

Some people saw the connection between humans and nature a long time ago. For example, on his second voyage, in 1494, Columbus was impressed with Jamaica's dark, misty forests and cloud-wrapped peaks. He noticed that every afternoon there was a rain storm that lasted for about an hour. Columbus compared Jamaica to other **tropical** islands he knew. Although those islands also once had great forests, they had been cut down. Columbus thought that those islands had less rain since the forests were cut.

As it turns out, Columbus's ideas were correct. Scientists have found that much local rainfall begins as water in the soil. Groundwater **evaporates** and forms clouds. Water in the clouds falls back to Earth as rain. When a forest is cut, the soil dries up. Then the **cycle** ends.

It is estimated that tropical forests are disappearing at a rate of two million acres a month! Almost half of the world's species of plants and animals live in tropical forests. The lack of rain causes these plants and animals to die. Biologists fear that many unidentified species will vanish with their **habitat**.

We have caused many living things to become extinct. We have placed thousands of species of animals in danger. Scientists estimate that by the year 2100, one-third of all species living today may no longer exist!

tropical (**trop**·i·kuhl)— located just north and south of the equator

evaporates (i·**vap**·uh·rayts)—turns from a liquid to gas

cycle (**sie**·kuhl)—a set of events that happens over and over in the same order

habitat (**hab**·i·tat)—the place where an animal or plant is normally found

Waste and Pollution

Humans have not always been careful with natural resources. For example, we waste water by letting faucets run and by watering lawns. We pollute rivers, streams, and groundwater with garbage and toxic wastes. Fumes from our vehicles and factories pollute the air. High levels of these fumes in the atmosphere may be changing the climate of the entire planet. Earth's temperature may be rising.

This "global warming" can create many problems. For instance, **glaciers** are shrinking, and the polar ice caps are melting. Rising sea levels may eventually flood coastal areas. Floods, drought, hurricanes, and tornadoes are among the natural disasters that can be caused by changes in the earth's climate.

Toxins in the air and other chemicals may be damaging the ozone layer. The ozone layer of the atmosphere protects living things from the sun's harmful rays. Without this protection, many life-forms—including humans—are in danger.

In the name of progress, we have changed the landscape. We have cut down whole forests for lumber and to create farmland. This action destroys wildlife habitat. It causes **erosion** and flooding. We have dammed rivers to produce electricity. Lakes formed by dams have flooded huge areas. Fish stopped by the dams can't reach their **breeding** grounds. We have changed the course of rivers to water farmland. This has formed deserts where the water used to flow. It has added salt to the soil, making the land **barren**. We have filled in swamps and built malls. The many animals and plants that lived in the swamps are gone.

Why have we been so careless? Part of the problem is that we often don't know the harm we are doing until it is too late. Two examples are the building of the Aswan Dam and the clearing of the Amazon rain forest.

glaciers (**glay·**shuhrz)— very large masses of ice and snow

erosion (i·**roh·**zhuhn)— the wearing away of soil by rain or wind

breeding—giving birth to young

barren (**bar·**uhn)—not producing crops or fruit

A destroyed rain forest

Aswan High Dam

In the 1960s, President Nasser of Egypt dammed the Nile River. The reason was to control its yearly flooding and to produce electricity. "The miracle has been wrought," he said. The dam did stop the floods. However, it also blocked the flow of **silt** that enriched the soil of farms along the Nile. This meant that farmers had to start using chemical fertilizers.

silt—tiny particles of soil or sand floating in or left by water

The lack of the silt that flowed from the Nile into the Mediterranean Sea caused many problems. It increased erosion along the coast and it harmed wildlife. Sardines and shrimp were two species that lived in the sea. After the dam was built, they could not get their normal food— **organic** matter in the silt. As a result, the fish died. Egypt's sardine industry failed.

organic (or·gan·ik)—of or coming from living things

Rodents that had been kept in control by the yearly floods increased in numbers. Sewage systems that were cleansed by the floods became clogged. Farmland below the dam no longer drained properly. It became salty and useless. Farm production was cut in half. The "miracle" turned out to be a disaster for Egypt.

Aswan High Dam, Egypt

Lush tropical rain forest

The Amazon Rain Forest

In Brazil, most people live in crowded cities along the coast. Decades ago, the government wanted people to move inland. Settlers were encouraged to clear land in the Amazon rain forest for farms. People thought that because the jungle was so **lush,** its soil must be rich. However, settlers found that when stripped of its trees, the forest's soil was poor. Crops did not grow well. Rain washed away the little soil there was. Many settlers gave up and returned to the cities. But the damage had been done.

lush—covered with thick, healthy growth

Much land was cleared by burning the trees. This added huge amounts of carbon dioxide to the air. Dense, black smoke clouds blocked the sun's light over vast areas. Many people in the area developed lung diseases. Even today, space shuttle astronauts can see the fires burning in the rain forest.

Why should anyone care? The Amazon rain forest plays a major role in the earth's climate. Its trees and other plants absorb the carbon dioxide that causes global warming. In turn, they give off oxygen, enriching the air we breathe. As the rain forest disappears, the atmosphere has more carbon dioxide and less oxygen.

Brazilian rain forest being burned to make farmland

Scientists have found important medicines in rain forest plants. Among these are powerful drugs used to fight different types of cancer. What other wonders have not yet been found? No one knows. Scientists worry that as plants are destroyed, many life-saving drugs may also be lost.

The Power of the People

Some people are still ignoring the damage that is being done to the earth. However, many others are taking responsibility for the care of the planet. Planet care and repair is a huge job, but it's not an impossible one, if enough people work at it.

It takes only a few people to create change. Ordinary people start things moving. Then the movement grows until it has the power to bring about changes. Here is one example.

Some years ago, news came out about tuna fishing. When fishers cast their nets to catch tuna, dolphins got caught in the nets, too. Each year more than 100,000 dolphins were accidentally drowned in nets. People began to protest this senseless killing. They **boycotted** the tuna-canning industry. Great numbers of people stopped buying tuna. The boycott was a success. In 1990, the three major canners of tuna sold in the United States made an announcement. They decided that they would no longer buy or sell tuna caught by methods that also killed dolphins. Tuna fishers had to change their ways or lose business. The power of the people worked, and dolphins' lives were saved.

boycotted
(**boy**·kot·id)—protested by refusing to buy or deal with

Student rally to support environmental concerns

It's Up to You

You may have heard the saying "A journey of a thousand miles begins with a single step." The task of repairing our planet can begin with a single act. This act can be as small as not letting the water run when you brush your teeth. It can be as big as passing a law to protect the environment.

You can put your efforts to work on behalf of the earth. Set a good example for others. Try not to waste water or electricity. Practice "precycling"—refusing to buy or use goods with **excess** packaging. Recycle glass, cans, plastic, and paper.

Share the information you have learned about planet Earth. Tell your parents, your friends, and your classmates. Urge them to learn more themselves and to begin caring for our planet.

Start changing the world with your own school. Ask whether the school's paper supplies are made of recycled paper. Find out what happens to the school's waste materials. Are glass, metal cans, and plastic used in the cafeteria recycled? How much food is wasted, and why? Put together and post a fact sheet with your class. Recommend changes that could be made. Write a letter to your local newspaper. Tell what you are doing to help care for Earth. Suggest ways that community members can help.

Go right to the top. Find out who your senators and representatives are. These leaders want to hear from people like you to help them make important decisions about our planet. You can even write to the President. Write on your own, or write with your whole class. Ask the school or local librarian for help in finding names and addresses.

Get involved with organizations that are trying to protect the environment. Some have narrow interests, such as preserving the rain forests or protecting wildlife. Others have broader interests. Write and ask whether they have special programs for students. If they don't, suggest that they start one.

These are just a few of the many, many steps we can take. There have always been people who have loved and taken care of the earth. You can be one of them.

Seventh graders sort materials as part of a recycling project.

excess (**ek**·ses)—more than what is needed

Put Your Habits to Work in

Literature	Social Studies	Science	Math

Before I Read Habit:
Check it out!

Identify the best features to preview the selection before you read a chapter in your math textbook. Look at the heads, diagrams, charts, graphs, and examples. Decide which are the most useful.

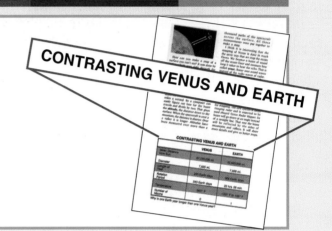

While I Read Habit:
Stop and ask, "Does it make sense?"

Don't forget to stop and ask yourself how the examples in your math book support a main point.

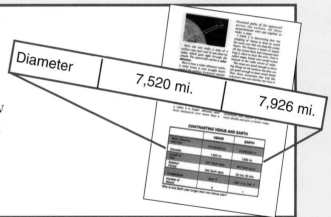

After I Read Habit:
Use what I've read.

When reading a math textbook, you're not finished until you use what you've read. You can do that by going back to recap the main points.

The main points are …

You may wish to use the **Put Your Habits to Work Sheet** (page 11 in your *Strategy Practice Book*) to practice these habits in your other reading.

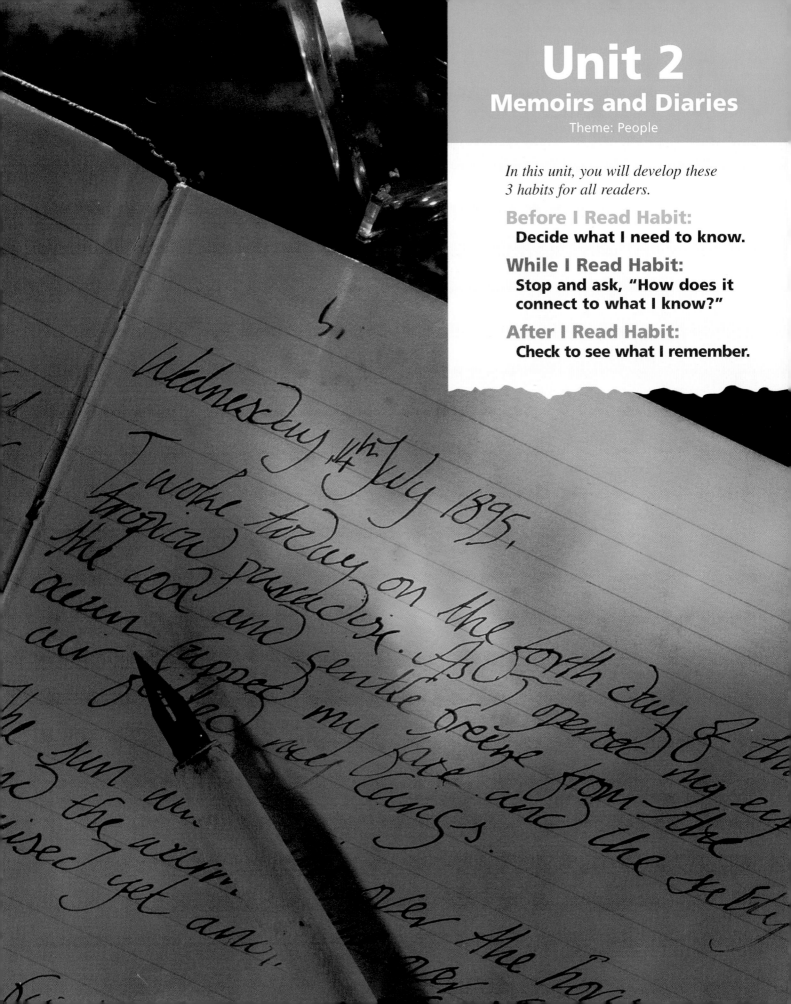

Unit 2
Memoirs and Diaries
Theme: People

*In this unit, you will develop these
3 habits for all readers.*

Before I Read Habit:
Decide what I need to know.

While I Read Habit:
Stop and ask, "How does it
connect to what I know?"

After I Read Habit:
Check to see what I remember.

In this unit, you will develop three habits—one for before you read, one for while you are reading, and one for after you finish reading. Start with **Before I Read**. Read the habit and strategy. Then read my notes below.

Before I Read

Which **HABIT** will I learn?
Decide what I need to know.
If I develop this habit, I will have a reason for reading. I will understand it better and remember more of what I read.

Which **STRATEGY** will I use to learn this habit?
Use the graphic aids and pictures to decide what the author wants me to understand.

My Notes

- Strategy says to use the graphic aids and pictures to decide what the author wants me to understand.

- I see a map and a diagram. The map shows a route that begins in Spain and goes across the Atlantic Ocean. It says it's Columbus's voyage. The diagram shows the parts of a ship.

- The pictures show Columbus and Columbus's ships.

- I think the story will be about Columbus's voyage when he first came to America.

Pedro was the name of a cabin boy who sailed with Christopher Columbus on his first voyage across the Atlantic. Did Pedro keep a diary? We don't know. This fictional diary describes the voyage from his point of view and is historically accurate. In it, Pedro recounts the dangers and adventures of six months at sea with Columbus.

Excerpts From

Pedro's Journal
A Voyage With Christopher Columbus
August 3, 1492–February 14, 1493
by Pam Conrad

Departure of Columbus from Palos, Spain, in 1492

August 3

The ship's **roster** of the *Santa María* has me down as Pedro de Salcedo, ship's boy. And the captain of this ship, who calls himself "Captain General of the Ocean Sea," has hired me not for my great love of the sea, nor for my seamanship, but because I have been taught to read and write, and he thinks it will be useful to have me along.

roster (ros•tuhr)—a list of people and their duties

Now read the habit and strategy for **While I Read**. When you see , read my notes in the margin.

While I Read

Which **HABIT** will I learn?

Stop and ask, "How does it connect to what I know?"
If I develop this habit, I will think about how what I'm reading fits with what I know. This helps me understand the new material and remember it better.

Which **STRATEGY** will I use to learn this habit?
Picture specific details.

Stop and Ask

How does it connect to what I know? Picture specific details.

. . . .

I can picture Pedro's mother on the dock watching his boat leave. I remember my mother saying good-bye to me when I went to visit my aunt.

mandarins (**man**·duh·rinz)—officials who served the Chinese emperor

brocade (broh·**kayd**)— heavy woven fabric with a raised design

Last night when I boarded the *Santa María* with forty others and made ready to begin this uncertain journey to India, I saw my mother standing alone on the dock wrapped in her black shawl. She lifted her hand to wave, and I turned away quickly. I have never been away from our home. I have never been on a ship as great as this one. I dedicate this journal, this parcel of letters and drawings, to my dear mother, who has lost so much and who I pray will not lose me as well—me, her young boy whom she calls *Pedro de mi corazón*, Pedro of my heart. **?** *Strategy Alert!*

We are a fleet of three ships, the *Niña* and *Pinta* with us, and this morning in the darkness, with no one watching or waving good-bye, we left the harbor at Palos and headed out for the sandbar on the Saltes River. There we waited for tide and wind and then made our way for the Canary Islands. We are to be the first ships ever to run a course west to the Indies, Marco Polo's land where palaces are built of gold, where **mandarins** wear silk **brocade** and pearls are the size of ripened grapes.

August 7

My mother would be pleased to know that each morning when the crew gathers on the deck, with the sails and lines rattling and clanking and the winds gusting above us, it is her own dear son who leads the morning prayers. She would also be amused to see the way the Captain says his rosary with such a fury, as if his prayers are orders to be carried out immediately.

I am learning the names and terms of all things to do with sailing and ships. In just a short time—given the Captain's lack of patience and fiery temper—I have learned to pretend that I know what everything means. I nod my head yes to his orders and then I search out someone who can explain what I must do. ❓ *Strategy Alert!*

Yesterday, after only four days out, the Captain was disturbed because the rudder broke on the *Pinta*. The rudder is the part that goes into the water to steer the ship, so of course we all had to wait.

I went with him to the *Pinta* in our ship's small **dinghy** to see what was wrong. The ocean tossed and threw us about, and I held onto the sides for dear life while Columbus and Martín Alonso Pinzón, the captain of the *Pinta*, shouted instructions back and forth to each other. We didn't get too close to the *Pinta* for fear of being crushed against her sides, but we were close enough to see what was wrong, and close enough to see that Martín Alonso was able to rig the broken rudder with rope.

Columbus was pleased for the moment that his captain had come up with an **ingenious** solution to the problem, and we returned to the *Santa María*. Last night Columbus wrote in his log that he believes it had been done on purpose, that there are men on board the *Pinta* who do not wish to make this journey.

Now those ropes on the rudder have all broken in a hard wind. More repairs must be made, or a replacement ship must be found. There is a brooding silence about the crew, and I am surprised to learn through mumblings and complaints that few of the men want to make this voyage. No one has much faith. And they whisper among themselves of sea monsters and how the sea will come to an abrupt end and we will go toppling off the edge of the world like a log **careening** over a waterfall.

Stop and Ask ❓

How does it connect to what I know? Picture specific details.

● ● ● ● ● ● ● ● ● ●

I can picture Pedro just nodding his head as though he knows what Columbus means. I sometimes pretend I understand what someone is telling me. I act like I do and then ask someone else.

dinghy (**ding**·ee)—a small boat with oars

ingenious (in·**jeen**·yuhs)—clever or skillful

careening (kuh·**ree**·ning)—lurching from side to side

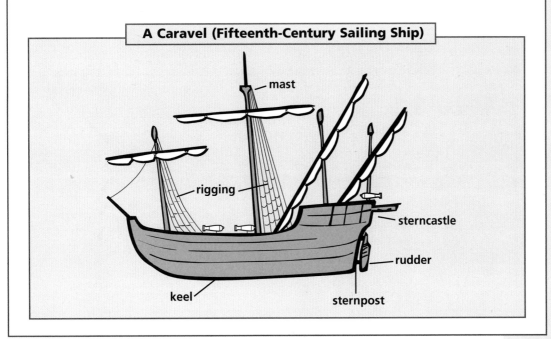

A Caravel (Fifteenth-Century Sailing Ship)

mast

rigging

sterncastle

rudder

keel

sternpost

My Captain seems like a smart man. I cannot believe he would do something so foolish. So I turn away from the men when they speak so, but late at night, when I lie sleeping beneath my covers, sometimes I bolt awake, sure we are falling through space and that we've left the world behind.

September 10

We finally lost sight of land as we sailed west. Some say it will be a long time before we see it again. If at all. A couple of the men were crying, and the Captain shamed them and then promised them all sorts of riches and fame. He has said that the first man to spot land will receive a reward of 10,000 **maravedis**.

The men listen to him **sullenly,** and I see them exchange glances. They don't believe him, and after what I saw this morning, I wonder if they should. I noted that the morning's slate said we made 180 miles, and yet the Captain recorded only 144 in his official log that the men see. I believe he is trying to make the crew believe that we are closer to home than is true. *Strategy Alert!*

But 10,000 maravedis! Ah, think of all I could buy for my mother. Even now I can picture a beautiful dress, a rich dress that she could wear to **Mass** at Easter. I will keep a sharp eye. I will be the first to spot land!

maravedis (mar·uh·**vay**·deez)—gold coins issued by the Spanish

sullenly (sul·uhn·lee)— in a bad mood

Stop and Ask ?

How does it connect to what I know? Picture specific details.

. . . .

I can picture the men looking at each other while Columbus is talking. Sometimes kids do that when they don't like or believe what an adult is saying.

Mass (mas)—a church service

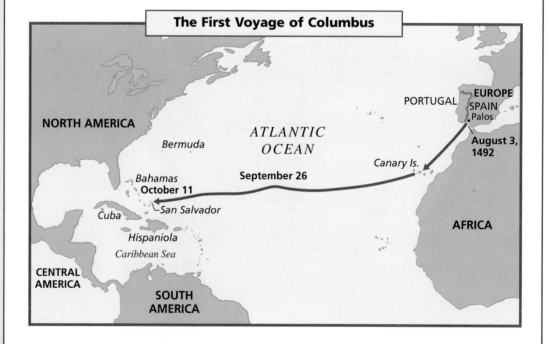

The First Voyage of Columbus

NORTH AMERICA

ATLANTIC OCEAN

Bermuda

Bahamas
October 11

September 26

San Salvador

Cuba

Hispaniola

Caribbean Sea

CENTRAL AMERICA

SOUTH AMERICA

PORTUGAL

EUROPE
SPAIN
Palos

August 3, 1492

Canary Is.

AFRICA

Columbus's ships—the *Niña, Pinta,* and *Santa María*

September 26

Last night nearing sunset, we were sailing alongside the *Pinta,* and our Captain and the *Pinta's* captain were calling back and forth, discussing the use of a certain chart. The sky was spectacular, striped with colors and softness, and all about us the sea was a quiet, slow river. Suddenly a cry went up on the *Pinta* that stunned us all.

"Land! Land, sir! I claim the reward! 10,000 maravedis are mine!"

An incredible sight! On all three ships the men scrambled up the rigging, higher and higher, wherever they could get a grip with their toes and their hands. Even I clambered as high as I could along the mast, which was not too high but high enough to see in the distance what appeared to be a tall mountain, clear and sharp like ice **chiseled** against the sky. We shielded our eyes against the setting sun, and in the soft pink air a great triple shout of joy went up across the small stretch of our sea. When I looked down at the deck, I saw the Captain on his knees in prayer.

I am sorry, however, to report this morning that after sailing all night in the southwesterly direction of that chiseled mountain, we have found nothing. Not even a sandbar. It had just been a **squall** cloud on the horizon at sunset. Nothing more. Nothing less. *Strategy Alert!*

Everyone is quiet. There is still a chance for each of us to win the reward.

⌒ ⌒

chiseled (**chiz**·uhld)— sharply cut

squall (skwawl)—a short, violent rainstorm

Stop and Ask ❓

How does it connect to what I know? Picture specific details.

• • • • • • • • • •

I can picture a cloud that looks like a mountain. I've seen clouds that look like all kinds of things.

leagues (leegz)—
measures of distance,
each equal to about three
miles

mutiny (myoot·nee)—
rebellion of a crew
against its captain

shrouds (shrowdz)—
a set of ropes connected
to the mast

October 10

This has been the worst day of all for the Captain. I am certain of this. We have doubled all previous records of days and **leagues** at sea, and we've gone way past the point where he originally said we would find land. There is nothing out here. Surely we are lost. And everyone is certain now as well.

This morning the men responded slowly to orders, scowling and slamming down their tools and lines. They whispered in pairs and small groups on deck and below. The air was thick with **mutiny** and betrayal, until finally everything came to a dead stop. The wind howled through the **shrouds,** and the men just stood there on deck and did not move aside when Columbus came.

"Enough," one of the men said to his face. "This is enough. Now we turn back."

The other men grumbled their assent and nodded, their fists clenched, their chests broad. And they remained motionless and unmoved while Columbus paced the deck, telling them how close he figured we must be, that land could be right over the next horizon. He told them again of the fame and fortune that would be theirs if they could only last a little longer. And they laughed at him, the cruel laughter of impatient and defeated men.

Columbus encourages his crew.

"All that aside," he added, "with the fresh easterly wind coming at us and the rising sea, we can't turn a course back to Spain right now. We would stand still in the water."

I looked up at the sails, full and straining, taking us farther and farther from Spain. What if a westerly wind never came? What if we were just blown away forever and ever? **?** *Strategy Alert!*

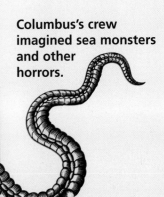

"Let me offer you this," Columbus finally said. "Do me this favor. Stay with me this day and night, and if I don't bring you to land before day, cut off my head, and you shall return."

The men glanced at each other. Some nodded. "One day," they said. "One day, and then we turn around."

"That is all I ask," Columbus said.

Later, when I went down to the cabin with the log, the Captain's door was bolted shut, and when I knocked he didn't answer, so I sat outside the door with the heavy journal in my lap and waited.

October 11

Through the day, the day that was to have been our last day traveling westward, many things were seen floating in the water, things that stirred everyone's hopes and had the men once again scanning the horizon. We saw birds in flocks, reeds and plants floating in the water, and a small floating board, and even a stick was recovered that had iron workings on it, obviously man-made. Suddenly no one wished to turn around. There was no further word on it.

At sunset, I led the prayers and the men sang the *Salve Regina* [**sal**·vay ri·**jee**·nuh]. Then the Captain spoke to the seamen from the sterncastle, doubling the night watch and urging everyone to keep a sharp lookout. No one asked about turning back. Then the Captain added a new bonus to his reward of 10,000 maravedis. He added a silk **doublet,** and some of the men joked with each other. Next the Captain nodded to me, and I sang for the changing of the watch, but my words were lost in the wind that was growing brisker and in the seas that were growing heavier and sounding like breakers all about us. The men **dispersed** to their watches and their bunks, and the Captain paced the deck. I don't know why, but this night I stayed with him. I stayed still by the **gunwale,** watching over the side. Once in a while he would stand beside me, silent, looking westward, always westward.

Then, an hour before moonrise, the Captain froze beside me. "Gutierrez!" he called to one of the king's men on board, who came running. He pointed across the water. "What do you see?"

Gutierrez peered into the west. "I don't see anything," he said. "What? What? What do you see?"

"Can't you see it?" the Captain whispered. "The light? Like a little wax candle rising and falling."

The man at his side was quiet. I was there beside him, too, straining my own eyes to the dark horizon.

Suddenly another seaman called out across the darkness, "Land! Land!"

"He's already seen it!" I shouted. "My master's already seen it!" And the Captain laughed and tousled my hair.

"Tierra! Tierra!" It was heard all across the water from all three ships.

I am below now in the Captain's cabin writing, while in the light of the rising moon, with our sails silver in the moonlight, we three exploring ships are rolling and plunging through the **swells** towards land. Tomorrow our feet will touch soil, and I can assure my dear mother in the hills of Spain that no one will get much sleep on board the *Santa María* tonight! **?** *Strategy Alert!*

Stop and Ask

How does it connect to what I know? Picture specific details.

. . . .

I think it would be hard to see by the light of the rising moon. I can picture boats plunging through the waves. I bet everyone on board was very excited. They must have wondered what they would find.

Congratulations! You finished reading. Now read the habit and strategy for **After I Read**. Then read my notes below.

After I Read

Which **HABIT** will I learn?

Check to see what I remember.

If I develop this habit, I will check to see what I remember as soon as I finish reading. It helps me see if I really understood what I read and helps me remember it better, too.

Which **STRATEGY** will I use to learn this habit?

Decide why certain events happened and whether they had to happen that way.

My Notes

- Strategy says to decide why certain things happened and whether they had to happen that way.

- The men on the ship wanted to turn back. This happened because they were afraid. They thought they were going to sail off the end of the earth!

- Columbus told them to give him one more day. If they didn't reach land, they could cut off his head and turn around. He had to say that, or there would have been a mutiny for sure.

Now it's time to practice the three habits and strategies you learned when you read "Pedro's Journal." Start with **Before I Read**. Look at the box below. It should look familiar! Reread the habit you will practice. Reread the strategy you will use—then do it!

Before I Read

Which **HABIT** will I practice?
Decide what I need to know.
If I develop this habit, I will have a reason for reading. I will understand it better and remember more of what I read.

Which **STRATEGY** will I use to practice this habit?
Use the graphic aids and photos to decide what the author wants me to understand.

Use the **Before I Read Strategy Sheet** for "The Sound of Drums and Gongs" (page 12 in your *Strategy Practice Book*) to decide what you need to know.

*In 1966, change came to China. Mao Ze-dong [**mow dzuh**‧dung], known as Chairman Mao, began a program of sweeping reform that came to be known as the Cultural Revolution. During this time, people lived in fear that their homes would be raided by Mao's Red Guards. These groups of young people would burst into houses and take valuable possessions. People weren't supposed to own anything beautiful or expensive.*

In the following chapter from her memoir, Red Scarf Girl, *Ji-li Jiang describes what it was like to live in China in 1966. At the time, she was 12 years old and living with her family in Shanghai [shang‧**hie**].*

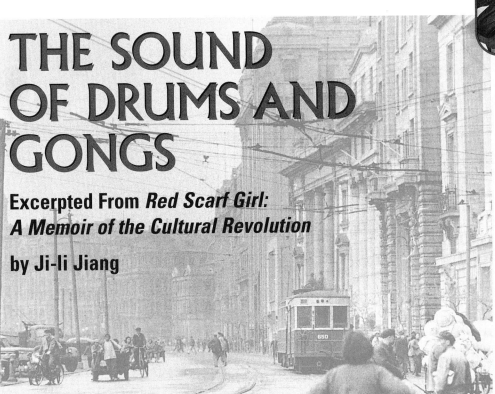

Mao Ze-dong

THE SOUND OF DRUMS AND GONGS

Excerpted From *Red Scarf Girl: A Memoir of the Cultural Revolution*

by Ji-li Jiang

Shanghai, 1961

The heat of summer had begun in earnest. At noon the sun scorched overhead, and the familiar slow **drone** of the popsicle man floated in through the open windows, accompanied by the rhythmic clap of a wooden block on a box: "Ice-cold popsicles. Green bean popsicles. Red bean popsicles. Ice-cold popsicles." My hands sweated so much holding the wool that I could not knit. Instead, I worked on embroidering a pillow sham as I waited for the cool of the evening. In the distance I could hear the sound of drums and gongs.

drone (drohn)—deep, humming sound

Read the habit and strategy below. Look for the *Strategy Alerts!* as you continue to read.

While I Read

Which **HABIT** will I practice?

Stop and ask, "How does it connect to what I know?
If I develop this habit, I will think about how what I'm reading fits with what I know. This helps me understand the new material and remember it better.

Which **STRATEGY** will I use to practice this habit?
Picture specific details.

Use the **While I Read Strategy Sheet** for "The Sound of Drums and Gongs" (page 13 in your *Strategy Practice Book*) as you read.

---

eradicate
(i·**rad**·i·kayt)—to get rid of

reactionary
(ree·**ak**·shuhn·er·ee)—against social or political changes

confiscate
(**kon**·fi·skayt)—to take by authority

How does it connect to what I know? Picture specific details.

There was a tension in the air that even we children felt. The newspapers and radio were full of the campaign to "Destroy the Four Olds" [old customs]. The campaign had been expanded to eliminate personal possessions. "If we do not completely eliminate the roots, the plant will grow back," we heard. "We must **eradicate** these relics of the past. . . . We must not allow the **reactionary** forces to hoard their treasures. . . ." And every day we heard the drums and gongs that meant the Red Guards were ransacking the houses of class enemies to find and **confiscate** their hoarded possessions. *Strategy Alert!*

One day the drums and gongs approached closer than I had ever heard them before. Ji-yun [author's younger sister] and her classmate Xiao Hong-yin ran into the house, full of the news. "It's a search party, all right," Ji-yun shouted. "They came from Old Man Rong's factory in trucks and they posted a *da-zi-bao* [notice]. Come on! Let's go see." She dragged me down the stairs.

A crowd was already gathering at Number Eleven, old Mr. Rong's house. Two dark trucks blocked the entry. The sides of the trucks were covered with red banners that said things like SWEEP AWAY ALL THE

REACTIONARY MONSTERS and DESTROY THE FOUR OLDS AND ESTABLISH THE FOUR NEWS. The big iron gate in front of the building was closed, but there was an unusual clamor coming from inside the house. The indistinct shouts of the Red Guards mingled with the furious barking of Mrs. Rong's huge dog. We could only imagine what was going on inside.

A *da-zi-bao* was posted on the gate, and a solemn crowd had gathered around to read it, wiping their faces with handkerchiefs and shading their heads with palm-leaf fans. Du Hai's mother was there along with another Neighborhood Party officer. I pushed my way between the people so I could read the *da-zi-bao*.

"Though the **capitalist** Rong De-feng has died, his widow still lives on his ill-gotten gains. The factories in which her husband **exploited** the masses have been returned to their rightful owners, the workers and the People's government. Yet the reactionary monster still lives on the blood of the workers. Instead of admitting her crimes and striving to atone for her sins, Old Lady Rong has sent her sons to Hong Kong, where they can continue to exploit the Chinese people, and she herself continues to **flaunt** her **bourgeois** life. The Red Guards have determined to eradicate the roots of this **noxious** weed in order to promote Chairman Mao's revolutionary cause."

I had never seen a search, except in the movies. I knew that they were the only way we were going to get rid of the Four Olds, once and for all. Still, there was something about the idea that made me nervous.

? *Strategy Alert!*

capitalist (cap·i·tl·ist)— owner of wealth used in business

exploited (ik·**sploy**·tid)—took advantage of

flaunt (flawnt)—to show off

bourgeois (boor·**zhwah**)—middle class

noxious (nok·shuhs)— poisonous

Stop and Ask ?

How does it connect to what I know? Picture specific details.

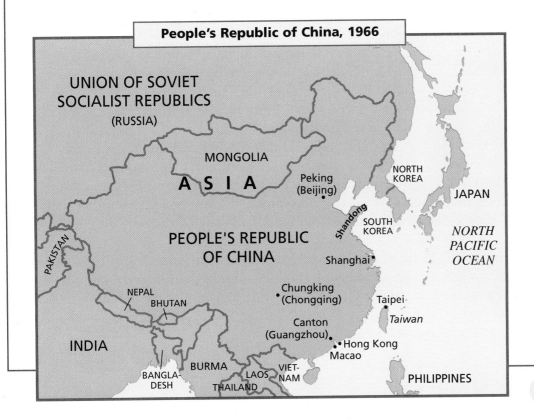

People's Republic of China, 1966

UNION OF SOVIET SOCIALIST REPUBLICS (RUSSIA)

MONGOLIA

A S I A

Peking (Beijing)

NORTH KOREA

JAPAN

Shandong

SOUTH KOREA

NORTH PACIFIC OCEAN

PEOPLE'S REPUBLIC OF CHINA

Shanghai

PAKISTAN

NEPAL

BHUTAN

Chungking (Chongqing)

Taipei

Taiwan

Canton (Guangzhou)

INDIA

Hong Kong

Macao

BANGLA-DESH

BURMA

LAOS

THAILAND

VIET-NAM

PHILIPPINES

A girl reading *da-zi-bao* **(notice)**

Ji-yun pulled on my arm. "Ji-li, what does 'noxious' mean?" Before I could answer her, Grandma was at my shoulder.

"Ji-li, help me carry this bag. Ji-yun, come along home now." She hustled us away. Ji-yun was still jabbering excitedly, but Grandma was stern. "You children stay in the house this afternoon, you hear? That's nothing for you to **gawk** at."

When Ji-yong [author's younger brother] came back in, he was thrilled too. He had spent part of the day in the park and had missed some of the excitement. "I saw them driving away a truck just full of stuff. I'm going back to see what else they got."

"You'll do nothing of the kind," Grandma said sharply. "Those poor people have enough to worry about without your going to stare at them." I was not sure who Grandma was worried about, the Red Guards or Mrs. Rong, but it was clear that she did not want us involved.

All that afternoon I was restless. I pictured Mrs. Rong, sitting under guard, cursing because her fourolds were being found. I imagined the searchers ransacking the trunks and drawers and drilling holes in the walls to look for hidden valuables. It seemed both inspiring and scary. When Grandma asked me [to] buy her some soy sauce, I could not help seizing the opportunity to go past Number Eleven and take another look.

People just getting home from work had swelled the crowd at the gate. Some of them were clustered in front of the *da-zi-bao*, but many more were talking in small groups. Children ran up and down the alley around and through the knots of people. One boy dared to hit a gong, and the clang startled everyone. The alley fell into silence. Everyone turned to look at the boy, and he scurried to stand behind his father. The conversation continued in hushed tones.  *Strategy Alert!*

Stop and Ask ?

How does it connect to what I know? Picture specific details.

"It's no surprise to me," said a woman I recognized as the housekeeper from Number Nine. "Every day when she went out all dolled up, I said to myself, she is heading for a fall."

"Last New Year's she went out with a new diamond ring bigger than I ever saw before," another old woman said. "Mrs. Feng's housekeeper told me it was over three carats. And the clothes she had made in Hong Kong! Every time somebody else got a new dress, you could be sure Mrs. Rong would get a prettier one."

"Yes, and the taxicabs and the dinners. . . . And **mah-jongg** all night sometimes."

I moved closer to the *da-zi-bao* on the gate.

"They said she had hundreds of thousands of **yuan** in the bank."

"I heard a million! My uncle worked in one of his factories before Liberation, and he knew all about Old Rong." This was Mr. Ni, the man we called Six-Fingers because of the extra finger on his right hand. He lived in one of the converted garages in our alley.

"The antiques they carried out a while ago must have been worth a million all by themselves."

"And there was that trunk full of gold bars. They could hardly carry it." There was satisfaction in their voices.

The gate opened with a loud clang and I jumped. Eight men struggled out with a huge mahogany four-poster bed. It was just like Mom and Dad's bed, with a mirror in the headboard surrounded by carved dragons. Most of the crowd murmured in admiration, but I also heard an **indignant** snort.

mah-jongg (**ma**-zhong)—a Chinese game played with tiles

yuan (**yoo**-ahn)—unit of Chinese money

indignant (in·**dig**·nuhnt)—angry; scornful

This ornate chest would have been unacceptable during the Cultural Revolution.

Stop and Ask ❓

How does it connect to what I know? Picture specific details.

riveting (riv·it·ing)— attention grabbing

posse (pahs·ee)—a group of people hired to keep order

"Typical capitalist," said a ragged-looking old woman.

I blushed. Our family had a capitalist bed, too. I turned and made my way out of the crowd.

The sound of drums and gongs drew near again. I saw Grandma wince. "Who is it this time?" she muttered. "You children stay in the house this afternoon." She wearily turned back to the kitchen.

Everyone could identify the sounds of a search, and we had grown expert at locating them in the neighborhood. After six more searches had been conducted in our alley, they were no longer exciting, but the adults I knew grew more and more tense. ❓ *Strategy Alert!*

Only Ji-yong was still enthusiastic about them. He always seemed to know the latest stories. "The housekeeper at Number Eighteen told the searchers that there were gold bars hidden in the toilet tank," he laughed. . . . And, most **riveting** of all, "They found real weapons at Number Thirty-eight." His voice was hushed with excitement. "They went up into the attic and looked in the old chimney, and they found a gun!"

"And do you know what else?" Song Po-po [the family's housekeeper] added, really speaking to Grandma rather than to us. "Six-Fingers is always at every search. He's too sick to work at the light bulb factory, but he's not too sick to go to every search and carry things out. He has all the roughest little children organized into a kind of **posse** to help keep order. He says he's proud to be doing his part." Grandma raised her head, but I heard no response.

Red Guards stage a pro-Mao march.

It was hard to imagine where Song Po-po heard so much news. When neighbors ran into each other, they did not stop to chat but just nodded and hurried on. Everyone felt **vulnerable,** and no one wanted to say anything that would cause trouble. We children were warned to stay close to home and come back at once if a search occurred. Only some of the few working-class people in the alley still seemed excited when they heard the drums and gongs.

In other years summer vacation had been a happy time. In the daytime we went to the pool or to the movies or to the park to turn somersaults and roll on the grass. Evenings we sat in the alley with the neighbors and listened to stories. We would watch the moon and sing and giggle until very late.

Now things were different. An Yi had been sent away to spend the summer with her grandparents in Shandong, away from Shanghai's **turbulence.** I missed her terribly. I saw hardly any kids in the neighborhood. No one came out to play. There seemed to be no laughter in the alley—just a growing, choking tension.

Shanghai street, 1960s

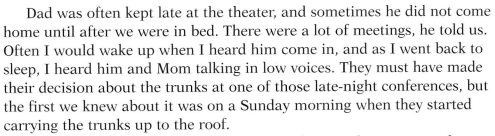

Dad was often kept late at the theater, and sometimes he did not come home until after we were in bed. There were a lot of meetings, he told us. Often I would wake up when I heard him come in, and as I went back to sleep, I heard him and Mom talking in low voices. They must have made their decision about the trunks at one of those late-night conferences, but the first we knew about it was on a Sunday morning when they started carrying the trunks up to the roof.

The four trunks were part of Grandma's **dowry**. They were a rich red leather, with a pattern stamped in gold. Each trunk had two sets of brass locks on its front and a round brass handle on each end. When they were stacked up on their rack, they made our room shine. Now Dad was going to dye them black so that they would not be considered fourolds.

vulnerable
(**vul**·nuhr·uh·buhl)—
in danger

turbulence
(**tur**·byuh·luhns)—
unrest; commotion;
disturbance

dowry (**dow**·ree)—
money and property a
woman gives to a man
when they marry

Four stools were waiting in the middle of the roof, and the first chest was placed upon them. The dark dye was already mixed. Dad set to work.

"Wait a minute," exclaimed Grandma. There was a dark stain about the size of a thumb print on one of the brass handles. She took out her handkerchief and rubbed the handle over and over until it was clean and bright. She looked at the chest with a dreamy expression and gently laid her hand on it. Against the deep red leather her skin seemed even paler.

"It won't look bad after it's painted," Dad said softly.

Grandma seemed to wake up. "Oh, I know," she said. "You go ahead." She went down to the room and did not come back.

"Her mother gave her these trunks when Grandma got married. That's why she's sad," Dad explained.

I thought of Grandma getting married so long ago, bringing the four beautiful trunks full of gifts her mother had sent from **Tianjin** to Shanghai. Grandma must have been excited and exhausted, traveling a thousand miles to marry a man she had never met.

Dad started to paint, wielding the brush awkwardly.

"Dad, it's too dry. Look how it's streaking."

Dad dipped the brush in the dye again.

"Look out! It's dripping, Dad."

Shouting advice, we ran around the trunks excitedly.

Eventually Dad's painting improved, and the first trunk was finished. But the original color could still be seen through the dye, and he had to put on a second coat. Ji-yun and I grew tired of watching and went back downstairs. Ji-yong stayed to help. *Strategy Alert!*

An amazing sight stopped the two of us in the doorway.

"Wow," Ji-yun said.

Glowing silks and satins spilled out of an old trunk. The whole room was alive with color.

Tianjin (**tyan**·jin)—a city in northern China

Stop and Ask ❓

How does it connect to what I know? Picture specific details.

Ji-yun grabbed a piece of silk. "Gorgeous! Are these costumes, Mom?"

They were old clothes, long gowns like the ones ancient courtiers and scholars wore in the movies. Many of them were embroidered with golden dragons or **phoenixes**. Some were printed with magnificent colorful patterns, and some were even crusted with pearls and gold sequins.

"These belonged to our ancestors. Grandma thought they were too nice to throw away, so we kept them in the bottom of this chest." Mom reached in and pulled out a bunch of colorful silk neckties. She threw them all on the floor.

I was worried. "Mom, aren't these all fourolds?"

"That's right. That's why Grandma and I decided to make comforter covers out of them. We can use the ties to make a mop."

"It seems terrible to just cut them all up. Why don't we just give them to the theater or to the Red Guards?" Ji-yun held a gown up in front of her. She was imagining what it would be like to wear it, I knew.

"The theater doesn't need them, and it's too late to turn them in now. The Red Guards would say that we were hiding them and waiting for New China to fall. Besides, even if we did turn them in, the Red Guards would just burn them anyway." Grandma looked at me and shook her head as she picked up her scissors. "I just couldn't bear to sell them," she said sadly. "Even when your father was in college and we needed money." She picked up a lovely gold-patterned robe and said softly, "This was a government official's uniform. I remember my grandfather wearing it."

"It *is* pretty, Grandma," I said, "but it is fourolds. Don't feel bad about it."

The long gowns were so large that the back of one was big enough for half a quilt cover. Mom and Grandma discussed the job while cutting: which parts could be used for covers and which parts for cushions. Ji-yun and I were enchanted by the pearls and gold sequins littering the floor. We pestered Grandma and Mom to let us have them, and finally Mom sighed and yielded.

Ji-yun and I were overjoyed. We sat amid the piles of silks, picking up pearls and putting them in a jar. Little White [author's cat] was happy too. She rolled over and over among the scraps of silk and batted pearls around the floor. ❓ *Strategy Alert!*

phoenixes (fee·niks·ez)— mythological birds

Stop and Ask ❓

How does it connect to what I know? Picture specific details.

While we played, Mom made two quilt covers out of the gowns, one deep purple and the other a bright gold. Then she made a pair of mops from the ties. We were delighted with them. You could not find anything like our tie mops in the stores.

Dad and Ji-yong finally finished the second coat of dye on the trunks. The gold stamping still **obstinately** showed through the layers, but the deep red had become a dark burgundy. The room seemed dressed up with the glowing new quilts and the repainted trunks. I felt good. We had really done what Chairman Mao asked, breaking with the old and establishing the new.

"You did a nice job on the trunks," Grandma said. "I don't think the Red Guards will notice them."

Ji-yun looked up from the bed where she was lying with her face in the silky new cover. "Are the Red Guards going to come and search our house?"

Everyone stood still. I stopped playing with the pearls. Even Little White stopped rolling around the floor.

"It's possible," Mom said slowly, "but you don't have to be afraid. You are just children, and a search would have nothing to do with you."

The new decor lost all its brightness. The pearls I had been playing with lost their **luster,** and I put them down.

Effects of Communism and the Cultural Revolution on China, 1949–1976

GOVERNMENT
- October 1, 1949: Communists, led by Mao Ze-dong, declare a new government called *People's Republic of China*.
- Mao supports radicals in the Communist Party who want to form a classless society. The Cultural Revolution, a 10-year period of political chaos and violence, begins.

ECONOMY
- Land is seized from landlords and organized into huge farming cooperatives.
- Hard labor is valued over technology. People and machines work overtime in the fields.
- Political upheaval destroys farm production. Schools close and the economy collapses.

PEOPLE
- People are told to dress and act alike and to turn away from the ancient culture (fourolds) of China.
- Intellectuals, professionals, and the wealthy are scorned. The common good is all-important.
- The Red Guard (groups of young people) carry banners that praise Mao and use violence to enforce the Cultural Revolution.

> Now that you've finished reading, review the **After I Read** habit below. Think about what you read in "The Sound of Drums and Gongs" as you practice the strategy.

After I Read

Which **HABIT** will I practice?
Check to see what I remember.
If I develop this habit, I will check to see what I remember as soon as I finish reading. It helps me see if I really understood what I read and helps me remember it better, too.

Which **STRATEGY** will I use to practice this habit?
Decide why certain events happened and whether they had to happen that way.

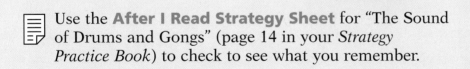 Use the **After I Read Strategy Sheet** for "The Sound of Drums and Gongs" (page 14 in your *Strategy Practice Book*) to check to see what you remember.

Apply 3 of the 9 Habits

Now read "Zlata's Diary" and apply these three habits and strategies.

Before I Read

Which **HABIT** will I apply?
Decide what I need to know.

Which **STRATEGY** will I use to apply this habit?
Use the graphic aids and pictures to decide what the author wants me to understand.

While I Read

Which **HABIT** will I apply?
Stop and ask, "How does it connect to what I know?"

Which **STRATEGY** will I use to apply this habit?
Picture specific details.

After I Read

Which **HABIT** will I apply?
Check to see what I remember.

Which **STRATEGY** will I use to apply this habit?
Decide why certain events happened and whether they had to happen that way.

 Use the **Self-Assessment Sheet** for "Zlata's Diary" on pages 15–16 of your *Strategy Practice Book* as you read to see how well you can apply the habits and strategies.

*In the spring of 1992 the civil war that was raging in other parts of Yugoslavia [yoo•goh•**slah**•vee•uh] reached Bosnia-Herzegovina. The city of Sarajevo [sahr•uh•**yay**•voh] was under attack. Many people fled. Others stayed, hoping that the war would soon end.*

Zlata Filipović, 11 years old at the start of the war, stayed with her parents in their apartment in Sarajevo. In her diary, Zlata described the fear, hope, and horror that she and her family experienced.

Excerpts From

ZLATA'S DIARY

A Child's Life in Sarajevo

by Zlata Filipović

Monday, March 30, 1992

Hey, Diary! You know what I think? Since Anne Frank called her diary Kitty, maybe I could give you a name too. What about:

ASFALTINA	PIDŽAMETA
ŠEFIKA	HIKMETA
ŠEVALA	MIMMY

or something else???
I'm thinking, thinking . . .
I've decided! I'm going to call you
MIMMY
All right, then, let's start.

Sarajevo before the war

half-term (haf turm)—
the middle of the school
term

Dear Mimmy,

It's almost **half-term**. We're all studying for our tests. Tomorrow we're supposed to go to a classical music concert at the Skenderija [**sken**·de·ree·yuh] Hall. Our teacher says we shouldn't go because there will be 10,000 people, pardon me, children, there, and somebody might take us as hostages or plant a bomb in the concert hall. Mommy says I shouldn't go. So I won't.

Hey! You know who won the Yugovision Song Contest?! EXTRA NENA!!!???

I'm afraid to say this next thing. Melica says she heard at the hairdresser's that on Saturday, April 4, 1992, there's going to be BOOM—BOOM, BANG—BANG, CRASH Sarajevo. Translation: they're going to bomb Sarajevo.

Love,
Zlata

Sunday, April 5, 1992

Dear Mimmy,

I'm trying to concentrate so I can do my homework (reading), but I simply can't. Something is going on in town. You can hear gunfire from the hills. Columns of people are spreading out from Dobrinja [doh·**brin**·ya]. They're trying to stop something, but they themselves don't know what. You can simply feel that something is coming, something very bad. On TV I see people in front of the **B-H parliament** building. The radio keeps playing the same song: "Sarajevo, My Love." That's all very nice, but my stomach is still in knots and I can't concentrate on my homework anymore.

Mimmy, I'm afraid of WAR!!!

Zlata

B-H—abbreviation for
Bosnia-Herzegovina (a
country in the Balkans),
also known as Bosnia

parliament
(**par**·luh·muhnt)—
a governing body

Thursday, April 9, 1992

Dear Mimmy,

I'm not going to school. All the schools in Sarajevo are closed. There's danger hiding in these hills above Sarajevo. But I think things are slowly calming down. The heavy **shelling** and explosions have stopped. There's occasional gunfire, but it quickly falls silent. Mommy and Daddy aren't going to work. They're buying food in huge quantities. Just in case, I guess. God forbid!

    Still, it's very tense. Mommy is beside herself, Daddy tries to calm her down. Mommy has long conversations on the phone. She calls, other people call, the phone is in constant use.

Zlata

shelling (shel·ing)— firing of explosive devices

Tuesday, April 14, 1992

Dear Mimmy,

People are leaving Sarajevo. The airport, train and bus stations are packed. I saw sad pictures on TV of people parting. Families, friends separating. Some are leaving, others staying. It's so sad. Why? These people and children aren't guilty of anything. Keka and Braco [author's family friends] came early this morning. They're in the kitchen with Mommy and Daddy, whispering. Keka and Mommy are crying. I don't think they know what to do—whether to stay or to go. Neither way is good.

Zlata

Crowds of refugees attempt to board buses near Tuzla Airport in Bosnia-Herzegovina.

A Sarajevo building destroyed in the Bosnian War

revolting (ri·**volt**·ing)— disgusting

Monday, April 20, 1992

Dear Mimmy,

War is no joke, it seems. It destroys, kills, burns, separates, brings unhappiness. Terrible shells fell today on Baščaršija, the old town center. Terrible explosions. We went down into the cellar, the cold, dark, **revolting** cellar. And ours isn't even all that safe. Mommy, Daddy and I just stood there, holding on to one another in a corner that looked safe. Standing there in the dark, in the warmth of my parents' arms, I thought about leaving Sarajevo. Everybody is thinking about it, and so am I. I couldn't bear to go alone, to leave behind Mommy and Daddy, Grandma and Granddad. And going with just Mommy isn't any good either. The best would be for all three of us to go. But Daddy can't. So I've decided we should stay here together. Tomorrow I'll tell Keka that you have to be brave and stay with those you love and those who love you. I can't leave my parents, and I don't like the other idea of leaving my father behind alone either.

Your Zlata

Saturday, May 2, 1992

Dear Mimmy,

Today was truly, absolutely the worst day ever in Sarajevo. The shooting started around noon. Mommy and I moved into the hall. Daddy was in his office, under our apartment, at the time. We told him on the intercom to run quickly to the downstairs lobby where we'd meet him. We brought Cicko [author's canary] with us. The gunfire was getting worse, and we couldn't get over the wall to the Bobars' [family friends and neighbors], so we ran down to our own cellar.

The cellar is ugly, dark, smelly. Mommy, who's terrified of mice, had two fears to cope with. The three of us were in the same corner as the other day. We listened to the pounding shells, the shooting, the thundering noise overhead. We even heard planes. At one moment I realized that this awful cellar was the only place that could save our lives. Suddenly, it started to look almost warm and nice. It was the only way we could defend ourselves against all this terrible shooting. We heard glass shattering in our street. Horrible. I put my fingers in my ears to block out the terrible sounds. I was worried about Cicko. We had left him behind in the lobby. Would he catch cold there? Would something hit him? I was terribly hungry and thirsty. We had left our half-cooked lunch in the kitchen.

When the shooting died down a bit, Daddy ran over to our apartment and brought us back some sandwiches. He said he could smell something burning and that the phones weren't working. He brought our TV set down to the cellar. That's when we learned that the main post office (near us) was on fire and that they had kidnapped our President. At around 8:00 we went back up to our apartment. Almost every window in our street was broken. Ours were all right, thank God. I saw the post office in flames. A terrible sight. The fire-fighters battled with the raging fire. Daddy took a few photos of the post office being **devoured** by the flames. He said they wouldn't come out because I had been fiddling with something on the camera. I was sorry. The whole apartment smelled of the burning fire. God, and I used to pass by there every day. It had just been done up. It was huge and beautiful, and now it was being swallowed up by the flames. It was disappearing. That's what this neighborhood of mine looks like, my Mimmy. I wonder what it's like in other parts of town? I heard on the radio that it was awful around the **Eternal Flame**. The place is knee-deep in glass. We're worried about Grandma and Granddad. They live there. Tomorrow, if we can go out, we'll see how they are. A terrible day. This has been the worst, most awful day in my eleven-year-old life. I hope it will be the only one. Mommy and Daddy are very edgy. I have to go to bed.

Ciao!
Zlata

devoured (di·**vowrd**)— ate hungrily

Eternal Flame (i·**tur**·nuhl flaym)— a monument to the former Yugoslavian president Tito

ciao (chow)—Italian word for "good-bye"

Bosnia-Herzegovina, 1992

Friday, June 5, 1992

Dear Mimmy,

There's been no electricity for quite some time and we keep thinking about the food in the freezer. There's not much left as it is. It would be a pity for all of it to go bad. There's meat and vegetables and fruit. How can we save it?

Daddy found an old wood-burning stove in the attic. It's so old it looks funny. In the cellar we found some wood, put the stove outside in the yard, lit it and are trying to save the food from the refrigerator. We cooked everything, and joining forces with the Bobars, enjoyed ourselves. There was veal and chicken, squid, cherry **strudel,** meat and potato pies. All sorts of things. It's a pity, though, that we had to eat everything so quickly. We even overate. WE HAD A MEAT STROKE.

We washed down our refrigerators and freezers. Who knows when we'll be able to cook like this again. Food is becoming a big problem in Sarajevo. There's nothing to buy, and even cigarettes and coffee are becoming a problem for grown-ups. The last reserves are being used up. God, are we going to go hungry to boot???

Zlata

strudel (strood·l)— a type of flaky cake

A Bosnian family pushes a water container in a handmade cart in war-torn Sarajevo.

Sunday, July 5, 1992

Dear Mimmy,

I don't remember when I last left the house. It must be almost two months ago now. I really miss Grandma and Granddad. I used to go there every day, and now I haven't seen them for such a long time.

I spend my days in the house and in the cellar. That's my wartime childhood. And it's summer. Other children are vacationing on the seaside, in the mountains, swimming, sunbathing, enjoying themselves. God, what did I do to deserve being in a war, spending my days in a way that no child should. I feel caged. All I can see through the broken windows is the park in front of my house. Empty, deserted, no children, no joy. I hear the sound of shells, and everything around me smells of war. War is now my life. OOHHH, I can't stand it anymore! I want to scream and cry. I wish I could play the piano at least, but I can't even do that because it's in "the dangerous room," where I'm not allowed. How long is this going to go on???

Zlata

———◆———

Saturday, July 11, 1992

Dear Mimmy,

Nedo brought us a little visitor today. A kitten. It followed him and he couldn't just leave it in the street so he picked it up and brought it home. We'll call it Skinny, Lanky, Kitty, Mikana, Persa, Cici . . .???? It's orange, has white socks and a white patch on its chest. It's cute, but a little wild.

Zlata

———◆———

Friday, July 17, 1992

Dear Mimmy,

We named the kitten Cici. Nedo gave it a bath, we feed it milk and biscuits, even rice. She has to get used to wartime food like the rest of us! She's cute. She has a beautiful head. We've all fallen in love with her and she is slowly getting used to us. Bojana [author's friend and neighbor] and I hold her in our lap, stroke her and she purrs. That means she likes it, she's happy. She must be lucky. Who knows whether she'd still be alive. She could have been hit by **shrapnel,** or died of hunger or been attacked by a stray dog. Nedo really did a good deed there. So, now we have a new member in this family we call THE NEIGHBORHOOD.
Ciao!

Zlata

shrapnel (shrap·nuhl)— pieces of a shell that scatter when it explodes

Thursday, September 3, 1992

Dear Mimmy,

The days are passing by more pleasantly. There's no shooting in our neighborhood, but we've been without electricity now for more than a month. If only the electricity would come back on. If only I could cross the bridge and at least go to Grandma and Granddad's! I'm working on it. I'm putting pressure on Mommy and Daddy. Will it work???? We'll find out!

Zlata

Sunday, September 20, 1992

Dear Mimmy,

YIPPEE! I crossed the bridge today. Finally I got to go out too! I can hardly believe it. The bridge hasn't changed. But it's sad, sad because of the post office, which looks even sadder. It's in the same place, but it's not the same old post office. The fire has left its mark. It stands there like a witness to **brutal** destruction.

The streets aren't the same, not many people are out, they're worried, sad, everybody rushing around with bowed heads. All the shop windows have been broken and looted. My school was hit by a shell and its top floor destroyed. The theater was also hit by some disgusting shells, and it's wounded. An awful lot of wonderful old Sarajevo buildings have been wounded.

I went to see Grandma and Granddad. Oh, how we hugged and kissed! They cried with joy. They've lost weight and aged since I last saw them four months ago. They told me I had grown, that I was now a big girl. That's nature at work. Children grow, the elderly age. That's how it is with those of us who are still alive.

brutal (**broot**·l)—cruel

A Sarajevo street shortly after the war

And there are lots and lots of people and children in Sarajevo who are no longer among the living. The war has claimed them. And all of them were innocent. Innocent victims of this disgusting war.

We ran into Marijana's mother. They didn't leave. They're alive and well. She told me that Ivana had gone to Zagreb [**zah**·greb]—with a Jewish **convoy**.

We also went to see our friend Doda. She, too, was surprised when she saw me. She cried. She says I've grown. Slobo (her husband) was wounded, but he's all right now. There's no news of Dejan (her son). It makes her sad.

Dear Mimmy, I have something to confess to you. I dressed up. I put on that nice plaid outfit. My shoes were a bit tight, because my feet have grown, but I survived.

So, that was my encounter with the bridge, the post office, Grandma, Granddad, and with a wounded Sarajevo. If only the war would stop, the wounds would heal!

Ciao!
Zlata

convoy (**kon**·voy)—
a group of vehicles traveling together

—————

Wednesday, October 21, 1992

Dear Mimmy,

Today is Daddy's birthday. I gave him a kiss and a "Happy Birthday, Daddy." We made little sweets *"à la Mirna."*

And now let me explain something to you Mimmy: as you know, I **confide** in you every day (almost). Well, you know the summer school in our community center? We had a wonderful time together there, did some acting, some reciting, and best of all, some writing too. It was all so nice, until that horrible shell killed our friend Eldin.

Maja [Bobar] is still working with our teacher Irena Vidovic. And the other day, Maja asks me: "Do you keep a diary, Fipa (my nickname)?"

I say: "Yes."

And Maja says: "Is it full of your own secrets or is it about the war?"

And I say: "Now, it's about the war."

And she says: "Fipa, you're terrific."

She said that because they want to publish a child's diary and it just might be mine, which means—YOU, MIMMY. And so I copied part of you into another notebook and you, Mimmy, went to the City Assembly to be looked at. And I've just heard, Mimmy, that you're going to be published! You're coming out for the **UNICEF** week! SUPER!

And now super good news: the electricity is back on. But it's 5:45 now and it's gone off already. Samra [neighbor] says it will come back on. Let's hope so.

Ciao!
Zlata

confide (kuhn·**fied**)—
to tell in trust

UNICEF—abbreviation for "United Nations International Children's Emergency Fund"

—————

Bosnian civilians, led by a policeman, use wrecked cars as shields from sniper fire.

Thursday, November 19, 1992

Dear Mimmy,

Nothing new on the political front. They are adopting some **resolutions,** the "kids" are **negotiating,** and we are dying, freezing, starving, crying, parting with our friends, leaving our loved ones.

I keep wanting to explain these stupid politics to myself, because it seems to me that politics caused this war, making it our everyday reality. War has crossed out the day and replaced it with horror, and now horrors are unfolding instead of days. It looks to me as though these politics mean Serbs, Croats and Muslims. But they are all people. They are all the same. They all look like people, there's no difference. They all have arms, legs and heads, they walk and talk, but now there's "something" that wants to make them different.

Among my girlfriends, among our friends, in our family, there are Serbs and Croats and Muslims. It's a mixed group and I never knew who was a Serb, a Croat or a Muslim. Now politics has started meddling around. It has put an "S" on Serbs, an "M" on Muslims and a "C" on Croats, it wants to separate them. And to do so it has chosen the worst, blackest pencil of all—the pencil of war which spells only misery and death.

resolutions
(rez·uh·**loo**·shuhns)—
courses of action decided
upon

negotiating
(ni·**goh**·shee·ayt·ing)—
talking, with the hope of
reaching an agreement

War in Bosnia

Zlata begins her diary.

September 1991

June 1991

Croatia and Slovenia declare
independence from Yugoslavia.
Fighting begins.

March 1992

Bosnians vote for
independence.
Bosnian Serbs resist.

Fighting has killed 17,000.
Thousands are evacuated
from Sarajevo.

November 1992

Why is politics making us unhappy, separating us, when we ourselves know who is good and who isn't? We mix with the good, not with the bad. And among the good there are Serbs and Croats and Muslims, just as there are among the bad. I simply don't understand it. Of course, I'm "young," and politics are conducted by "grown-ups." But I think we "young" would do it better. We certainly wouldn't have chosen war.

The "kids" really are playing, which is why us kids are not playing, we are living in fear, we are suffering, we are not enjoying the sun and flowers, we are not enjoying our childhood. WE ARE CRYING.

A bit of **philosophizing** on my part, but I was alone and felt I could write this to you, Mimmy. You understand me. Fortunately, I've got you to talk to.

And now,

Love,
Zlata

philosophizing
(fi·**los**·uh·fie·zing)—
trying to explain things

━━◆◆━━

Wednesday, August 18, 1993

Dear Mimmy,

Yesterday I heard some optimistic news. The "kids" have signed an agreement in Geneva on the **demilitarization** of Sarajevo. What can I say? That I hope, that I believe it???? I don't know how I could. Whenever I believed and hoped for something it didn't happen, and whenever I didn't believe or expect anything it did happen.

Today some Italian journalists asked me what I thought about the idea of "Sarajevo—an Open City." I gave them some answer, but I think the "kids" are just playing and I don't believe them at all and I've had enough of everything. Because, I know there is no electricity, no water, no food, that people keep getting killed, that we no longer have even candles, that smuggling and crime are **rife,** that the days are getting shorter and soon it will be what the whole of Sarajevo fears most: WINTER. The mere thought of it gives me the chills.

Mommy and Daddy often say: *"Post nubila, Phoebus,"* which is Latin, Mimmy, and it means: "After the clouds comes the sun." But when????

Zlata

demilitarization
(dee·**mil**·i·tuh·riz·**ay**·
shuhn)—replacing
military control with
civilian control

rife (rief)—widespread

Sarajevo is declared a "safe area" under UN protection.

May 1993

Zlata and her family fly to the safety of Paris, France.

December 23, 1993

December 3, 1992

Zlata's 12th birthday

July 23, 1993

Zlata's Diary is promoted. Zlata is compared to Anne Frank.

July 23, 1993

The Dayton agreement is signed in Paris, France, bringing peace to the area.

Put Your Habits to Work in

Literature | **Social Studies** | **Science** | **Math**

Before I Read Habit:
Decide what I need to know.

Decide what you need to know by looking at the maps, charts, time lines, and pictures that are a part of the chapter or chapters you are about to read in your social studies book.

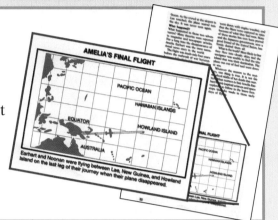

While I Read Habit:
Stop and ask, "How does it connect to what I know?"

Try to make mental pictures of what you are reading. Picturing specific details will help you connect what you are reading to personal experience or to other books or movies with which you are familiar.

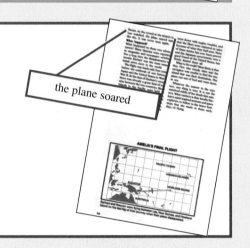

the plane soared

After I Read Habit:
Check to see what I remember.

Think about why certain events happened. Ask yourself whether those events had to happen that way, or whether things could have turned out differently.

That event happened because...

 You may wish to use the **Put Your Habits to Work Sheet** (page 17 in your *Strategy Practice Book*) to practice these habits in your other reading.

Unit 3
Their Thoughts Changed Our Lives
Theme: Imagination

In this unit, you will develop these 3 habits for all readers.

Before I Read Habit:
Think about what I know about the subject.

While I Read Habit:
Stop and ask, "Does it make sense?"

After I Read Habit:
Use what I've read.

Learn 3 of the 9 Habits

In this unit, you will develop three habits—one for before you read, one for while you are reading, and one for after you finish reading. Start with **Before I Read**. Read the habit and strategy. Then read my notes below.

Before I Read

Which **HABIT** will I learn?
Think about what I know about the subject.
If I develop this habit, I will bring to mind what I already know about the subject. This gets me ready to connect what I read to what I know so I will understand it better.

Which **STRATEGY** will I use to learn this habit?
Read the questions, introduction, and/or summary to decide what I know about this.

My Notes

- Strategy says to look at questions, introduction, and/or summary.

- Read the introduction. I've heard of a man named Gandhi but I didn't know that "Mahatma" means "Great Soul." I knew that Gandhi was from India.

- There's a question at the end of the introduction and at the end of some sections. The question in the introduction is about how Gandhi became a beloved leader. I think he was in politics.

- I don't see a summary.

Mahatma Gandhi

Great Soul of India

Introduction

He was a great leader who
led India from British rule
to self-rule. Not a president
or a soldier, he did not rise to power
in the usual ways. He simply worked
to help the poor—and became one
of the greatest leaders in the world.
His name was Mohandas Gandhi [**gon**·dee].
The poor he helped called him *Mahatma* [muh·**haht**·muh],
or *Great Soul*. How did Gandhi become one of the most
beloved leaders the world has ever known?

Now read the habit and strategy for **While I Read**. When you see ❓, read my notes in the margin.

While I Read

Which **HABIT** will I learn?
> **Stop and ask, "Does it make sense?"**
> If I develop this habit, I will stop now and then to make sure I understand what I'm reading.

Which **STRATEGY** will I use to learn this habit?
> See if I can explain important words.

Early Years

Mohandas Gandhi was born in 1869 in India. He was the youngest child in a large Hindu family. As Hindus, the family lived under the caste [kast] system. In this system, people are born into a certain level of society. They may not move from caste to caste. The Gandhis were members of the **merchant** caste. This caste was neither the richest nor the poorest caste in India.

Gandhi's father worked for the government. His mother was deeply religious. As a child, young Mohandas was shy and quiet. He was very close to his mother and always tried to do as she wished. She expected her son to follow the **traditional** ways of the Hindu religion.

Traditional Ways

According to Hindu custom, Mohandas's family picked a bride for him when they were both children. When they were 13, Mohandas and Kasturba were married. Then, also according to custom, they each went home to finish school. They would stay married for the rest of their lives.

When he was 19, Gandhi's family decided to send him to London to study law. Leaving India to study was unusual for members of the

merchant
(**mur**·chuhnt)—a person who buys and sells things

traditional
(truh·**dish**·uh·nuhl)—accepted; according to custom

merchant caste. The caste leader tried to stop him from going, but Gandhi stood up to him. Even when the caste leader threatened to throw Gandhi out of his caste, he chose to follow his family's wishes. His mother asked him to promise not to return to India until he had his law **degree**. She also made him promise to live up to his Hindu ideals by not eating meat or drinking alcohol. What would life outside India be like for a young Hindu?

Gandhi Leaves Home

In London, Gandhi felt lost and out of place. So he decided to make himself into an English gentleman. He took lessons in speaking, dancing, and playing the violin. This period of trying to "fit in" did not last long, however. He soon decided he was happier living a quiet, **solitary** life.

It took him a long time to find a restaurant where he could avoid eating meat. For a while he lived on oatmeal that he made in his room. Finally he found a place that served only vegetarian food. He made friends there and learned more about being a vegetarian. For the rest of his life, he ate only vegetables, fruits, and grains.

When he graduated from law school three years later, Gandhi returned to India and found work as a lawyer. At first, he was so shy that he would lose his voice when he opened his mouth. He wondered if he would ever be able to practice law. Then a company in South Africa offered him a job. He could work in their office and not have to speak in court. He accepted and again left India, this time with his wife. How would he manage in South Africa? Gandhi found out quickly.

Working for Civil Rights

Almost as soon as he got there, Gandhi met with racism. South Africa was part of the British Empire and was ruled by white people. Gandhi had dark skin. Because of his color, he was thrown out of a first-class train compartment even though he had a ticket! When he refused to give up his seat on a stagecoach, he was beaten. Gandhi was not used to being treated this way. This unfair treatment aroused his sense of right and wrong. He decided to use legal means to end racism.

 Strategy Alert!

Gandhi and staff at his law office in South Africa, 1905

degree (di·**gree**)—a title earned by a student who finishes a course of study

solitary (sol·i·ter·ee)— living or being alone

Stop and Ask ?

Does it make sense? See if I can explain important words.

Racism is an important term. It means "treating people differently because of their color or race."

petitions
(puh·**tish**·uhnz)—letters
signed by many people

Stop and Ask

Does it make sense?
See if I can explain
important words.

· · · · · · · · · · · · · · ·

Civil disobedience is
important here. It
means "refusing in a
nonviolent way to
obey unjust laws."
Gandhi told his
followers to do this.

Gandhi sent **petitions** to the South African government asking for better treatment for Indians. But he saw that the Indians in South Africa would have to organize politically to get better treatment. He became their leader. He left his job to be able to give more time to gaining justice in everyday life for the Indian people. He traveled to India to tell Indians there about the problems of Indians in South Africa. He also started a newspaper to keep Indians in South Africa informed.

Gandhi's commitment to work for social justice was growing stronger. By now, he and Kasturba had four sons. He was a caring father. But he began to feel that his duty to his people was more important than his duty to his family. He withdrew from family life in order to have more time for the cause of social justice.

Responding to Injustice

Gandhi had always been deeply religious. The Hindu belief in service to others without thought for self became his guiding principle. Gandhi told his followers that they must resist unfair laws. This was to be more than just passive resistance. People should refuse to obey unjust laws. But their refusal must be nonviolent, and they must always accept responsibility for their actions. If this meant going to prison, they must do so gladly. Gandhi called this way of responding to injustice *satyagraha* [suh·**tyah**·gruh·huh], which means "holding on to the truth." We know it as civil disobedience. Years later, another young man would admire Gandhi and study his ideas. Martin Luther King, Jr., the great leader of the Civil Rights movement in the United States, would preach civil disobedience and nonviolent action.

 *Strategy Alert!*

Gandhi was arrested for participating in illegal acts of *satyagraha*. He was given a sentence of hard labor. He was treated badly, both by his jailers and by other prisoners. He endured through faith and by observing all prison rules with good grace as long as they were not at odds with his religion. Once he was out of prison, he went back to work with new strength. His hard work finally met with success. South Africa passed a law granting more rights to Indian people. Gandhi's work in South Africa was finished. He returned to India in 1914.

**Gandhi and wife
Kasturba in 1922**

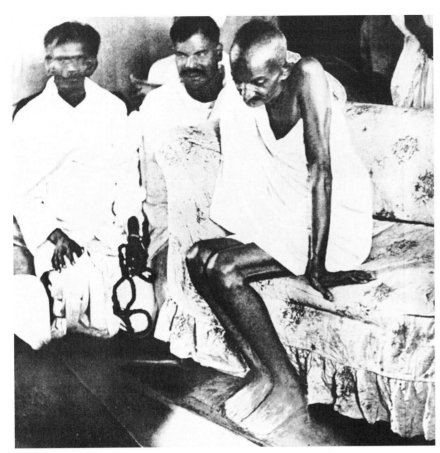

Gandhi meets with delegates of Unity Conference after ending a fast in 1924.

Bringing Civil Disobedience to India

Gandhi was no longer the shy young lawyer who had left years before. He was now a powerful political leader. Gandhi stayed out of the public eye for a while. He did, however, set up a place where he could teach the principles of *satyagraha*, or civil disobedience. More and more people came to learn from him.

In 1919, the government passed laws that called for harsh punishments for political violence. To protest, Gandhi called for people across India to close down businesses. When police came to arrest him, rioting broke out. The police killed hundreds of Indians. Hundreds more were arrested and punished under the new laws. Gandhi felt that things had gone too far. He called for an end to the protests. Then he began a fast to **atone** for what had happened. He would take neither food nor water for 72 hours. In the Hindu religion, fasting is a way to cleanse the mind of impure thoughts and feelings. In the future, Gandhi would undertake many more fasts. *Strategy Alert!*

atone (uh·**tohn**)— to make up for

Stop and Ask ?

Does it make sense? See if I can explain important words.

• • • • • • • • • •

Fast is an important term here. It means "to go without food, often for religious reasons." Gandhi fasted to atone for what had happened. It was part of the Hindu religion. That makes sense because he was Hindu.

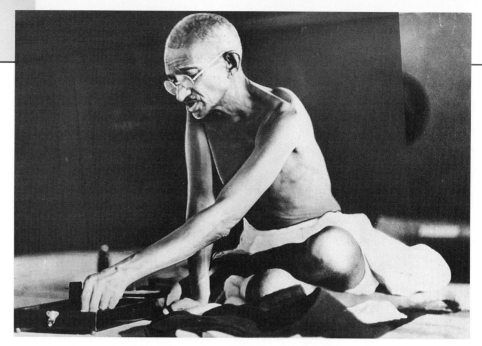

Gandhi gave up Western clothing and wore simple Hindu attire.

A Simple Life

The violence and the killings had been a bitter experience. Gandhi began calling for the Indian people to take back their country from the British. He began a new program. Under this program, each village would become independent through crafts and farming. Their independence would become the model for national independence. Gandhi decided to stop buying and using foreign-made goods. He gave up wearing European suits. He also started to spin his own thread to make cloth. Instead of suits, he wore a Hindu *dhoti* [**doh**·tee], a garment made of plain white cloth worn around the waist and hips.

Besides independence, two other issues troubled Gandhi. One was the caste system, which labeled some people as "untouchable." The untouchable caste did all the dirty work in India. People looked down on them and treated them badly. Gandhi felt that all people were children of God. He also felt that as long as one part of Indian society looked down on another, the society could not come together and succeed. He fasted often to show the strength of his beliefs.

The other issue that troubled him was the frequent violence in India between Hindus and Muslims, another large religious group. Some Muslims wanted to break away from India and form a new country. Although Gandhi, like most Indians, did not want to see India divided into more than one country, he realized that he must accept partition.  *Strategy Alert!*

People saw that Gandhi was **devoted** to helping them. They began to come around to his way of thinking. By the 1920s, people had begun to call Gandhi *Mahatma*, a title for someone wise and holy. People in India had come to love this good and gentle man who cared so deeply about his country.

Stop and Ask ?

Does it make sense? See if I can explain important words.

. . . .

Partition seems like an important term. Partition means "to divide into parts." That makes sense because it says they wanted to divide India up into more than one country.

devoted (di·**voh**·tid)— strongly loyal

Movement Toward Independence

The movement toward independence from Britain became stronger. Around 1930, a British law raised the price of salt. People were not allowed to dig salt themselves or to make it from seawater. This law made it very hard for the poor to get salt. And India's hot weather makes salt important for health. So Gandhi led people to the sea to get salt from saltwater. This act was illegal, and tens of thousands were arrested and put in prison. Finally, the British government agreed to relax the laws about salt-making.

Gandhi's popularity worried the British rulers. His presence seemed to encourage people to stand up to the government. The rulers tried putting him in prison, and things got worse. They made his political party illegal and shut down the newspapers. Many of Gandhi's followers wanted to take up armed protest. This was against everything Gandhi believed. Gandhi gave up membership in the group and focused again on helping villages become **self-sufficient**. But the movement toward Indian independence continued. *Strategy Alert!*

In 1939, World War II broke out. The Japanese were threatening India. Gandhi wanted immediate independence for Indians. That way they would be fighting for their own country, not Britain. Gandhi called for a mass protest, in which all Indians would demonstrate for independence. He and other leaders were arrested.

While he was in prison, the people demonstrated violently. The British rulers of India would not grant independence. They blamed Gandhi for the outbreak. From prison, he could do little to stop the violence. Finally, at the age of 73, he began another long fast. Gandhi was now an old man. His wife had died, and his earlier fasts had weakened his body. After three weeks without food, his health began to fail. Afraid that he would die in prison, the British released him.

Supporters of Mahatma Gandhi breaking salt laws by taking seawater

self-sufficient (self suh·**fish**·uhnt)—able to take care of all needs without outside help

Stop and Ask ❓

Does it make sense? See if I can explain important words.

· · · · · · · · · ·

Independence is an important term. It means "being free of another country's rule." The Indian people wanted independence from Britain.

Stop and Ask ❓

Does it make sense?
See if I can explain
important words.

・・・・・・・・・・

*Assassinated is an
important term. It
means "murdered a
well-known person."
Gandhi was certainly
well known.*

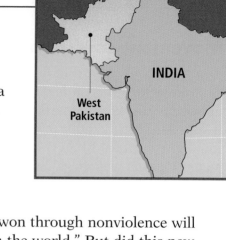

Independence at Last

In 1947, Britain granted India its independence. As part of the agreement, India was split into two countries. India would be the country for Hindus, and Pakistan would be the country for Muslims. Referring to India's new independence, Gandhi said, "The freedom of India means everything for us, but it also means much for the world. For freedom won through nonviolence will mean the **inauguration** of a new order in the world." But did this new-found freedom mean peace would follow?

Problems Persist

Although India was now free of British rule, the Indian people fought the partition plan that would divide the country. Fighting grew between the Hindus and Muslims. Gandhi undertook another fast, vowing not to eat or drink until all people agreed to make peace. Three days later, all the religious leaders agreed to stop fighting. Gandhi's fast ended.

Despite this coming together of Hindu, Muslim, and Christian leaders, the country did divide. This was a very difficult period for all Indians. It meant that millions were forced to leave their homes. Muslims went to Pakistan, Hindus to India. Gandhi felt that he had not done enough to keep the country from splitting. He continued to pray and live a simple life.

On January 30, 1948, while making his way to a platform where he would lead a prayer meeting, Gandhi was approached by a young Hindu. This man believed that Gandhi had **betrayed** India by accepting the division of the country. He walked up to the Mahatma, pulled out a gun, and assassinated him. Around the world, people mourned a great leader, who died as he had lived, in prayer and in hope of peace. ❓ *Strategy Alert!*

Thousands flocked to see
Mahatma Gandhi's ashes.

Gone But Not Forgotten

Today, more than half a century after his death, the world continues to remember Gandhi. Through example, he taught the importance of using nonviolence to bring about change. Scientist Albert Einstein spoke for all when he said of Mahatma Gandhi, "Generations to come, it may be, will scarce believe that such a one as this ever in flesh and blood walked upon this earth."

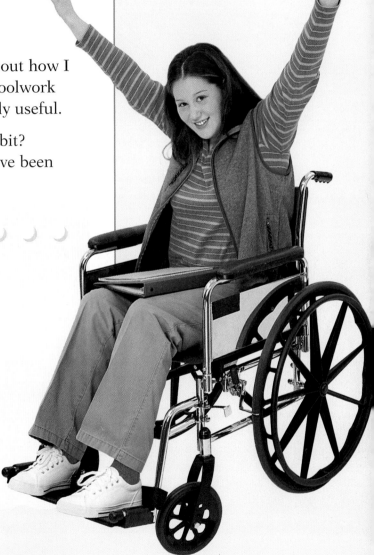

Congratulations! You finished reading. Now read the habit and strategy for **After I Read**. Then read my notes below.

After I Read

Which **HABIT** will I learn?
Use what I've read.
If I develop this habit, I will think about how I can apply what I just read to my schoolwork and my life. This makes reading really useful.

Which **STRATEGY** will I use to learn this habit?
Describe ways the selection could have been made better.

My Notes

• Strategy says to think about how the article could have been better.

• I have never heard of the caste system before. It sounds really interesting. The article would have been better if there had been more information about different castes.

Now it's time to practice the three habits and strategies you learned when you read "Mahatma Gandhi: Great Soul of India." Start with **Before I Read**. Look at the box below. It should look familiar! Reread the habit you will practice. Reread the strategy you will use—then do it!

Before I Read

Which **HABIT** will I practice?
Think about what I know about the subject.
If I develop this habit, I will bring to mind what I already know about the subject. This gets me ready to connect what I read to what I know so I will understand it better.

Which **STRATEGY** will I use to practice this habit?
Read the questions, introduction, and/or summary to decide what I know about this.

Use the **Before I Read Strategy Sheet** for "Albert Einstein: Man of the Century" (page 18 in your *Strategy Practice Book*) to decide what you know about the subject.

Albert Einstein

Man of the Century

$$E=MC^2$$

matter (**mat**•uhr)—what all things are made of

Albert and his sister Maja

Introduction

When Albert Einstein was five years old, his father showed him a compass. The boy thought about it for a long time, wondering what invisible force kept the needle pointing north. For the rest of his life, Einstein tried to figure out such hidden secrets of nature. The answers he found changed the way we understand the universe and everything in it.

What did Einstein discover about time, space, energy, and **matter**? What were the beginnings of this young man whose thinking had such a huge impact?

Reread the habit and strategy below. Look for the *Strategy Alerts!* as you continue to read.

While I Read

Which **HABIT** will I practice?
> **Stop and ask, "Does it make sense?"**
> If I develop this habit, I will stop now and then to make sure I understand what I'm reading.

Which **STRATEGY** will I use to practice this habit?
> See if I can explain important words.

Use the **While I Read Strategy Sheet** for "Albert Einstein: Man of the Century" (page 19 in your *Strategy Practice Book*) as you read.

Family Influences

Albert Einstein was born in Ulm, Germany, on March 14, 1879. His family was Jewish. Soon after his birth, the Einsteins moved to nearby Munich where Albert attended elementary school. Albert's father, Hermann, managed an electrical machinery firm. He encouraged Albert's interest in science and math. Albert's mother, Pauline, was an excellent pianist who gave her son a deep love of music. Albert began to play the violin at the age of six. In later years, he turned to the violin whenever his work became too much for him.

A Slow Learner?

Einstein's childhood was by no means a success story. Now Einstein is recognized as one of the most brilliant people who ever lived. As a young boy, however, Albert seemed slow to learn. When he was six he still could not speak well. Albert did not speak well until he was nine years old. Both his parents and his teachers were afraid that he was "backward." This did not prevent Einstein's uncle, Jakob, from bringing him science and math books. Jakob introduced him to algebra,* a branch of mathematics that uses both numbers and letters to solve problems. *Strategy Alert!*

Albert's family moved to Italy when he was 15 years old. Albert, however, stayed behind in Germany to finish school. As he grew older, Albert became an **unruly** student. He did not like the strict discipline of his

Stop and Ask ?

Does it make sense?
See if I can explain important words like *algebra*.

---

unruly (un·**roo**·lee)—hard to keep under control

secondary school, and he was always questioning what he was taught. His teachers felt he was a "**disruptive** influence in class." Albert was finally expelled from school at the age of 15. When asked what line of work the boy was best suited for, one of Einstein's teachers answered that it didn't matter—he would never make a success of anything.

disruptive (dis·**rup**·tiv)— causing trouble

At Home in Switzerland

After he left school, Albert joined his family in their new home in Italy. Although he did not stay there long, Albert enjoyed his time in Italy. He especially enjoyed the sense of freedom he felt there. And, in his opinion, Italy had the culture that was missing in Germany. Within a year, Albert moved to Switzerland and attended the Federal Institute of Technology (F.I.T.) in Zurich [**zoor**·ik]. Einstein liked Switzerland and its breathtaking views. The relaxed atmosphere of the F.I.T. also suited him. He spent many evenings playing violin with his friends. On a nearby lake, he discovered the joy of sailing.

At the institute, Albert met Mileva Maric, a brilliant mathematician. The two fell deeply in love, married, and had three children together. Later, Mileva helped her husband conduct important research.

Einstein with Mileva

The Young Physicist

Einstein always carried a pen and paper with him. He used them to jot down any ideas that came into his head. More and more, he thought about physics,* the study of matter and energy. In recent years, some scientists had noticed a number of things about the universe that did not seem to make sense. They could not understand how light travels, how planets move, and how matter is composed. Always curious and imaginative, Einstein wanted to find answers to these puzzles. *Strategy Alert!*

Stop and Ask ?

Does it make sense? See if I can explain important words like *physics*.

Professor Albert Einstein as a young man

Stop and Ask

Does it make sense? See if I can explain important words like *hypotheses*.

speed of light—the speed at which light from the sun travels

equation (i·**kway**·zhuhn)— a mathematical statement that shows that two things are equal

After graduating from the institute in 1900, Einstein worked first as a private math tutor and then as a clerk in the Swiss patent office. His job was to look at new inventions and describe how they worked. His scientific research, which he did in his free time, was very similar to his work in the patent office. Einstein studied the experiments of other scientists and tried to explain their findings. Many of the things he tried to explain, like the movement of light, were hard to see. Einstein had to imagine how they worked, and he made hypotheses.* Then, he and his wife used mathematics to see if those creative guesses made sense. Slowly, Einstein gained new and valuable insights. **?** *Strategy Alert!*

Three Significant Papers

It was not long before his work paid off. In 1905, at the age of 26, Einstein published a series of papers that changed the world. In one paper, Einstein proved that all matter is made up of tiny particles called atoms. He showed that atoms could combine to form molecules. He also explained how molecules can be counted and how their movement affects temperature. The study of atoms, molecules, and even smaller particles became a whole new branch of physics. This new knowledge would have important consequences for medicine and industry.

In another paper, Einstein argued that light travels in quanta, or small packets of energy. He used this theory to explain the photoelectric effect. The photoelectric effect deals with how metal reacts to light. This work later earned him the Nobel Prize. Among other results, his ideas made possible the invention of television and movies with sound.

Einstein is even more famous for another idea. His Special Theory of Relativity changed our understanding of space, light, motion, and time. According to this theory, the closer an object gets to moving at the **speed of light,** the more energy it takes to move the object. Einstein also used his theory to show that time passes more slowly for an object traveling at or near the speed of light. This proves that even time is relative. In other words, time does not pass at the same rate for all things.

The Special Theory of Relativity also relates matter to energy. Einstein proved that vast amounts of energy are stored in the tiniest bits of matter. He did not know it then, but this discovery would be used to make the world's first nuclear weapons. Einstein expressed many of his ideas in one simple **equation** about energy, mass, and the speed of light: $E = mc^2$.

Einstein's Circle Expands

Before 1905, most scientists had never heard of Albert Einstein. His publications quickly changed that. In honor of his work, he was awarded another degree from the F.I.T. He was also promoted at the patent office. By 1909, he was a full-time professor at Zurich University. However, the university could not keep him for long. With his wife and sons, Einstein moved first to Prague, then back to Zurich, and finally to Berlin. Here, he worked as Research Director of the new Kaiser Wilhelm Institute of Physics.

These were not **idle** years for Einstein. He spent a good deal of time making friends in the scientific community and soon knew most of the brightest scientists in Europe. He also began working on a new explanation of gravity.* This study of the force that pulls objects toward the earth took him 10 years to complete. ⑦ *Strategy Alert!*

World Events Interrupt

The future seemed bright for the Einstein family, but events soon took a turn for the worse. World War I began in 1914, and troops from all over Europe joined the fight. Many Europeans saw the war as a good thing. Einstein, however, feared mass **slaughter**.

Events soon confirmed his worst fears. Millions of young men died in the **trenches**. Einstein was also horrified by the poisonous gases that scientists invented to use in the war. Believing this was a misuse of science, Einstein urged his countrymen to end the war. He joined a political party that stood for peace. Einstein was fast becoming a political figure. But he had not forgotten his research.

idle (ied'l)—not busy

Stop and Ask

Does it make sense? See if I can explain important words like *gravity*.

slaughter (slaw·tuhr)— the killing of a large number of people, usually in battle

trenches (trench·iz)— long ditches used to protect soldiers

American troops caught in gas attack during World War I

"Light Caught Bending!"

In 1916, Einstein published his General Theory of Relativity. This theory has been called "the greatest single achievement of human thought." It is so complex that very few people can understand all of it. The theory explains how the stars and planets affect space and time. Einstein proposed the existence of **black holes,** the exact size of the universe, and the expanding nature of the universe. While none of these ideas have been proven, Einstein's theory is supported by much evidence. For example, the theory explains the exact orbit of Mercury, which no one could describe before.

Following World War I, in 1919, British scientists in Brazil and Africa observed a **total eclipse of the sun**. Their observations showed that light was bent by the mass of the sun. This proved one of the predictions of Einstein's relativity theory and made him famous around the world. Headlines everywhere read "Light caught bending!" People wanted to know more about relativity and the brilliant man who explained it.

black holes—small areas in the universe with powerful amounts of gravity

total eclipse (i·**klips**) **of the sun**—the complete blocking of the sun by the moon

Einstein (third from left) gathers with other Nobel Prize winners Sinclair Lewis, Frank Kellogg, and Irving Langmuir.

A World Figure

The next few years brought many changes. Einstein and Mileva were divorced in 1919, and Einstein remarried soon after. He spent much of his time giving talks around the world, and his wild white hair, worn coat, and baggy trousers made him an easily recognized figure. In 1922, he was awarded the **Nobel Prize** in Physics for his theory of quanta. Einstein gave all the money from this award to his former wife, Mileva Maric, who had helped her husband with his early research.

At about this time, Einstein became interested in Zionism. Zionists favored the creation of a Jewish state in Palestine. Einstein actively supported the cause and encouraged others to join him. In 1923, he officially opened the new Hebrew University in Jerusalem. Remembering the lessons of World War I, Einstein also spoke out in favor of world peace. He asked the people of the world to throw away their weapons, so that peace could be assured.

The Refugee

In the early 1930s, Adolf Hitler and his Nazi party came to power in Germany. Their actions would make Einstein think again about weapons and world peace. As a well-known Jew, Einstein had long been a target of prejudice against Jews. But Hitler's breed of anti-Semitism* was something new and terrible. In 1933, while Einstein was in California, Nazis broke into his home in Germany and took or destroyed everything they found. His books were burned, and his face appeared on the first page of a book of Nazi "enemies." Underneath, the caption read, "Not Yet Hanged." ❓ *Strategy Alert!*

Afraid of returning to Germany, Einstein became a **refugee**. He lived for a short while with his friends, the King and Queen of Belgium. As Hitler's power grew, it was clear that Einstein's friends could no longer protect him. Einstein moved to England and soon decided to leave Europe entirely.

At the end of 1933 Einstein moved to the United States where he was forced to make a choice. Although he believed in world peace, he was afraid of what might happen if Hitler ever got his hands on a powerful nuclear weapon like the atomic bomb. Einstein spoke with President Roosevelt about this possibility. This meeting led to the beginning of The Manhattan Project and to the creation of the atomic bomb.

Atomic bomb cloud over Nagasaki, Japan, 1945

Nobel Prize—one of six international prizes given every year for outstanding work

Stop and Ask ❓

Does it make sense? See if I can explain important words like *anti-Semitism*.

refugee (ref•yoo•**jee**)— a person who runs away, usually to another country, for protection

Later Years

In the United States, Einstein taught at Princeton University. In 1940, he became a U.S. citizen. He spent the rest of his life working on yet another theory, which he never completed. This brilliant thinker knew how to refresh himself with music and with time to daydream and **contemplate**. Whenever possible, he would spend an evening with his violin or an afternoon in a sailboat.

Einstein remained a pacifist* who used his fame to speak out for world peace. He was asked to be President of Israel in 1952, but refused. On April 18, 1955, Albert Einstein died at the age of 76. ⓦ *Strategy Alert!*

To many people, Albert Einstein was, and remains, "an artist of science." His theories were creative and new. In an interview, Einstein once said, "I am enough of an artist to draw freely upon my imagination. Imagination is more important than knowledge. Knowledge is limited. Imagination encircles the world."

contemplate
(**kon**·tuhm·playt)—to think about carefully

Stop and Ask ❓

Does it make sense? See if I can explain important words like *pacifist*.

Albert Einstein taking an oath of U.S. citizenship on October 1, 1940

> Now that you've finished reading, review the **After I Read** habit below. Think about what you read in "Albert Einstein: Man of the Century" as you practice the strategy.

After I Read

Which **HABIT** will I practice?
Use what I've read.
If I develop this habit, I will think about how I can apply what I just read to my schoolwork and my life. This makes reading really useful.

Which **STRATEGY** will I use to practice this habit?
Describe ways the selection could have been made better.

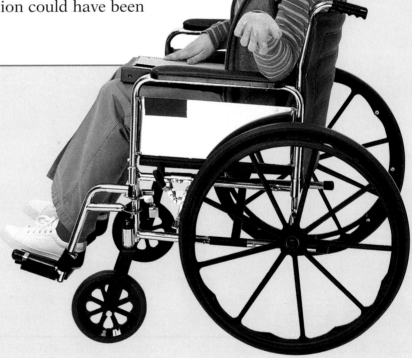

Use the **After I Read Strategy Sheet** for "Albert Einstein: Man of the Century" (page 20 in your *Strategy Practice Book*) to use what you've read.

Apply 3 of the 9 Habits

Now read "Rachel Carson: Environmental Pioneer" and apply these three habits and strategies.

Before I Read

Which **HABIT** will I apply?
Think about what I know about the subject.

Which **STRATEGY** will I use to apply this habit?
Read the questions, introduction, and/or summary to decide what I know about this.

While I Read

Which **HABIT** will I apply?
Stop and ask, "Does it make sense?"

Which **STRATEGY** will I use to apply this habit?
See if I can explain important words.

After I Read

Which **HABIT** will I apply?
Use what I've read.

Which **STRATEGY** will I use to apply this habit?
Describe ways the selection could have been made better.

 Use the **Self-Assessment Sheet** for "Rachel Carson: Environmental Pioneer" on pages 21–22 in your *Strategy Practice Book* as you read to see how well you can apply the habits and strategies.

Rachel Carson
ENVIRONMENTAL PIONEER

Introduction

You probably know that the air we breathe, the water we drink, and the land where we grow our vegetables are all affected by pollutants. But do you know that we have not always understood the link between the environment and the substances that people leave in the air, water, and land? Rachel Carson understood that our environment is a fragile place, and that its delicate balance can be upset by harmful pollutants. She wrote an important book that changed the way people think about the environment. As a result of her work, the government made many changes that protect animals, plants, and people from harmful chemicals.

How did Carson's childhood affect her lifelong interest in nature? Why were Carson's contributions important? Why did her work attract enemies? How is Carson's work important today?

Some harmful chemicals commonly used in the 1950s

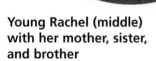

A Childhood Surrounded by Nature

Rachel Carson was born in 1907 in Springdale, Pennsylvania, near Pittsburgh. She was the youngest of three children. The Carsons owned a large piece of land with woods and fields. It was a wonderful place for a child with a rich imagination. While Rachel's older brother and sister were at school, Rachel had her mother's full attention. Together they listened to bird songs and watched butterflies. The Carsons had a cow, chickens, and pigs. Rachel got to know all of the creatures around her, both wild and tame. Rachel liked school, but she was often absent. Her mother worried that Rachel would get sick. If other children were sick, Rachel's mother kept Rachel home. Maria Carson had been a teacher, and she helped Rachel with her lessons at home. Rachel loved reading. Soon she began to write her own stories and poems. When she was ten, she began sending stories to *St. Nicholas*, a magazine that published children's writing. In September 1918, she opened the magazine to find one of her stories. Later that month, she received payment— a check for ten dollars. Rachel submitted more stories to *St. Nicholas*, and in the next year, two more were published. She was determined to become a writer.

Young Rachel (middle) with her mother, sister, and brother

Rachel with her dog

Rachel's childhood home

A Serious Student

In high school, Rachel was quiet and serious. She worked hard at her studies. Because she lived far from the center of town, she went out less than most of her classmates. However, she did have good friends. With them she shared her interests in books, music, and the outdoors. When she had free time, Rachel loved to go into the woods. There she would find flowers, birds, animal tracks, and signs of the changing seasons.

After high school, Rachel went to Pennsylvania College for Women, now Chatham College, in Pittsburgh. The college had only about 300 students. It was close to her home, and it had high academic standards. Best of all, it offered **scholarships**. Rachel's family had enough money to live comfortably, but not enough for college, so she needed financial help. She was able to get a scholarship, and the school also gave her loans.

Rachel discovered her love of science as a college student.

scholarships (**skol**·uhr·ships)— financial aid awarded by a school

annual (**an**·yoo·uhl)— yearly

Discovering Her Love of Biology

At college, Rachel studied hard. She had to get good grades to keep her scholarship, and she had no money to waste. She wrote for the school's literary magazine. The story she submitted at the end of her sophomore year won the **annual** prize. Rachel was delighted. She was on her way to becoming a writer. Then, in her junior year, she took a biology course. She liked it so much that she changed her major from literature to biology. Although she still loved writing, she loved science more.

Rachel graduated with high honors. She still owed the college money, which she knew she would have to pay back. But first, the college had arranged for her to take a summer course at the Marine Biology Laboratory at Woods Hole, Massachusetts. She would finally get to see the ocean, the home of many of the creatures she had been studying. For the fall, she had a scholarship to Johns Hopkins University. She would be a graduate student in zoology, the study of animal life.

Carson at Woods Hole in 1929

Rachel Carson began her graduate work at Johns Hopkins in 1929.

brochures
(broh•**shoorz**)—small pamphlets or booklets

A Career in Marine Biology

Rachel Carson loved her summer at Woods Hole. She decided on a career in marine biology, the study of sea life. In the fall of 1929, she went to Johns Hopkins. She had just started school when the United States plunged into The Great Depression—a period in which many people were out of work. Carson managed to get a job as a teaching assistant for the summer. The next year, she was hired as a lab assistant. With the money that she earned from these jobs, she could meet her daily needs. But she didn't make enough money to pay her college debts. She took a second job, as a teaching assistant at the University of Maryland. While working two jobs, she completed the work for her Master's degree.

Working for the U.S. Government

In 1935, Carson's father died. Now responsible for her mother as well as herself, Carson needed a full-time job. The Bureau of Fisheries was looking for a scientist who could write scripts about marine biology for radio broadcasts. They had to be written so that people with no background in science could understand them. Carson knew that she was perfect for the job. She soon proved she was. When she finished that job, the bureau found other work for her. Then Carson heard that an exam would be given for a full-time job at the bureau. When she took the test, she got the highest score of all those taking it. In 1936 she became a full-time employee of the U.S. government, writing **brochures** and answering letters. One of the pieces she wrote was so good that her boss told her to send it to a magazine. Carson didn't take him seriously. She put the article aside. She did, however, add to her income by selling articles to a local newspaper.

Carson (right) with colleagues at the Fish and Wildlife Service office

Finding a Wider Audience

When her sister died, Carson asked her two young nieces to live with her. Now Carson needed more **income**. She dug out the article that she had put away the year before and sent it to the *Atlantic Monthly* magazine. It was accepted. The money was welcome, and Carson now had a national audience. Her boss suggested that she expand the article into a book, and Carson decided to try. She wrote after work and on weekends. Her first book, *Under the Sea-Wind*, was published in late 1941. Although it received good reviews, *Under the Sea-Wind* did not sell well.

At work, Carson won steady **promotions**. Eventually, she became editor-in-chief of the Information Division of the Fish and Wildlife Service. In those days, women rarely rose to become the head of a department.

Carson decided to write another book about the sea. She called it *The Sea Around Us*. This book was a huge success even before it was published. Magazines, including *The Reader's Digest*, paid to reprint parts of it. *The Sea Around Us* was published in 1951. It was an instant best-seller. Carson succeeded because her writing was clear and could be easily understood by people without a science background. *The Sea Around Us* remained on the Best-Seller list for 81 weeks. Rachel Carson was suddenly one of the most famous women in America.

Carson at her typewriter

income (**in**·kum)— money received in return for work or services

promotions (pruh·**moh**·shuhnz)— advancements at work

Becoming a Full-time Writer

Carson no longer needed her government job, so she **resigned** to become a full-time author. She wrote *The Edge of the Sea*, published in 1955. It, too, was successful. She was able to buy a home in Maine near the sea. She also built a new home in Maryland. But she faced difficulties, too. Her mother was old and frail. Her niece died, leaving her young son Roger. When she was 48 years old, Carson legally adopted Roger.

resigned (ri·**ziend**)—quit

Rachel Carson checking specimens for *The Edge of the Sea*, early 1950s

horrified (**hor**·uh·fied)—
shocked; terribly upset

But Rachel Carson had not yet done her most important work. In 1958, she received a letter from a friend in Massachusetts. Her friend, Olga Huckins, described how a plane had flown overhead, spraying for mosquitoes. Within a few hours, birds began dying. Huckins found seven dead birds. The next day, there were three more, and three more the day after that. Olga Huckins was **horrified** by what had happened. Carson had planned to write another book about the sea, but she decided, instead, to write about the environment.

Chemicals That Kill

The planes that Olga Huckins had seen flying over her property were spraying the chemical DDT. DDT is a pesticide, used to kill crop-destroying insects. When used as a powder on people, it killed body lice that could spread illness. DDT killed mosquitoes that carried malaria and typhoid fever, two deadly diseases. The makers of DDT and other pesticides advertised them as "Bad News for Bugs." People rushed to buy them for their homes and gardens. They were widely used around the world.

As a scientist, Rachel Carson knew that DDT and other pesticides were also dangerous. When rain carried them into lakes and rivers, fish died by the thousands. These pesticides killed not only harmful insects, but also good ones. These chemicals also killed the birds that ate the insects, as well as other small animals. Birds that survived often laid eggs that would not hatch, or hatched baby birds that could not live.

There were dangers to people, too. They ate vegetables and fruits that had been sprayed with pesticides. Even meat was not safe. Cattle ate grass containing pesticides. Chicken ate grains. Fish **absorbed** the pesticides from the water. When people ate foods sprayed with pesticides, the pesticides entered their bodies. People who were exposed to large amounts of these **toxic** chemicals could suffer damage to their nerves or to body organs. They might even die.

Mother sprays DDT over crib in the 1950s.

absorbed (uhb·**zorbd**)— took in and made part of themselves

toxic (**tok**·sik)— poisonous

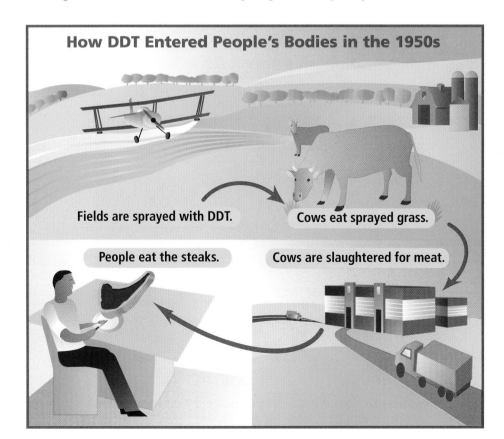

How DDT Entered People's Bodies in the 1950s

Fields are sprayed with DDT.

Cows eat sprayed grass.

People eat the steaks.

Cows are slaughtered for meat.

Carson's Important Work

When Rachel Carson sat down to write her book, she knew it would be the most important thing she had ever written. Ecology, the balance of nature, was not her main field. In addition, Carson knew that this book would attract enemies—the chemical companies and even the United States government, which recommended pesticides. Her facts had to be perfect. She did endless research. She wrote and rewrote.

It took Carson more than three years to write the book. She had to stop several times. Her mother died. Her adopted son, Roger, needed her attention. Then she developed breast cancer. She had surgery, but continued her work. Finally, in 1962, her book *Silent Spring* was published. It quickly became a best-seller.

Mixed Reactions—Great Impact

Despite the book's success, Carson found herself with a fight on her hands. People attacked her for trying to stop progress, for being a troublemaker and a **sentimental** bird-lover. The chemical companies were especially vicious, but she was ready for them. She had checked and double-checked every fact. Her publisher backed her up. The earth was in danger from the chemicals that were polluting its soil, its water, and its air.

Carson was invited to give numerous speeches and interviews. She received thousands of letters. President John F. Kennedy ordered a committee to explore the questions that Carson had raised in *Silent Spring*. On May 15, 1963, the President's Science Advisory Committee released its report. It supported Carson's views. By the time she appeared as a star witness before the Senate committee examining the use of pesticides, her ideas were being accepted.

Rachel Carson testifies to Kennedy's Science Advisory Committee, 1963.

sentimental
(sen·tuh·**men**·tl)—overly emotional

While she fought for her ideas, Carson also fought cancer. The disease had returned. Rachel Carson died of cancer within a year. She had not lived a long life. But with *Silent Spring*, she had changed our understanding of the environment. Because of Carson's work, the government more closely **regulates** pesticides today. Many of the birds that were threatened by the use of DDT have increased in number and are now producing healthy eggs and chicks. There is still a danger from pesticide pollution, but we no longer live under the threat of a silent spring.

regulates
(**reg**·yuh·layts)—controls according to a rule

Summary

Rachel Carson devoted her life to understanding the natural world. She began her career as a marine biologist. She wrote several books about the sea. In 1958, Carson received an important letter from a friend. Her friend described finding dead birds just hours after an airplane had sprayed DDT, a chemical used to kill insects. Carson decided to dedicate herself to studying the environment and the dangers of pesticides. What she found caused a huge change in the way we understand our environment. Because of Carson's discoveries, we now treat our air, land, and water with greater respect.

Rachel Carson, seated in the middle, at Cobb Island, VA, 1946

Put Your Habits to Work in

| Literature | Social Studies | Science | Math |

Before I Read Habit:
Think about what I know about the subject.

Remember to read the questions, introduction, and/or summary to decide what you know about the subject **before** you read a chapter in your science textbook.

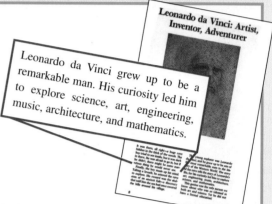

Leonardo da Vinci: Artist, Inventor, Adventurer

Leonardo da Vinci grew up to be a remarkable man. His curiosity led him to explore science, art, engineering, music, architecture, and mathematics.

While I Read Habit:
Stop and ask, "Does it make sense?"

Don't read a whole chapter in your science textbook straight through! Stop and ask yourself if what you're reading makes sense. One way to find out if it makes sense is to try to explain important words to yourself.

Leonardo da Vinci: Artist, Inventor, Adventurer

architecture

After I Read Habit:
Use what I've read.

Remember, you're not finished reading the chapter in your science textbook until you use what you've read. You can do that by describing ways the chapter could have been made better.

A diagram would have helped.

You may wish to use the **Put Your Habits to Work Sheet** (page 23 in your *Strategy Practice Book*) to practice these habits in your other reading.

Unit 4
Myths of the World
Theme: Classics

In this unit, you will develop these 3 habits for all readers.

Before I Read Habit:
Think about what I know about the subject.

While I Read Habit:
Stop and ask, "If it doesn't make sense, what can I do?"

After I Read Habit:
Check to see what I remember.

Learn 3 of the 9 Habits

In this unit, you will develop three strategies—one for before you read, one for while you are reading, and one for after you finish reading. Start with **Before I Read**. Read the habit and strategy. Then read my notes below.

Before I Read

Which **HABIT** will I learn?
Think about what I know about the subject.
If I develop this habit, I will bring to mind what I already know about the subject. This gets me ready to connect what I read to what I know so I will understand it better.

Which **STRATEGY** will I use to learn this habit?
Identify the genre and decide what I know about this genre.

My Notes

- Strategy says to identify the genre and decide what I know about this genre.

- Genre is a kind of writing like a story, poem, or play. From the title and pictures, I think that this story is a myth.

- A myth is an ancient story. It usually tries to explain something. Myths also tell about things that can't happen in real life.

RAINBOW SNAKE
An Australian Myth

Retold by Geraldine McCaughrean

AUSTRALIA

In dreamtime, our ancestors walked the Song Lines of the Earth, and thought about us, though we did not even exist. The Earth they walked was a brown flatness, its only features a few humpy huts built to keep off the sun, the dark, monsters and falling stars. Little tribes of people talked together in their own languages, and sometimes got up and danced their own magic dances. But even magic in those days was brown, drab and unremarkable, for there were no colors to **conjure** with.

The only colors shone in the sky. Sometimes, after a storm, as rain gave way to sun, a **distillation** of colors hung in the air, spanning Australia: the Rainbow. And that rainbow, like the people below it, dreamed, thought and had longings in its heart. "I will go down," it thought, "and find a tribe of people who think as I think, and dance as I dance, and we shall enjoy each other's company."

So the Rainbow drank all its own magic, and writhed into life. Whereas before it had been made only of falling rain and sunlight, each raindrop turned into a scale and each **glimmer** into a sinew of muscle. In short, it transformed itself into a snake. Twisting and flexing, its body a blaze of color, it snaked its way down the sky to the edge of the Earth. Its jaws were red, its tail violet, and in between, its overlapping scales passed through every other shade.

conjure (**kon**·juhr)— to make a spell

distillation (dis·tuh·**lay**·shuhn)— the process of turning a liquid into a vapor

glimmer (**glim**·uhr)— a small amount of light

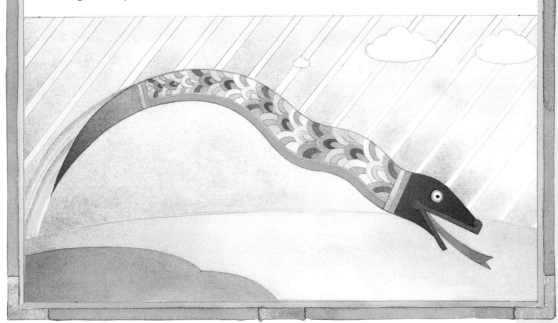

Now read the habit and strategy for **While I Read**. When you see ❓, read my notes in the margin.

While I Read

Which **HABIT** will I learn?

Stop and ask, "If it doesn't make sense, what can I do?"

If I develop this habit, I will stop and figure out what to do so what I'm reading makes sense. Then I can keep reading and not be lost.

Which **STRATEGY** will I use to learn this habit?

Use context clues to help me understand words.

But the Rainbow Snake was massively heavy. As it slithered along, it carved a trench through the featureless countryside, and threw aside mounds of mud. Because it was so huge, the trenches were valleys, and the mounds mountains. The next rain which fell was channeled into rivers, and puddling pools, so that already the world was altered by the presence of the Snake.

Rainbow Snake traveled from the Bamaga Point southward through the bush, and every now and then raised its scarlet head and tasted the air with its flickering tongue. It listened too, with its lobeless ears. Sometimes it heard voices, but did not understand them. Sometimes it heard music, but the music moved it neither to tears nor laughter. "These are not my kind of people," it thought, and went on southward, always south.

Then one day, it found a happy, laughing people whose language it partly understood and whose music made it sway—rear and sway, sway and dance—to the rhythm of the **didgeridoo**.

didgeridoo
(**di**·juh·ree·doo)—
a large bamboo or wooden trumpet

rapture (rap·chuhr)—
a state of great emotion

Stop and Ask

If it doesn't make sense, what can I do? Use context clues to help me understand words.

I don't understand faltered. But it says the dancers "froze." So faltered must mean "slowed" or "stopped."

The dancing faltered. The dancers froze. The music died away. For towering high above them, jaws agape, the people saw a gigantic snake with scales of every color in the rainbow. Its eyes closed in **rapture,** it swayed its sinuous body in time to the music. *Strategy Alert!*

When the music fell silent, it opened its gigantic eyes and looked down at them. Mothers drew their children close. Warriors fingered their spears. The Snake opened its mouth . . .

"I am Rainbow Snake, and you are my kin, for you speak the same language I think in, and make the music I have heard in my dreams."

An elder of the tribe, still balanced on one foot in mid-dance, looked up from under his hand. His bright teeth shone as his face broke into a smile. "In that case, you're welcome, friend! Lay yourself down and rest, or lift yourself up and dance—but don't let's waste another moment's fun!" The people gave a great shout of welcome, and went back to feasting.

Next day, Rainbow Snake coiled itself around the village, and sheltered it from the wind. Its flanks shaped the land during daylight hours, and in the evening it ate and drank and talked with the villagers. It was a happy time. Even afterward, it was remembered as a happy time. *Strategy Alert!*

After all its travels, the Snake knew more dances than the people did, and from its place in the sky, it had seen more wonders. It taught them all it knew, and in honor of Rainbow Snake, the people decorated their bodies with feathers and patterned their skin, as the snake was patterned (though in plain, stark white).

Then it happened, the terrible mistake.

Dozing one night, mouth wide open, Rainbow Snake felt the pleasant tickle of rain trickling down its back and splashing in its nostrils. The patter of something sweet on its rolled tongue it mistook for rain, and closed its mouth and swallowed. Too late, it realized that the shapes in its mouth were solid.

Stop and Ask

If it doesn't make sense, what can I do? Use context clues to help me understand words.

What does coiled mean? It says the snake "coiled itself around the village" and "sheltered it." It must have wrapped itself around the village.

foregoing
(for·**goh**·ing)—
giving up

shale (shayl)—
a claylike rock that is
easily broken

escarpments
(i·**skahrp**·muhnts)—
steep slopes or cliffs

Stop and Ask

If it doesn't make
sense, what can I do?
Use context clues to
help me understand
words.

. . . .

What does
treacherous mean?
It says "Boulders
tumbled." That
would be dangerous!
Treacherous must
mean "dangerous."

Two boys, looking for shelter from the rain, had mistaken the Snake's huge mouth for a cave and crept inside. Now they were deep in its coiling stomach, and the Snake could not fetch them back. What to do?

Keep silent and hope the boys were not missed? No. The tribe were certain to notice, and would guess what had become of the lost boys. Admit to eating them, and listen to the mothers weep and reproach it? No. Better to slip away noiselessly, **foregoing** old friends and seeking out new ones.

Away it went, slithering silently, slowly and sleepily away over the wet ground, colorless in the starlight. It wrapped itself around Bora-bunara Mountain and slept.

Waking to find Rainbow Snake gone and the two boys lost, the tribe did indeed guess what had happened. They did not shrug their shoulders and they did not sit down and weep. Instead, they grabbed their spears and hollered, *"Murder!"* Then they followed the Snake's tracks, plain to see in the wet earth. They sped along the valley carved by its leaving, and had no difficulty in finding its resting place on the peak of Bora-bunara.

The Snake's dreams were pleasant and deep. Its stomach was full, and its contented snores rolled like thunder down every side of the mountain. Boulders tumbled, and **shale** cascaded, making a climb treacherous. But three brothers clambered nimbly up the rocky **escarpments,** knives clenched in their teeth. They slit open the side of Rainbow Snake; scales fell in a rain of indigo, green and blue. They opened the wound and shouted inside to the boys . . . ⓐ *Strategy Alert!*

But the great magic of which the Snake was made had partly digested the children. Out past the rescuers fluttered—not boys, but two brightly colored birds. Their plumage was indigo, green and blue. Soaring high in the sky, they circled the mountain twice, then flew off, singing joyfully in the language of the birds.

The three brothers looked at one another and shrugged. Why grieve for boys who have been turned into birds? Their story has ended happily, after all. Only when they turned to make their descent did they see their friends and neighbors at the bottom of the mountain, jumping, gesticulating and pointing up at the Snake. *Strategy Alert!*

The Snake had opened its eyes.

Feeling a pain in its side like a stitch, the Rainbow Snake experienced a sudden drafty coldness in its stomach. It felt, too, a leaking away of its magic, like blood. And worst of all, it felt *betrayed*. *Strategy Alert!*

"I knew my little mistake might end our friendship," it hissed, "but I never realized it would stir you up to such **insolence**! Attack the Rainbow Spirit? Cut open your **benefactor**? Shed the scales of a Sky Creature? I'm hungrier now than I was before. And how do you think I shall satisfy that hunger, eh? I know! *I'LL EAT YOU, EVERY ONE!*"

The tongue that darted from its mouth was forked lightning. Its tail drummed up thunder. It crushed the mountain like bread into bread crumbs, and thrashed the **outback** inside out and back to front.

Stop and Ask

If it doesn't make sense, what can I do? Use context clues to help me understand words.

I don't understand gesticulating. It says the people were jumping and pointing. So gesticulating must mean "waving around."

insolence (in·suh·lens)— rudeness

benefactor (ben·uh·fak·tuhr)— one who does good for someone else

Stop and Ask

If it doesn't make sense, what can I do? Use context clues to help me understand words.

What does betrayed mean? The snake felt bad. The people had hurt it. Betrayed must mean something like "hurt" or "let down."

outback (owt·bak)— remote, rural part of Australia

Stop and Ask

If it doesn't make
sense, what can I do?
Use context clues to
help me understand
words.

· · · · · · · · · · ·

*What does rampage
mean? The snake
was out of control. I
think that rampage
must mean "wild
and crazy behavior."*

miasma (mie·**az**·muh)—
a vapor

In their terror, some people froze, some ran. Some even escaped. Some wanted so much to get away that they ran on all fours and wore down their legs to the thinness of **jumbuck**. Some leapt so far and so high that they turned into kangaroos. Some, in hiding under rocks, became tortoises and turtles. Others, who stood stock-still with fright, put down roots and turned into trees; others climbed them and turned into koalas with big frightened eyes. Some leapt off Bora-bunara and flew away as birds. And some burrowed deep and became **platypuses**.

To escape the rampage of venomous Rainbow Snake, they became anything and everything, transforming the landscape almost as much as the angry serpent was doing with its lashing tail. ❓ *Strategy Alert!*

At last Rainbow Snake exhausted itself and, leaving behind a trail of destruction, hurled itself headlong into the sea. Through the half-circle of the setting sun it slithered, like an eel swallowed down the world's throat.

And next morning, it was back in place again, as though it had never left: the Rainbow, spanning the sky like a breath of peace; a **miasma** of rain and sunlight, a trick of the light. A reminder of stormy nights.

But when the airy Rainbow Spirit looked down on the Earth below, the landscape it saw was transformed. So too were the lives of our ancestors, for some were animals and some were plants, and those who were still men and women were wiser men and women by far.

Now read the habit and strategy for **After I Read**. Then read my notes below.

After I Read

Which **HABIT** will I learn?
Check to see what I remember.
If I develop this habit, I will check to see what I remember as soon as I finish reading. It helps me see if I really understood what I read and helps me remember it better, too.

Which **STRATEGY** will I use to learn this habit?
Decide why the story ended the way it did.

My Notes

- Strategy says I should tell why the story ended the way it did.

- In the end, the Rainbow Snake was back in the sky. Most of the people became other things, like animals and plants.

- I noticed that the story ended the way it began.

- The story also showed how the world came to be the way it is. Myths often try to explain things like that.

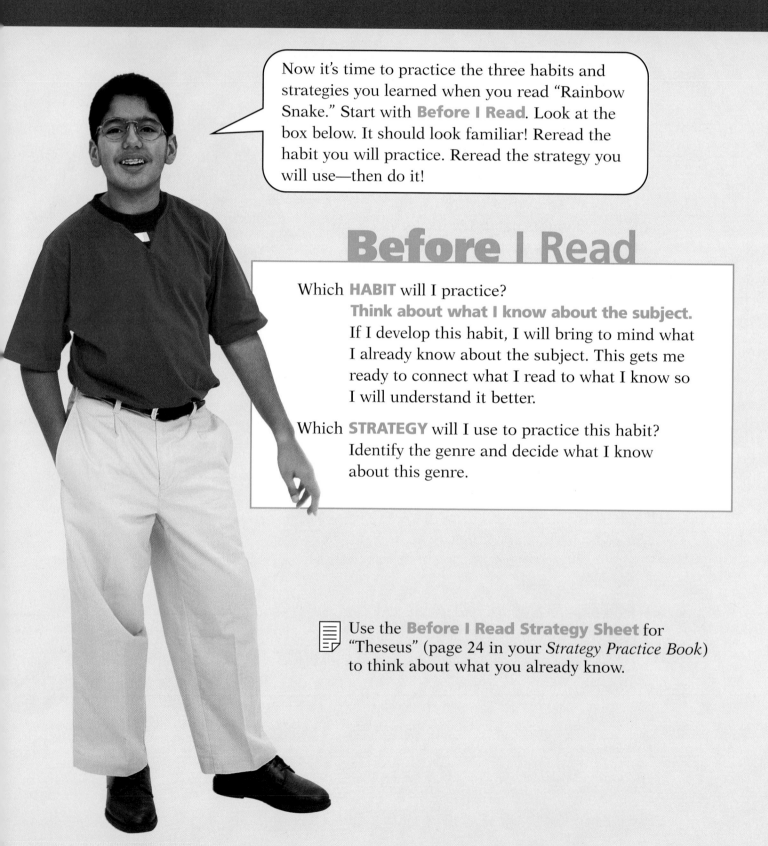

Now it's time to practice the three habits and strategies you learned when you read "Rainbow Snake." Start with **Before I Read**. Look at the box below. It should look familiar! Reread the habit you will practice. Reread the strategy you will use—then do it!

Before I Read

Which **HABIT** will I practice?
   Think about what I know about the subject.
   If I develop this habit, I will bring to mind what I already know about the subject. This gets me ready to connect what I read to what I know so I will understand it better.

Which **STRATEGY** will I use to practice this habit?
   Identify the genre and decide what I know about this genre.

Use the **Before I Read Strategy Sheet** for "Theseus" (page 24 in your *Strategy Practice Book*) to think about what you already know.

THESEUS
Hero of Athens

Many, many years ago there was a brave hero named Theseus [**thee**·see·uhs]. His feats were so many that people used to say, "Nothing happens without Theseus."

His life began far from the places where he earned his fame. He was raised in the kingdom of Troezen [**tree**·zuhn] by his mother, Aethra [**ee**·thruh], who was the daughter of the Troezen king. Theseus' father was King Aegeus [**ee**·jee·uhs] of Athens. He had returned to his own kingdom after Theseus' birth. Before he left, Aegeus had placed his sword and a pair of sandals under a heavy rock.

"Aethra," Aegeus said, "the world holds many rewards for those prepared to seek them out and fight for them. When the time comes for our son to seek his fortune, bring him here. Let him try to move this mighty stone. If he is strong enough, let him take the things he finds. They will help him make his way to me in Athens."

The time came for Aethra to test the strength of her son. She brought him to the great rock. Would he be able to move it? He crouched low to grasp the stone in his powerful arms. Aethra was amazed to see him easily lift the stone and roll it aside. To his great wonder, Theseus found a fine pair of sandals and a sword with a gold hilt* that fit his hand. His mother told him that the shoes and the sword with the golden handle belonged to his father. Theseus was now ready to meet him! *Strategy Alert!*

Stop and Ask

If it doesn't make sense, what can I do? Use context clues to help me understand words like *hilt*.

Did you see that *Strategy Alert!* on the last page? Did you remember to use context clues to help you understand the word *hilt*? Review the **While I Read** habit and strategy below and continue.

While I Read

Which **HABIT** will I practice?

Stop and ask, "If it doesn't make sense, what can I do?"
If I develop this habit, I will stop and figure out what to do so what I'm reading makes sense. Then I can keep reading and not be lost.

Which **STRATEGY** will I use to practice this habit?
Use context clues to help me understand words.

Use the **While I Read Strategy Sheet** for "Theseus" (page 25 in your *Strategy Practice Book*) as you read.

Stop and Ask

If it doesn't make sense, what can I do? Use context clues to help me understand words like *vowed*.

---

barbaric (bahr·**bar**·ik)— beastly, wild, cruel

Aethra feared for her son's life on his journey. "I beg you, my dear son, to travel by boat. Robbers and cutthroats are known to endanger the roads to Athens." But Theseus was not afraid. For him, going by sea would be running away from danger. He wanted to fight all evildoers and make the roads safe. Wearing the sandals and carrying the sword, he felt ready for anything! He said good-bye to his mother and vowed* to make her proud. He would not break his promise. *Strategy Alert!*

Theseus' journey to Athens was full of adventures. The robbers he met were **barbaric**. The first robber was Pityocamptes [pit·ee·oh·**kamp**·teez], who liked to strap travelers between two bent-over pine trees. He would cut the trees loose, tearing his victims in two. Theseus fought this cruel man and killed him with his sword. Next, Theseus met Sciron [**sie**·ron], who would kick people into the sea where they were eaten by a huge turtle. Theseus fought Sciron and hurled him over a cliff to his death. Then Theseus defeated Cercyon [**sur**·see·uhn]. This robber had forced travelers to wrestle with him until they were dead. Theseus' final stop before Athens gave him one of his greatest challenges. It was at this time that he met Procrustes [proh·**krus**·teez], who liked to tie people to a bed. If people were too short for the bed, Procrustes would stretch them. If people were too tall, he would chop off their legs! When Procrustes tried to tie Theseus to the bed, Theseus killed him with his sword.

By the time Theseus reached Aegeus' court in Athens, he was known as a great hero. But only Medea [mi•**dee**•uh], Aegeus' new wife, knew that he was also the true prince of Athens. Her magic powers revealed the truth about Theseus to her, but she kept silent.

"I cannot allow Aegeus to learn that this brave young man is his son," Medea thought. "He will make him king instead of my own son." So Medea told the king that Theseus was planning to kill him and steal the throne.

At a banquet, Medea and Aegeus put poison in Theseus' cup. As Theseus was about to take a sip, Aegeus saw his sandals and sword. He had left those things under the rock for his son! He knocked the cup from Theseus' hands and **embraced** him.

embraced
(em•**braysd**)—hugged

"Theseus, beloved son of Aethra! You are the joy of my life!" he exclaimed. "How could I not have recognized you! May the gods be praised that you are here with me now. And a curse upon the evil forces that would have me destroy you!"

reunion
(ree·**yoon**·yuhn)—
a gathering of people
who had been separated

Stop and Ask

If it doesn't make
sense, what can I do?
Use context clues to
help me understand
words like *avenge*.

sacrifice (**sak**·ruh·fies)—
an offering

Aegeus punished Medea and her son by sending them far away. That night Theseus and his father celebrated their **reunion** with a great feast.

Despite their joy, all was not well in Athens. Aegeus told his son this story to explain his terrible problem:

King Minos [**mie**·nuhs] of Crete had conquered Athens to avenge* the death of his son, who had died in the Athenian athletic games. This king demanded a terrible price to further punish the people of Athens. Minos possessed a horrible monster called the Minotaur [**min**·uh·tor]. It was half man and half bull. The monster needed to eat seven young men and seven young women every nine years. Minos kept it locked up in the center of a maze built by the great craftsman Daedalus [**ded**·l·uhs]. This maze had so many twists and turns that no one could find the way out. ⑦ *Strategy Alert!*

At this point in the story, Aegeus' voice began to tremble. With a shaking voice, he told Theseus that the 14 victims must come from Athens. "To my great sorrow, I have twice sent youths to Crete to feed the horrible Minotaur, and now it is time for the third **sacrifice**."

Theseus begged his father to let him be one of the youths sent to feed the Minotaur. Aegeus refused at first, but Theseus was able to change his mind.

"Great king, I have come so far and destroyed many enemies to feel the joy of being with you!" Theseus exclaimed. "But I see a great sadness in the people of Athens. Let me go and destroy this Minotaur so your people may feel the joy of freedom once again."

A few days later, the people of Athens came together to say good-bye to Theseus and the other youths. Before the ship left, Aegeus and Theseus made a plan. Usually the ship carrying the unlucky youths came back to Athens with a black sail. This meant that all 14 youths had been killed. Theseus' ship would also carry white sails. If Theseus and the others survived, they would raise the white sails.

When the ship reached Crete, the youths were paraded before the king. Ariadne [ar·ee·**ad**·nee], the daughter of King Minos, was in the crowd watching with other spectators.* She fell in love with Theseus the moment she saw him. Theseus had bravely hidden his sword in his cloak, but the guards found it and grabbed it from him. Ariadne froze when they said, "For this foolishness, you will be the first to be eaten." *Strategy Alert!*

Stop and Ask ?

If it doesn't make sense, what can I do? Use context clues to help me understand words like *spectators*.

The youths were taken to the dungeon deep within the castle. That night, Ariadne sneaked into the dungeon and found Theseus' dark cell. She unlocked the door and stepped into the room. Theseus was instantly charmed by the beautiful young princess. She told him of her love and said she would help him escape.

"But I cannot run away and leave my friends to be eaten," objected Theseus. "I must face the Minotaur and kill it!"

Ariadne pleaded, "I can help you kill the Minotaur. Look, I have stolen back your sword from the guards. Take it now and kill the horrible monster."

Ariadne also knew how to lead Theseus out of the maze. She had asked Daedalus for the way out, and he told her to give a ball of silk thread to Theseus.

"I will stay at the entrance to the maze and hold one end of the thread," Ariadne explained. "You hold the ball of silk and let it **unravel** as you move through the maze. Once you kill the monster, follow the thread back to me."

unravel (un·**rav**·uhl)— to undo or separate

bellowing (bel·oh·ing)— a very loud roaring

Theseus' heart was moved by her goodness and daring. He felt a tender love grow within him. He told her that once his terrible task was done, he would take her to Athens as his bride.

That night, Ariadne and Theseus sneaked past the sleeping guards. They stood at the entrance to the maze. A frightful **bellowing** within the maze made their blood run cold. Ariadne held onto her end of the ball of thread while Theseus entered the huge maze. After many twists and turns, Theseus reached the center.

An awful scene lay before him: Human bones littered the ground. The Minotaur, a giant with the massive head of a bull, turned on him. Theseus was frozen by the wild power in the glaring eyes of the beast. Without realizing it, he dropped the ball of silk. Furiously stomping the ground, the Minotaur lowered his huge horns and leaped forward. Theseus dodged the attack but did not flee. The monster whirled and, snorting, came nose to nose with Theseus. Its foul breath sickened Theseus. He knew he had to reach deep inside himself to find courage. He had to match the strength of the creature. Then, the Minotaur slowly swung away and kicked some bones aside. Theseus stayed alert. Suddenly, the beast gave an awful roar and charged.

Theseus was ready with his sword. He slashed low at the charging beast and cut off one of its legs. The beast fell hard, howling in pain and anger. It rolled in agony.* Then it launched itself at Theseus with its deadly sharp horns. But Theseus threw himself to the ground to avoid the attack, jabbed upward, and pierced the heart of the raging beast. The Minotaur dropped to its knees, and with a terrible groan, fell dead.

 Strategy Alert!

Stop and Ask

If it doesn't make sense, what can I do? Use context clues to help me understand words like *agony*.

Theseus found the ball of silk that he had dropped. He followed the thread back to Ariadne. They returned to the dungeon to free the other youths. Then Ariadne led Theseus and the youths to the harbor where they boarded the ship and left for Athens.

In their haste to leave, they failed to bring food or drink. They stopped at the island of Naxos [**nak**·sos] for refreshment.* After eating and drinking, they all fell into a deep sleep on the beach. As Theseus slept, Dionysus [die·uh·**nie**·suhs], the god of wine, came to him in his dreams. *Strategy Alert!*

"Theseus, Ariadne must stay on the island when you leave for Athens," he ordered. "I have long loved her and want her as my wife. Don't be a fool and try to trick me. You may be smart enough to kill the Minotaur, but you cannot outsmart a god!"

Theseus knew that it was dangerous to anger a god. He woke his companions, and they quickly boarded the ship. Ariadne, still sleeping, was left on the island.

Theseus was upset about leaving Ariadne. He had felt great joy and hope about his new life with her. Now he felt only despair. Lost in sadness and pain, he forgot to change the ship's black sail to the white one.

Stop and Ask

If it doesn't make sense, what can I do? Use context clues to help me understand words like *refreshment*.

In Athens, Aegeus was waiting for the ship. Would the sail be black or white? As the boat came into view, he saw to his great horror that the sail was black. He thought that his son had been killed by the Minotaur. Filled with grief, Aegeus threw himself off the edge of the cliff and drowned in the sea below. That sea became known as the Aegean Sea.

Theseus and his companions reached the shore safely, but their joy was spoiled by news of Aegeus' death. Theseus' anguish* was great, for he felt that his father's death was his fault.

With Aegeus' death, Theseus became king. He was a wise ruler but soon stepped down from the throne. Theseus wanted all the people to have a voice in their government. He thought this could happen only if the people ruled themselves. So Theseus built a hall where the citizens could come together and vote. Thus, Athens became a true democracy.

 Strategy Alert!

Stop and Ask ❓

If it doesn't make sense, what can I do? Use context clues to help me understand words like *anguish*.

> Now that you've finished reading, review the **After I Read** habit and strategy below. Think about what you read in "Theseus" as you practice the strategy.

After I Read

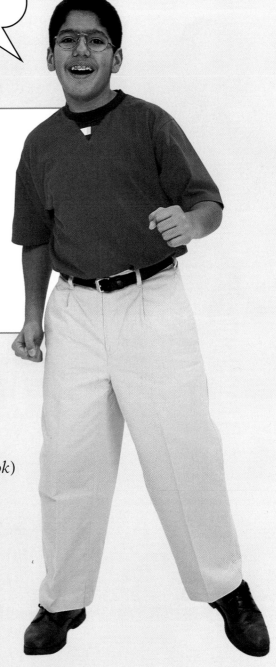

Which **HABIT** will I practice?
Check to see what I remember.
If I develop this habit, I will check to see what I remember as soon as I finish reading. It helps me see if I really understood what I read and helps me remember it better, too.

Which **STRATEGY** will I use to practice this habit?
Decide why the story ended the way it did.

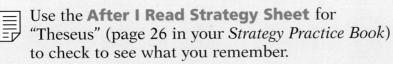 Use the **After I Read Strategy Sheet** for "Theseus" (page 26 in your *Strategy Practice Book*) to check to see what you remember.

Apply 3 of the 9 Habits

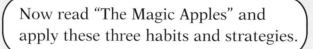

Now read "The Magic Apples" and apply these three habits and strategies.

Before I Read

Which **HABIT** will I apply?
Think about what I know about the subject.

Which **STRATEGY** will I use to apply this habit?
Identify the genre and decide what I know about this genre.

While I Read

Which **HABIT** will I apply?
Stop and ask, "If it doesn't make sense, what can I do?"

Which **STRATEGY** will I use to apply this habit?
Use context clues to help me understand words.

After I Read

Which **HABIT** will I apply?
Check to see what I remember.

Which **STRATEGY** will I use to apply this habit?
Decide why the story ended the way it did.

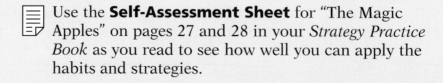

Use the **Self-Assessment Sheet** for "The Magic Apples" on pages 27 and 28 in your *Strategy Practice Book* as you read to see how well you can apply the habits and strategies.

The Magic Apples

A Norse Myth

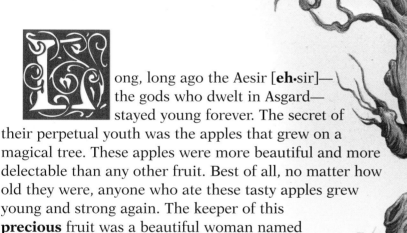

Long, long ago the Aesir [**eh**·sir]—the gods who dwelt in Asgard—stayed young forever. The secret of their perpetual youth was the apples that grew on a magical tree. These apples were more beautiful and more delectable than any other fruit. Best of all, no matter how old they were, anyone who ate these tasty apples grew young and strong again. The keeper of this **precious** fruit was a beautiful woman named Idun [**ee**·thuhn]. Only Idun could gather the fruit, for only she knew where the magical tree grew. Each morning, all of the Aesir came to Idun for a bite of the wonderful fruit. As long as Idun protected the life-giving fruit, the Aesir would stay strong and youthful.

Life in Asgard was pleasant. However, Odin [**oh**·duhn], the king of the gods, often grew bored sitting on his throne and would invite his brothers, Hoenir [**huh**·nir] and Loki [**loh**·kee], to join him in a **quest** for adventure. Together they would slip out of the palace and cross over the rainbow bridge which led to the lands of humans, giants, and dwarfs. Clever Loki, known among the Aesir for his **mischievous** ways, never failed to lead the others into exciting pranks.

precious (**pre**·shuhs)—having a high value

quest (kwest)—search

mischievous (**mis**·chuh·vuhs)—naughty in a fun way

talons (**tal**·unz)—claws

On one of these journeys, after Odin, Hoenir, and Loki had been wandering all night over mountains and across rivers, they paused in a valley for respite and food. Suddenly, Thiasse [**thie**·uhs] the giant, disguised as a huge eagle, swooped down to where the three Aesir sat, snatched up Loki in its huge **talons,** and soared into the sky. "Help!" Loki shrieked, as the eagle carried him off, ascending high over treetops and mountain peaks.

"No one can help you, Loki," said the eagle. "I have you in my power now. But if you promise to do what I ask, I shall set you free."

"Oh, Lord Eagle, if you tell me who you really are and let me go, I will promise whatever you wish," the terrified Loki pleaded.

"I am the giant Thiasse," answered the eagle. "I am growing old, and I want the magic apples that Idun guards so that I can recapture my youth. I have long heard of your cleverness, Loki, and know that if anyone can get those apples for me, you can—and you must!"

"I can't!" Loki cried. "To steal the apples from Idun is impossible!"

"Then you must bring me Idun herself, apples and all," the eagle replied.

Crying and pleading, Loki finally agreed to the eagle's demand. The eagle returned Loki to his friends who joyfully rushed to his side and asked what had happened. Of course, Loki could not tell the truth of his adventure, so instead, he made up a story to explain why the eagle had let him go. The three brothers then returned home to Asgard, having had enough excitement.

Soon after his return, Loki looked for Idun. She sat beside a stream of clear, pure water. Holding her basket of apples on her lap, she combed out her long, golden hair. Spread about her were the silken folds of her green robe, embroidered all over with flowers and leaves sewn from silk thread. Around her head was a wreath of spring flowers. Smiling up at Loki, Idun held out an apple. "Have a bite to refresh yourself," she said welcomingly.

"Thank you, Idun," said Loki. "However, I no longer have need of your apples. I've found a tree that **yields** apples that are sweeter and more beneficial than yours."

yields (yeeldz)—gives

"Impossible!" Idun protested. "There are no apples anywhere as helpful as mine. Where is this tree you say you've found?"

"Oh, I can't tell you," Loki said with a laugh. "It's my secret, and mine alone."

"I'd very much like to compare your apples with mine," Idun said. "Won't you bring *me* some?"

"Oh, no," responded Loki. "Then you might start giving people bites of *my* apples instead of your own. I want people to come to me for their refreshment!"

"Please, Loki," Idun coaxed. "Just take me to see your apple tree."

"Oh, very well," said Loki, pretending to give in. "I will take you to the place where the tree grows, but it must be a secret. I want no one else to know where my special apples come from."

"Thank you, Loki," Idun cried. "Let's go now, while no one is around."

Now, this was just what Loki had hoped for. "Bring along your basket of apples, so that you may compare them with mine," he told Idun. "I'm sure you'll discover that mine are far better."

So off the two went, with Loki leading the way and Idun with the basket of apples under her arm. Loki led her farther and farther from Asgard. "Where are you taking me, Loki?" Idun asked fearfully. "I see no evidence of an apple tree anywhere."

"Just a few more steps and you'll see the proof," Loki replied, trying to reassure Idun. "Come, just a little way more."

But those few more steps took Idun across the border of Asgard and into the land of the giants. With a whir of wings, down flew Thiasse in his eagle disguise. Idun screamed and turned to run back to the safety of Asgard, but it was too late. Before she could take another step, the gigantic bird clasped her in his talons and transported her and her magic apples to his castle high atop a mountain.

Loki sneaked back to Asgard, thinking himself safe from discovery. As time passed, the Aesir slowly began to show signs of aging and became aware of Idun's absence. The Aesir looked in the places where Idun used to roam, and one by one they returned, having failed to find her. As their hair turned gray and wrinkles formed on their faces, the Aesir felt fear for the first time in their long lives. Asgard itself began to show signs of aging in its fading flowers and its withering grass. Its eternal springtime gave way to fall. If Idun and her apples were not found soon, the gods themselves might blow away like autumn leaves.

Odin called a council to try to determine what had happened to Idun. He asked of the group, "Who was the last to see Idun before she disappeared?" As it turned out, Heimdal [**haym**·duhl] had observed Loki strolling out of Asgard with Idun. Angrily, the gods confronted Loki and accused him of causing Idun's disappearance. Frightened by their threats, Loki confessed and explained what Thiasse had forced him to do.

The gods became truly horrified at the thought of Idun and her apples in the power of an evil giant! Idun was lost to them forever, and Asgard was growing older by the minute. Filled with fury, Thor, the mighty god of thunder and lightning, **seized** Loki and hurled him high into the sky. Thor threw Loki so high that he crashed into the moon and bounced back to Earth! You can still see the marks of Loki's boots on the moon's face. "You must bring Idun back from the land of that wicked giant!" Thor roared.

seized (seezd)—grabbed

Loki crouched before Thor and asked with a shaking voice, "How can I do that?"

"That is for you to figure out," Thor growled. "Go—and do not return without her!"

Loki **contemplated** his **dilemma** until at last an idea came to him. "The giant disguises himself as an eagle," he explained to the Aesir. "If I disguise myself as a bird, perhaps I will be able to rescue Idun. To do this, however, I will need to borrow Freia's [**fray**·uhz] falcon robe."

Now, Freia, the goddess of love and **fertility,** loved to dress in her feather robe and soar like a falcon above the clouds. Reluctantly, Freia finally agreed to lend her precious garment to Loki. Loki put on the robe, and looking exactly like a great, brown falcon, lifted from the ground with a flap of his new wings. Flying across valleys and rivers and high above mountains, he at last came to the castle of Thiasse the giant. Fortunately for Loki, Thiasse had gone off to fish in the sea, leaving Idun unattended in his mountaintop home. She gave a little shriek when Loki, in his guise as a falcon, peered in the window at her. "Fear not, Idun," the bird squawked. "It is I, Loki. I have come to rescue you and return you to Asgard."

contemplated (kon·tuhm·**play**·tid)— thought over

dilemma (di·**lem**·uh)— a problem or difficult choice

fertility (fer·**til**·uh·tee)— the ability to have children

"Loki!" Idun cried. "You say you want to rescue me, but you are the reason I am here. Is this another of your tricks?"

"It's no trick," Loki answered. "Please forgive me for what I did. I was captured by Thiasse and was frightened. I had no choice but to do as he wished. But I am indeed here to save you."

"And how do you plan to do that?" Idun asked doubtfully. "I am locked in here, and the window bars are close together. I can't slip through them."

"I shall turn you into a nut," Loki replied. "Then I can carry you easily in my talons."

"What about my basket of apples?" Idun asked. "Must I leave it behind with Thiasse?"

Loki laughed heartily at that thought.

"How welcome do you think I would be in Asgard without the apples?" he cried. "Of course I will take them as well!"

Using his magical powers, Loki turned Idun into a nut. Then, seizing her and the basket of apples in his talons, he hurried away from the giant's castle.

Not long after Loki flew off with Idun, Thiasse returned home to find his captive and her magical apples gone. Enraged, Thiasse put on his eagle feathers and flew in swift pursuit of the falcon. Now, an eagle is far larger and stronger than all other birds. In a race it can overtake even the fastest of falcons. As Loki neared Asgard, he heard behind him the shrill scream of a mighty eagle. The wind raised by the beat of its powerful wings ruffled his feathers. Loki's heart sickened as he realized the escape might fail. His strength fading, he dove toward the walls of Asgard.

On the rainbow bridge leading to Asgard, the aged gods were gathered, watching for Loki's return. A cheer went up when Loki and his precious **burden** were seen. They grew suddenly quiet, however, when they saw the eagle close behind, its sharp talons reaching out toward the fleeing falcon.

Shouting commands, Odin told the other gods to pile wood upon Asgard's walls. As soon as Loki fluttered feebly over the wall, he dropped to the ground, weak and tired. The Aesir lighted the piles of wood, sending flames upward into the path of the eagle. Thiasse was moving too quickly to stop and flew straight into the wall of the roaring fire. He shrieked in rage and fear as flames surrounded him, sending him to the ground inside the walls. The mighty Thor fell on the helpless Thiasse, and with one blow of his sword, slew the giant so that he could never trouble the Aesir again!

Restored by Loki to her human form, Idun passed among the Aesir. To each of the gods, she gave a bite of her youth-giving apples until all of the aging Aesir grew young again. Around them, flowers bloomed as spring-time returned to Asgard.

No one, however, forgot that it was Loki who had brought all the troubles upon them. The memory of Loki's **treachery** lay buried deep in the hearts of the Aesir, and any honor that had once been attached to Loki's name was forever lost.

burden (burd·n)—anything that is carried

treachery (trech·uh·ree)—an act of disloyalty to a trusting person

Put Your Habits to Work in

Before I Read Habit:
Think about what I know about the subject.

Remember to think about personal experiences you have had or things you have already read **before** you read a chapter in your social studies textbook.

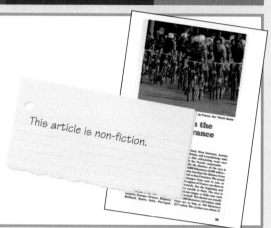

This article is non-fiction.

While I Read Habit:
Stop and ask, "If it doesn't make sense, what can I do?"

Don't forget to stop and ask yourself if what you're reading makes sense. One way to find out if it makes sense is to use context clues to help you understand words.

*Difficult climbs, dizzying **descents***

After I Read Habit:
Check to see what I remember.

When you read your social studies book, you're not finished until you see what you remember. You can do that by deciding why events happened as they did.

It ends this way because...

You may wish to use the **Put Your Habits to Work Sheet** (page 29 in your *Strategy Practice Book*) to practice these habits in your other reading.

Unit 5
Unsolved Mysteries in History
Theme: Mystery

In this unit, you will develop these 3 habits for all readers.

Before I Read Habit:
Check it out!

While I Read Habit:
Stop and ask, "How does it connect to what I know?"

After I Read Habit:
React to what I've read.

In this unit, you will develop three habits—one for before you read, one for while you are reading, and one for after you finish reading. Start with **Before I Read**. Read the habit and strategy. Then read my notes below.

Before I Read

Which **HABIT** will I learn?
Check it out!
If I develop this habit, I can find out something about what I am going to read so that I know what to expect.

Which **STRATEGY** will I use to learn this habit?
Decide what the internal organization of the selection is.

My Notes

- Strategy says to look at how the article is organized. Writers can organize in different ways. Some articles are organized in time order. Some explain why things happen. That's cause-and-effect organization. Some say how things are alike and different. That's comparing and contrasting.

- When I look at the headings in this selection, it looks like the article is comparing stories and facts to find out whether two places were real or imaginary.

Lost Cities of Legend

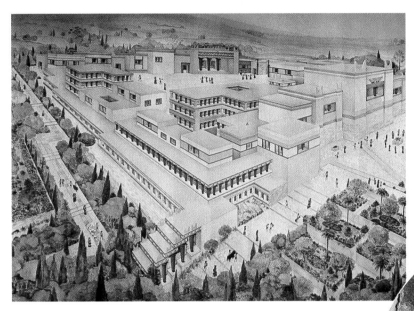

Modern drawing of the Palace of Knossos

golden age
(**gohl·**duhn ayj)—a time in which there is peace, prosperity, and happiness

evidence (**ev·i·**duhns)—something that proves what is true or not true

philosopher (fi·**los·**uh·fuhr)—a person who studies wisdom and knowledge

According to legend, there was a **golden age** of civilization on the islands of the Aegean [i·**jee·**uhn] Sea. Rich and powerful people lived in grand palaces. Their fleets of ships roamed the seas. These people made fine works of art. They also had a system for writing. Yet about 3,500 years ago, the people and their cities vanished.

What happened? Did the cities of the Aegean really exist? The legends have lasted over time. Researchers have tried to find the truth behind these stories. Different sets of **evidence** will be compared and contrasted in this article.

Two of the oldest stories are about the city of Knossos [**nos·**uhs] and the continent of Atlantis. A 2,500-year-old Greek myth tells the story of Knossos and its king, Minos. Around the same time, 500 B.C., the Greek **philosopher** Plato wrote about the wonders of Atlantis. Here are those stories.

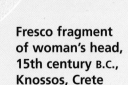

Fresco fragment of woman's head, 15th century B.C., Knossos, Crete

Now read the habit and strategy for **While I Read**. When you see ❓, read my notes in the margin.

While I Read

Which **HABIT** will I learn?

Stop and ask, "How does it connect to what I know?"
If I develop this habit, I will think about how what I'm reading fits with what I know. This helps me understand the new material and remember it better.

Which **STRATEGY** will I use to learn this habit?
Identify things the author is comparing and contrasting.

Knossos

According to legend, a powerful king named Minos once lived on the island of Crete. He had a large palace in Knossos, the capital city. King Minos had a Minotaur [**min·oh·tor**], a half-man, half-bull monster that lived in the **Labyrinth**. The neighboring city of Athens was under Minos' power. He forced the king of Athens to send 14 young men and women each year to feed to the Minotaur.

Did the Minotaur really exist? Could a person as evil as Minos have lived?

Atlantis

According to Plato, Atlantis was an island nation in the Atlantic. On this island lived a race of wealthy people. Their land was a center of trade. From their ports, swift ships roved the world. The island itself was beautiful and lush. Its tall mountains rose above clear lakes and green meadows. Fruits, nuts, and crops of all kinds grew there.

The people of Atlantis lived in a golden age. However, they became greedy. As a result, the gods punished them. Explosions shook the ground, and mountains tumbled. Buildings broke apart and crashed. Then the island, its people, and all its treasures sank beneath the ocean waters.

To this day, people are struck by the story of this lost land. Was it real? If so, where was it located? What caused its sudden end? Some say that one day Atlantis

Labyrinth
(**lab·uh·rinth**)—a maze

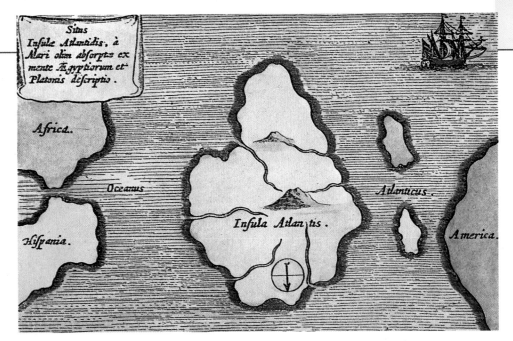

Early maps were drawn with north at the bottom. In this map from 1687, Atlantis is shown as a continent between Africa (left) and America (right).

will rise from the sea. Then a new golden age will begin for all people.

Knossos and Atlantis: Fact or Fiction?

Is there any truth to the legends of Knossos and Atlantis? The Greek poet Homer wrote about Minos more than two thousand years ago. So did the Greek historian Thucydides [thoo·**sid**·i·deez]. It seems likely that Minos was a real king. But what is the truth about Atlantis? Many people believe that the story of Atlantis is just a legend. They say that Plato created the tale to make a point. On the other hand, some people think that the story is true. They believe that Atlantis did exist, just as Plato described it. Still others say that the story was inspired by long-ago events in the Aegean. They say that Plato's Atlantis was really an island called Thera. *Strategy Alert!*

Digging Out Knossos

The legends of King Minos and the golden age of the Aegean interested an Englishman named Sir Arthur Evans. Evans decided to find out if the stories were based on fact. He began his search in Greece in 1893.

While in Athens, Evans saw women wearing small stones as charms. Evans was very near-sighted. He had to hold things very close to his eyes to see any details. When he peered at these stones, he noticed something strange. The stones were carved with shapes that looked like picture writing. Evans was told that the stones came from Crete.

Other things had been dug up on this island south of the Greek mainland. Huge jars had been found at a large mound called Kephala [ke·**fah**·luh]. Tradition held that this mound was the site of Knossos, the palace of the legendary King Minos.

Stop and Ask ?

How does it connect to what I know? Identify things the author is comparing and contrasting.

· · · · · · · · · ·

I think I've heard of Atlantis. The author is comparing Knossos and Atlantis. They are alike because they both are told about in ancient legends. They're different because we think King Minos was real. I'm not sure about Atlantis.

Palace of Knossos throne room

excavate
(**ek**·skuh·vayt)—to
remove by digging or
scooping out

frescoes (**fres**·kohz)—
paintings that are made
on moist plaster with
water paint

In 1894, Evans bought the right to **excavate** the mound. By 1900, he had gathered a team of workers and was ready to dig. Evans was to spend most of his life excavating and restoring the city he found. He would also spend many years writing a four-volume book about his findings.

From the very start, the mound at Kephala was a wonder. Four days after digging began, Evans wrote in his diary that he was finding something amazing.

Was Knossos King Minos' Palace?

For 25 years, Evans and his team dug out the remains of a huge building. It had twisting corridors, dead-end passages, many stairways, and some 1,400 rooms around a central courtyard. The building was indeed a maze. **Frescoes** showed young girls and boys jumping over the horns of bulls. Pictures of bulls appeared throughout the building. Could these bulls have been pictures of the Minotaur? Evans was sure he had found the remains of the palace of King Minos.

One finely decorated room was lined with stone benches. Among them stood a high-backed chair carved from stone. Its seat, higher than those of the others, must have been Minos' throne. From this room, Minos and the kings who followed him had ruled a great sea empire.

The people who lived in the palace had every luxury. They even had modern plumbing! A system of pipes carried hot and cold water throughout the building. Other pipes carried waste water and sewage away from the palace. The drainage system was still in working order after more than 3,000 years!

Palace of Knossos guard room

Ruins of the Palace of Knossos

Among the many things Evans found were hundreds of clay **tablets**. Carved in them were rows of picture writing. Evans thought they were palace records. Evans found that there were two types of picture writing. However, he could not figure out the meaning of the writing. In spite of years of trying, he would never succeed.

To help with the work, Evans had brought along an architect and a Swiss artist. The architect helped Evans rebuild the walls, floors, staircases, and columns. The team's artist helped put together the pieces of broken frescoes and fill in missing parts.

More digging showed that the palace had not been built all at once. Kings who came after the original Minos took that same name. In their turn, each added to the palace. Then, around 1450 B.C., Knossos and other cities of the Aegean burned. The Minoan [mi·**noh**·uhn] culture—as it was called in honor of Minos— disappeared.

What ended this golden age? Did the same cause sink Atlantis?

Digging Out Thera

A volcanic island named Thera lies about 70 miles north of Crete. Excavations begun there in 1870 found ancient houses under volcanic debris. One hundred years later, more excavations were made. This digging showed that hidden under the ash were the remains of an advanced culture.

Workers found thousands of stone tools, utensils, and pottery. They unearthed pieces of broken furniture. Colorful paintings came to light. With each new discovery, a picture of life on Thera emerged.

Strategy Alert!

tablets (**tab**·lits)—slabs of stone that are used to write on

Stop and Ask

How does it connect to what I know? Identify things the author is comparing and contrasting.

Now the author is starting to compare Knossos to Thera. Thera and Knossos are alike because they're close to each other. I can see that on the map. There were lots of paintings in each place, too. And they were both destroyed.

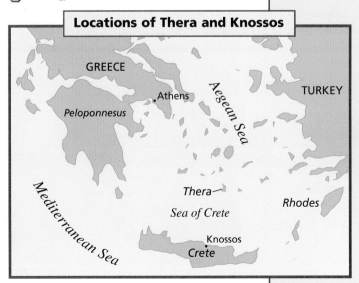

Locations of Thera and Knossos

GREECE

Athens

Peloponnesus

Aegean Sea

TURKEY

Thera

Sea of Crete

Rhodes

Mediterranean Sea

Knossos

Crete

Palace of Knossos, queen's bathroom

extinct (ik·**stingkt**)—no longer living or existing

inspiration (in·spuh·**ray**·shuhn)—something that moves someone to create or invent

Stop and Ask

How does it connect to what I know? Identify things the author is comparing and contrasting.

Thera and Atlantis seem to have lots in common! Thera is like Plato said Atlantis was. He said Atlantis sank. Thera was destroyed by a volcano and then sank.

The Therans lived in tall, well-built houses. Bathrooms had earthenware tubs and stone toilets. Clay pipes linked the bathrooms to a drainage system that ran beneath the city streets. The Therans' homes were filled with goods of all kinds. On the walls were fine paintings of flowers, animals, and people.

Amid the natural beauty of their island, the people of Thera lived a peaceful life. They grew rich from trade with lands as far away as Egypt. In their workshops, they made fabrics, tools, pottery, and other goods for trade. From Thera's seaport, ships went to visit all the lands of the known world. If you think this sounds much like Plato's description of Atlantis, so do many other people.

Was Thera Atlantis?

Unfortunately, the forces that formed Thera also destroyed it.

Millions of years ago, volcanoes had erupted at the bottom of the sea. With each eruption, their crests grew and rose a little more above the waters. They formed the islands of the Aegean. Over time, most of these volcanoes became **extinct**. Under Thera, however, a time bomb was waiting to go off.

Around 1600 B.C., Thera's volcano awoke. In a violent burst, the island blew apart. The force of the eruption flung debris 20 miles into the air! The volcanic cone collapsed inward. It formed a basin into which the sea poured. A large part of Thera sank beneath the waves, just as Atlantis supposedly had. Later eruptions turned Thera into three separate islands. A thick layer of ash settled over what was left of the once-beautiful island.

Was Thera Plato's **inspiration** for the lost continent of Atlantis? Weigh the evidence. You be the judge. ❓ *Strategy Alert!*

Today a thriving town exists on the island of Thera.

Thera and Knossos may have been destroyed by a volcano such as the one shown above.

Knossos and Thera: Linked in Disaster?

Scholars long believed that the event that destroyed Thera was also the force that destroyed Knossos. They dated the eruption to 1500 B.C. This was about the same time that Minoan **culture** collapsed.

Sir Arthur Evans himself thought that Knossos had fallen to a natural disaster. Crete is prone to earthquakes. During Evans's digs, he saw signs that Minos' palace had been damaged by tremors several times. In the end, a great fire had burned the structure. Many walls and ceilings had fallen. To Evans, these were signs that a violent event had brought down the Minoan world.

That may indeed have been the case. However, wood and seeds buried in the fall of ash on Thera have been **carbon-dated** to no later than 1600 B.C. Further evidence of the date of Thera's end comes from as far away as California. Wind currents carried the cloud of ash from the eruption around the world. Analysis of ancient wood samples shows that around 1620 B.C., trees in many parts of the world were stunted. An ash cloud blocking the sun may have caused global cooling. This could have kept the trees from growing. Ice samples from Greenland of about the same date show high levels of acidity. High acid levels in ice are a sign of volcanic activity somewhere in the world. ⑦ *Strategy Alert!*

culture (**kul**·chuhr)— people's arts, beliefs, and other products of work and thought

carbon-dated (**kahr**·buhn **day**·tid)— determined the age of an ancient object by measuring the amount of carbon 14 in it

Stop and Ask

How does it connect to what I know? Identify things the author is comparing and contrasting.

The author is comparing the ways Knossos and Thera were destroyed. It looks like both were destroyed by a volcano. I've seen volcanoes on TV.

seismic (siez·mik)—
caused by an earthquake
or earth vibration

Stop and Ask

How does it connect
to what I know?
Identify things the
author is comparing
and contrasting.

● ● ● ● ● ● ● ● ● ● ●

The author com-
pared the legends
of Knossos and
Atlantis. They are
both ancient leg-
endary places that
were probably
destroyed by volca-
noes. I think they
were real.

What can we conclude? The end of Thera took place at least one hundred years before the fall of Knossos. This does not mean, however, that the events could not have been linked. Thera's eruption may have signaled the beginning of a period of **seismic** activity. Further eruptions may have occurred. Destructive earthquakes may have followed. These later earthquakes may have destroyed the Minoan world.

History or Legend?

Until the discoveries at Knossos and Thera, this glorious past was known only in myths and legends—like the myth of the Minotaur and the Labyrinth. People were not even sure whether these worlds really existed. Now scientists have uncovered many facts that seem to solve the mysteries. Or do they? Knossos and Atlantis—history or legend? You decide. ❓ *Strategy Alert!*

This picture shows one artist's idea of the famous Labyrinth. Theseus, who eventually slew the Minotaur, is also pictured.

Congratulations! You finished reading. Now read the habit and strategy for **After I Read**. Then read my notes below.

After I Read

Which **HABIT** will I learn?
React to what I've read.
If I develop this habit, I will take time to think about what I've just read. Deciding what I think and what I feel helps me remember it better.

Which **STRATEGY** will I use to learn this habit?
Weigh the evidence to draw conclusions.

My Notes

- Strategy says to weigh the evidence in what I've read and then decide for myself what I think about the subject. I need to draw my own conclusions.

- First, I think Knossos was real. Evans found the palace. The Minotaur was probably just a fierce bull, like the ones in the pictures Evans found. Then legends grew up about it.

- I think Atlantis was really Thera. There's enough evidence of that. I don't know why Thera would be called Atlantis.

Practice 3 of the 9 Habits

Now it's time to practice the three habits and strategies you learned when you read "Lost Cities of Legend." Start with **Before I Read**. Look at the box below. It should look familiar! Reread the habit you will practice. Reread the strategy you will use—then do it!

Before I Read

Which **HABIT** will I practice?
Check it out!
If I develop this habit, I can find out something about what I am going to read so that I know what to expect.

Which **STRATEGY** will I use to practice this habit?
Decide what the internal organization of the selection is.

 Use the **Before I Read Strategy Sheet** for "The Mysteries of Easter Island" (page 30 in your *Strategy Practice Book*) to check out the article.

The Mysteries of Easter Island

In this article, you will consider the mysteries of Easter Island: Where did the first people come from? How did they move the huge statues that still stand there? Experts have different ideas about the answers to these questions. The ideas are based on different sets of evidence. Compare and contrast the evidence. Then decide the answers to these questions for yourself. Maybe you will solve the mysteries of Easter Island.

The Dutch Land on a Remote Island

Imagine you are aboard a Dutch sailing ship with explorer Jacob Roggeveen. It's Easter Sunday, 1722. You sight land. Your ship arrives at a small island in the middle of the Pacific Ocean. Roggeveen dubs the isle of land "Easter Island" in honor of the day it was first seen. This island of stony soil is shaped like a triangle. There is an extinct volcano in each corner. About 47 square miles in size, this island is one of the most **remote** places in the world. The nearest land is another small island 1,400 miles west. The nearest continent, South America, is 2,300 miles to the east.

remote (ri·**moht**)—far away from land

Reread the habit and strategy below. Look for the *Strategy Alerts!* as you continue to read.

While I Read

Which **HABIT** will I practice?

Stop and ask, "How does it connect to what I know?"
If I develop this habit, I will think about how what I'm reading fits with what I know. This helps me understand the new material and remember it better.

Which **STRATEGY** will I use to practice this habit?
Identify things the author is comparing and contrasting.

 Use the **While I Read Strategy Sheet** for "The Mysteries of Easter Island" (page 31 in your *Strategy Practice Book*) as you read.

cultivate (kul·ti·vayt)— to raise crops

It is stormy, so Roggeveen decides to wait until the next day to land. When you do land, you see huge stone statues—11 to 40 feet tall. Each statue must weigh as much as 50 tons. Some stand on platforms; others lie on their sides. The statues have carved faces. Empty eye sockets stare into the distance. Carved arms end in hands with long fingers. The standing statues are topped with red, hat-like stones.

With the crew, you explore the land. You meet thousands of islanders. Some are dark-skinned, some lighter. Others are reddish, as if they've been tanned by the sun. Grasses and reeds grow wild on the island. The people **cultivate** bananas, sugar cane, and a few other crops. The only boats you see are small rafts made from reeds. The rafts hold just one person who paddles with his hands.

Suddenly, you find yourself with many questions. You wonder where these first settlers on Easter Island came from. You're puzzled about how they got to this island, so far from other lands. You wonder how the people moved their huge stone statues. You are not alone in your questions.

Statues on Easter Island

For hundreds of years, people have asked questions like these. Scientists have tried to find answers. But even today, much about Easter Island remains a mystery.

Where Did They Come From?

Jump ahead about 50 years to the late 1700s. By this time, much of South America had been **colonized** by Spain. In 1770, the Viceroy of Peru sent an expedition to Easter Island. These Spanish explorers noticed some interesting things. They noted that some islanders were lighter skinned than others. The people didn't look like South American Indians the explorers knew. But they did grow many of the same crops as those distant farmers. The Spanish also recognized some of the language they heard. Some words were similar to those of the Polynesians [pol·uh·**nee**·zhuhns] who lived miles away in the South Pacific. But, the Easter Islanders also had made picture-like markings on stone tablets—a written language. The Polynesians' language was strictly **oral**.

Four years after the Spanish explorers, James Cook, an English **navigator,** landed on Easter Island. Many of the great statues he had heard about had been knocked over and broken. The Spanish had found thousands of people. But Cook found only 600–700 islanders. Like the Spanish, Captain Cook compared the islanders to people of the South Pacific. He thought the islanders looked like the Maoris [**mow**·reez] of New Zealand and the Polynesians of Tahiti. He also compared the islanders' language with those spoken in the South Pacific. He found that the Easter Islanders' words for numbers were much like those of the Tahitians. A mystery was born: Did the first people on Easter Island come from South America or the South Pacific?

(?) *Strategy Alert!*

Captain James Cook

colonized
(**kol**·uh·niezd)—set up land separate from, but under the rule of, another country

oral (**or**·uhl)—spoken

navigator
(**nav**·uh·gay·tuhr)—a person who explores by ship

Stop and Ask (?)

How does it connect to what I know? Identify things the author is comparing and contrasting.

Stone carving on Easter Island

balsa (**bawl**·suh)—
a type of very light
wood

Stop and Ask ⬡❓

How does it
connect to what I
know? Identify
things the author
is comparing and
contrasting.

how to read the writing on the old stone tablets. What people carved those words? Where did the first settlers come from? Legends help to answer these questions.

One legend tells of a chief who came from east of the island, or the west coast of South America. That's a journey of 2,300 miles! Before modern ships and navigation, sailing that distance would have been an amazing feat. But, the Norwegian explorer Thor Heyerdahl [**hay**·uhr·dahl] thinks that's what happened. In 1947 he, and five others, sailed a **balsa** raft from Peru to the South Pacific. This proved that ancient peoples could have made such a long trip in similar craft. The voyage supported his theory that the Polynesians' ancestors came from South America. ❓*Strategy Alert!*

Unraveling the Mystery

More than 2,000 people live on Easter Island today. Most people speak Spanish. Some speak Rapanui [rah·puh·**noo**·ee], the Polynesian language. No one knows

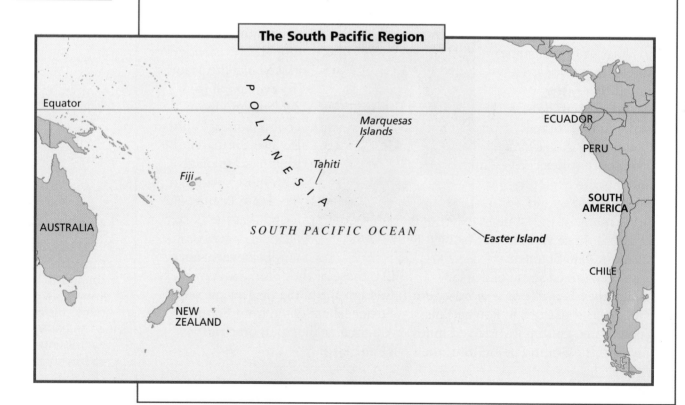

The South Pacific Region

Equator

POLYNESIA

Marquesas Islands

Tahiti

Fiji

ECUADOR

PERU

SOUTH AMERICA

AUSTRALIA

SOUTH PACIFIC OCEAN

Easter Island

CHILE

NEW ZEALAND

Sculpture wall at an early South American site

In the 1950s, Heyerdahl began studying Easter Island. The first settlers, he thought, may have been related to the early people of Peru. These light-skinned people ruled what became the **Inca** Empire. Early Spanish explorers heard Incan legends about these people. The legends told of people who left South America and sailed west into the Pacific. Heyerdahl compared these legends to the picture carvings of ships found on some Easter Island statues. He believed these carvings showed the reed ships those people had sailed.

Heyerdahl also found pollen of reeds and palm trees on Easter Island. Both, he said, were native to South America. The palm grew only in Chile. If palm seed had never naturally spread as far as Peru, he did not think it could have drifted 2,300 miles across the ocean! It must have been carried by people.

The reeds were used to build the long narrow rafts the islanders paddled out to sea. These reed rafts were also used in coastal Peru.

Pictures of the rafts and men with bird-like heads are common in Incan art, but they are not found in Polynesian art. The same designs are also found in the art of the Easter Islanders.

Heyerdahl had another striking thought. He believed that the raised platforms on which the statues stood came from the cultures of the South Americans. He compared them to the stone altars in Bolivia, which may have been the center of the pre-Incan empire.

The stone tablets filled with writing are similar to Egyptian **hieroglyphics** and to ancient writing from India. Forms of script were also used by **pre-Columbian** Americans. But script was not used on the islands of the South Pacific. All this led Heyerdahl to believe that the first people to live on Easter Island came from South America. A later group, he thought, may have come from the South Pacific. The two groups may have had a war. This could explain the population drop that Cook noticed in 1786. *Strategy Alert!*

Inca (**ing**·kuh)—Indian tribes that ruled Peru before the Spanish conquered them

hieroglyphics (hie·ruh·**glif**·iks)—a system of writing that uses pictures or symbols

pre-Columbian (pree·kuh·**lum**·bee·uhn) —the time before Columbus came to the Americas in 1492

Stop and Ask ❓

How does it connect to what I know? Identify things the author is comparing and contrasting.

Newer Evidence Casts Doubts

In recent years, scientists have questioned Heyerdahl's theories. Heyerdahl thought that the reeds on Easter Island had to have come from South America. New technology has proved that the reeds had actually grown on Easter Island for 30,000 years. This was long before the first settlers came. New information about the people has surfaced, too. A study in the 1980s looked at stone altars, ovens, statues, and house foundations on Easter Island. They all seem to have Polynesian **origins**. The stone altars especially were much more like those seen in Polynesia than those seen in South America.

This new evidence seems to support those who think the Easter Islanders came from Polynesia. The Polynesian people were adventurous. They were resourceful and good explorers. Most likely, they adapted their culture to fit the resources they found on the island. As the population grew, the people might have fought over land and natural resources. The drop in population in the 1700s may have been caused by **clan** warfare.

And the stone tablets? Easter Island is the only island in the area where ancient writing has been found. Many scientists believe this is because writing was not brought to Easter Island by other people. Instead, the writing developed on Easter Island. These "notes" helped the people pass along their stories orally. The writing developed because the people were **isolated**.
❓ *Strategy Alert!*

origins (**or**·uh·jinz)— beginnings

clan—a group of families with the same ancestors

isolated (ie·suh·**lay**·tid)—living separate from others

Stop and Ask ❓

How does it connect to what I know? Identify things the author is comparing and contrasting.

Some statues on Easter Island still have their red, hat-like stones.

Archaeologists carefully assemble the parts of a statue that had never been erected on Easter Island.

The Mystery of the Statues

How the islanders built and moved the great stone statues is another mystery. Both legend and science say the statues were carved by hand from volcanic rock. The remains of 400 statues still line the walls of the volcano's crater. But how were nearly 600 statues moved from the volcano's rim to the edge of the Pacific Ocean? Scientists have compared several ideas.

"Walking" Wonders?

Most people believed that the giant statues were dragged or rolled to the coast. These methods were commonly used by ancient people to move heavy objects. Easter Island legend, however, says that the statues were lowered down the side of the volcano with ropes. Then, they "walked." Was this possible? Did the statues "walk"? An engineer explained how this might have been done. First, ropes were tied to opposite sides of a statue's head and base. Then, pulling in turn, four groups of people tipped the statue slightly and wiggled the base forward. This made the statue shuffle along, the way a penguin walks. The movement became smoother once the pullers developed a rhythm.

Walking the statues might have worked. But some scientists think that this was not likely. The risk of damaging the statues was too great. Remember, the largest ones weighed as much as 50 tons! The statues could have tipped over too easily. Contact with the rocky ground would have worn away the bases. The process would have been slow and taken large numbers of people. Some experts thought there must have been another way.

"Sailing" Statues?

In 1999, archaeologist Jo Anne Van Tilburg **demonstrated** another method. After watching how the islanders moved their canoes across the land, she had a thought. She proposed that the statues might have been moved the same way. With the help of native artists, she made a cement copy of a statue. The 12-ton model was tied to a

demonstrated (de·muhn·stray·tid)— showed how something works

wooden rig shaped like a canoe. Then it "sailed" across the land on a grid of logs made slippery with water and ground-up banana trees. It took only 40 people pulling to "sail" the statue this way. Then 20 people used ropes, wooden **levers,** and stones to raise the model until it stood. Van Tilburg can't prove that the statues were "sailed" this way. But she believes it is a good possibility. *Strategy Alert!*

Comparing the Evidence

So, what are the answers to the ancient mysteries of Easter Island? Did the first settlers come from South America or Polynesia? Experts cannot agree. Information about the islanders' appearance, legends, crops, boats, and language seems to support both theories. Did the massive statues walk or sail? Both methods seem possible, but no one knows for sure.

These questions remain unanswered. Scientists may continue to be puzzled for centuries to come unless some new evidence helps them unravel the mysteries of Easter Island. What do you think the answers to the mysteries are?

Statues continue to stand guard on Easter Island.

Now that you've finished reading, review the **After I Read** habit below. Think about what you read in "The Mysteries of Easter Island" as you practice the strategy.

After I Read

Which **HABIT** will I practice?
React to what I've read.
If I develop this habit, I will take time to think about what I've just read. Deciding what I think and what I feel helps me remember it better.

Which **STRATEGY** will I use to practice this habit?
Weigh the evidence to draw conclusions.

Use the **After I Read Strategy Sheet** for "The Mysteries of Easter Island" (page 32 in your *Strategy Practice Book*) to react to what you've read.

Apply 3 of the 9 Habits

Now read "Lost: One Colony" and apply these three habits and strategies.

Before I Read

Which **HABIT** will I apply?
Check it out!

Which **STRATEGY** will I use to apply this habit?
Decide what the internal organization of the selection is.

While I Read

Which **HABIT** will I apply?
Stop and ask, "How does it connect to what I know?"

Which **STRATEGY** will I use to apply this habit?
Identify things the author is comparing and contrasting.

After I Read

Which **HABIT** will I apply?
React to what I've read.

Which **STRATEGY** will I use to apply this habit?
Weigh the evidence to draw conclusions.

Use the **Self-Assessment Sheet** for "Lost: One Colony" on pages 33 and 34 in your *Strategy Practice Book* as you read to see how well you can apply the habits and strategies.

Lost:
One Colony

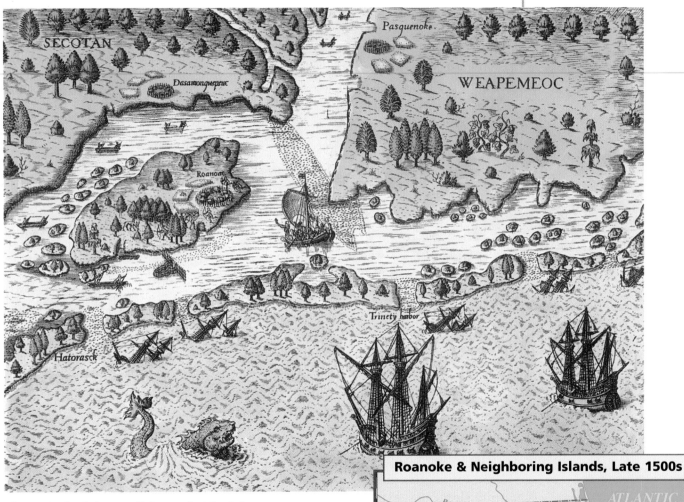

The arrival of the Englishmen in Virginia

Roanoke & Neighboring Islands, Late 1500s

At some point between 1587 and 1590, a colony of settlers disappeared from a small island off the coast of what is now North Carolina. More than 400 years later, we still don't know what happened to this colony. Read about the colony and compare the theories about how it became the "lost colony."

Sir Walter Raleigh

Queen Elizabeth I

Settling Roanoke Island

In 1584, Sir Walter Raleigh sent two ships to the New World to look for a place for a colony. European navigators had long been sailing up and down the Atlantic coast. But no country had built a settlement there. Queen Elizabeth I of England wanted to claim land in the New World. She knew that the Spanish had found gold in South America, and she wanted such treasure for England. She also wanted a base in the New World to support English ships that attacked Spanish ships loaded with gold. If the base were hidden, these **privateers** could surprise the Spanish.

This scouting trip was a success. The English were pleased with the apparent richness of the land. The Croatoans and Roanokes—the two groups of Indians who lived on the island—had treated them warmly. When the ships returned to England in the fall, two Indians sailed with them. The stage was set for a permanent English base in the New World.

The First Colony

The next year, Raleigh sent another group to build a settlement. Seven ships and 118 men set off with three purposes: to build a privateer base, to search for gold, and to study plant and animal life. John White, an artist who had made the trip the year before, would record what they saw in paintings. These men, however, were not farmers interested in setting up a colony. They were adventurers who wanted to find gold to please their queen.

privateers
(prie·vuh·**teers**)—ships sent by a government to capture enemy ships

On the north end of the island, some of the men built a small fort. They hoped it would be hidden from the Spanish. The ocean off Roanoke and the outer islands was very shallow. Rough seas often shifted the sand, blocking passages between the islands. This stopped ships from sailing directly to Roanoke Island. Anyone coming to the island had to row a small boat in from the large ships a mile or two to shore. The natives mentioned the Chesapeake Bay, 150 miles north of the island. This sounded appealing because ships trying to reach the mainland would not experience these same difficulties.

As the winter passed and spring came, food became **scarce**. The English sent word back to England to send ships with food. In the meantime, they asked the Roanoke Indians for food. The Roanokes became tired of the English demands and began to withhold food. Thinking the Roanokes were about to attack, the English struck first and killed a chief. Since they now could expect no help from the Roanokes, they hoped the supply ships would come soon. However, the English explorer Sir Francis Drake arrived with his ships first, and the colonists returned to England with him.

The English supply ships came several weeks later. Fifteen men from these ships stayed to guard the fort. They had enough supplies for two years. These men were **ambushed** by natives. One was killed. The others may have died while trying to escape in a small boat.

This first colony had lasted only one year.

Colonists landing on Roanoke Island

The Second Colony

In 1587 Raleigh sent a second group of colonists to what is now Virginia. John White, the artist, was named governor. This group, which included women and children, planned to settle in the Chesapeake Bay area. The soil there was not sandy as it was on Roanoke Island, so it was better for farming. Large ships could also anchor close to shore.

These ships stopped to bring supplies to the 15 men left on Roanoke Island before sailing north to the Chesapeake. They found no sign of life, only the skeleton of one guard. The ships' pilot and sailors refused to carry the colonists any farther. Instead they wanted to look for enemy Spanish ships.

The settlers stayed on Roanoke and rebuilt the fort. They tried to make peace with both groups of Indians—the Roanokes and the Croatoans on nearby Croatoan Island. Even though there were some misunderstandings, the colonists did eventually make peace with the Croatoans. On August 18, 1587, Virginia Dare, John White's granddaughter, was born. She was the first child of English parents born in the New World. Soon after that, John White returned to England for supplies.

The Lost Colony

England's war with Spain prevented White from returning to the island for three years. When he did, he found the colony deserted. Some buildings were knocked down and covered with grass and weeds. A large **barricade** had been built.

barricade (**bar·i·**kayd)— something set up to block others from getting in or out

The baptism of Virginia Dare

On his return to the island, John White found *Croatoan* carved on a post.

"Croatoan" had been carved on a post and "Cro" on a tree.

Except for the barricade, John White found no sign of war at the colony. Before he sailed for England, the colonists had agreed to carve clues to where they were going if they left. They would carve crosses over the clues if they left in danger. From the clues they had left, White was sure they had gone to Croatoan Island and planned to join them. The weather was stormy, however, and White's ships lost several anchors. With the hurricane season coming, White was forced to return to England.

At home, White tried to keep the English interested in the fate of the colony. But he could not find anyone to **finance** another trip. After 1593, he stopped trying.

What happened to the colonists? Many different theories have been suggested. Consider each theory. How do they compare? How are they different? Which one do you think makes sense?

finance (fie·nans)— to pay for

Did Unfriendly Natives Destroy the Colony?

The Roanoke Indians were good farmers and were well supplied with food. At first they were friendly toward the first colonists. But in 1585, the first group of English had destroyed a native village because they thought the Roanokes had stolen a small silver cup. Later they held the son of a chief hostage while they looked for a mine the chief had told them about. But food became scarce on the island. The natives' supply was stretched. The English had arrived too late in the year to grow their own food. Their constant demands made the Roanokes angry. And killing the Roanoke chief during an attack cut off any hope for peace. Out of supplies and without allies, the colonists left with Sir Francis Drake. Indians ambushed the 15 men from the supply ships who had stayed behind to guard the fort.

When White and the second group of colonists came in 1587, they found signs of Indian hostility and the skeleton of one man. White hoped to make friends with the Croatoans. After all, these were the people of Manteo, an Indian who had made two trips to England. Manteo's first trip was with the

Sir Francis Drake

1584 scouting party; the second was with the men who returned to England with Drake.

The Croatoans were helpful but **cautious**. They too had been badly treated by the first group of colonists. The Croatoans did arrange a meeting between the English and the Roanokes. When the Roanokes didn't show up, the English attacked their village. The people in that village, however, were Croatoans. They had come to look for food the Roanokes had left behind. Did the Roanokes return and kill the colonists?

Did the Colonists Move to Chesapeake Bay?

Maybe natives actually helped the settlers. When the colonists left England, they planned to move to Chesapeake Bay. Some historians think they did. The Jamestown colonists, who arrived 17 years later, asked about the first settlers. Stories were shared of people who had made friends with a Chesapeake tribe. These people were like the English in appearance and dress. Their houses were said to be built like English houses; some even had two stories.

The Jamestown settlers never met these people. About the time the Jamestown colony was being established, the Chesapeake

cautious (**kaw**•shuhs)—careful

Spanish Armada

were attacked by Powhatan. He was the leader of the tribe that later helped the settlers at Jamestown. Powhatan was said to have utensils that had belonged to the colonists. This supports the theory that the first colonists did in fact move to Chesapeake Bay. Perhaps members of the Chesapeake tribe were given utensils from the colonists in exchange for food and other supplies. Later, when Powhatan attacked the Chesapeake, he must have taken these utensils.

Did the Spanish Invade Roanoke?

Maybe natives were not involved at all. While England was trying to build a colony on Roanoke Island, it was **competing** with Spain. Both countries had strong navies, and both wanted to **claim** land in the New World. Spain already had claims in South America and north of what is now Florida. From these claims, Spain had gotten huge riches. War with Spain kept John White from returning to Roanoke Island in 1588.

The fort on Roanoke Island in 1585 was a base for privateers hunting Spanish ships. The builders of the fort thought it was hidden from the Spanish. Spanish records show, however, that the Spanish knew the fort was there. Spanish officers in Florida had asked their king for more troops to help them find and destroy an English settlement they had heard about. Spain needed the New World riches to pay for its navy, so an English base was a big threat. However, King Philip II of Spain was preparing to attack England. He did not send troops to Florida. Philip's attack resulted in the defeat of the **Spanish Armada** in 1588. It was this war that had prevented John White's return to Roanoke Island.

competing (kuhm·**pee**·ting)—trying to beat others for some sort of prize or profit

claim (klaym)—to name as one's own

Spanish Armada (ahr·**mah**·duh)—a large group of warships owned by Spain

Did the Spanish from Florida invade Roanoke Island on their own? Did they capture and kill the colonists? Most historians believe the Spanish did not attack the colony. Spanish records show that the Spanish were still searching the coast for a settlement as late as 1600.

Did the Colonists Try to Sail for England?

Maybe the colonists destroyed themselves. When John White returned to Roanoke Island, he found no boats. The colonists had no large sailing ships, but they did have smaller boats. Perhaps the colonists tried to return to England on their own. They might have lost faith in White when he did not come back with supplies. Their smaller boats might have made the crossing, but they were more likely to have been overturned by waves.

Lumbee Indians in ceremonial headdress (shown here and above right)

Did the Colonists Join the Croatoans?

Maybe the colonists never really left. John White believed that the colonists had gone to Croatoan Island, an island south of Roanoke. They had, after all, left "Croatoan" carved on a post. If most of the colonists left for the Chesapeake, some may have stayed. They might have chosen to wait for White and the supplies. Or, all the colonists may have joined the Croatoans and moved with them inland.

A group of Indians known today as the Lumbee were called *Croatan* or *Croatoan* in the 1800s. Early reports of the Lumbee describe them as living like white settlers but looking like Indians. Other reports said they spoke English and had light skin. Many Lumbee today have the same last names as the Roanoke Island colonists. They believe they are the **descendants** of the English settlers of the Lost Colony.

descendants (di·**sen**·duhnts)— offspring

Comparing the Theories

Today, the mystery of the lost colonists remains. Based on the facts known, a number of theories and new questions have been formed: Did unfriendly natives destroy the colony or did the settlers simply move to Chesapeake Bay? Did the Spanish invade Roanoke Island or did the colonists try to sail back to England and fail? Or, did the colonists survive by living with the Croatoans and moving inland? Unfortunately, answers to these questions may never be found. As time passes, Roanoke Island gets smaller and smaller. The tides and storms have eaten away at the island. Sixteen miles long at the time the colonists arrived, Roanoke is now only 12 miles long! Clues that once lay on the island may have been swallowed up by the sea.

Roanoke Island Today

Roanoke Island is now **linked** to the mainland and the Outer Banks islands by bridges. A small fort made of earth was rebuilt 50 years ago and named Fort Raleigh. Had the original fort been built by the first group of colonists? Or was it one of the forts made by the 15 men left behind in 1586? This is another mystery that may never be solved. Today Fort Raleigh and more than 500 acres on Roanoke Island are a National Historic Site.

linked (linkd)— connected

Reenactment of Lost Colony story

Put Your Habits to Work in

| Literature | Social Studies | Science | Math |

Before I Read Habit:
Check it out!

Remember to look at how the sections are organized **before** you read a chapter in your science textbook.

While I Read Habit:
Stop and ask, "How does it connect to what I know?"

While you read your science book, don't forget to identify information that the author is comparing and contrasting.

After I Read Habit:
React to what I've read.

When you read your science textbook, you're **not** finished until you react to what you've read. You can do that by weighing the evidence to draw conclusions.

You may wish to use the **Put Your Habits to Work Sheet** (page 35 in your *Strategy Practice Book*) to practice these habits in your other reading.

Unit 6
Dangerous Journeys
Theme: People on the Move

In this unit, you will develop these 3 habits for all readers.

Before I Read Habit:
Decide what I need to know.

While I Read Habit:
Stop and ask, "If it doesn't make sense, what can I do?"

After I Read Habit:
Check to see what I remember.

Learn 3 of the 9 Habits

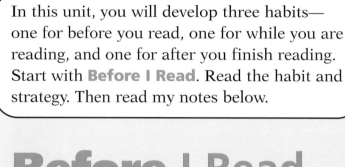

In this unit, you will develop three habits—one for before you read, one for while you are reading, and one for after you finish reading. Start with **Before I Read**. Read the habit and strategy. Then read my notes below.

Before I Read

Which **HABIT** will I learn?
Decide what I need to know.
If I develop this habit, I will have a reason for reading. I will understand it better and remember more of what I read.

Which **STRATEGY** will I use to learn this habit?
Use the introduction and summary to ask purpose-setting questions.

My Notes

- Strategy says to look at the introduction and summary and to ask purpose-setting questions. These questions will help guide my reading.

- The introduction tells me that this will be about a woman named Sacajawea. It also says she was important to American history. Here are my questions: What role in history did Sacajawea play? Why is she important?

- The summary says she traveled with Lewis and Clark. Here's another question I have: Why did Sacajawea go with Lewis and Clark?

HER NAME WAS SACAJAWEA

Lewis and Clark with Sacajawea, 1805

Map drawn by William Clark of a section of the Missouri River

Introduction

Sacajawea [sah·cuh·juh·**wee**·uh] was probably born around 1789 in what is now Idaho. She was part of the Shoshoni [shoh·**shoh**·nee] tribe. The Shoshoni hunted buffalo, elk, and other animals. They traveled across the mountains to fish for salmon. They also gathered fruits, berries, and the roots of the camas plant, which was ground into flour for bread. Like all Shoshoni girls, Sacajawea learned to make clothing from animal skins. She also learned to find and prepare the foods her family ate.

Now read the habit and strategy for **While I Read**. When you see ❓, read my notes in the margin.

While I Read

Which **HABIT** will I learn?

> **Stop and ask, "If it doesn't make sense, what can I do?"**
> If I develop this habit, I will stop and figure out what to do so what I'm reading makes sense. Then I can keep reading and not be lost.

Which **STRATEGY** will I use to learn this habit?

> Go to the introduction and/or summary for help.

When she was 10 or 11, warriors from the Hidatsa [hi·**daht**·suh] tribe attacked Sacajawea's village. They killed many villagers and kidnapped Sacajawea. They took her to a Hidatsa village in what is now North Dakota, more than 500 miles from her home. The Hidatsas called her Sacajawea, which meant "Bird Woman." Her Shoshoni name has been lost. The Hidatsas kept Sacajawea as their slave. Would Sacajawea ever return to her village, or would she spend the rest of her life with the Hidatsas? Little did Sacajawea know what an important role she would play in American history.

The Lewis and Clark Expedition

In 1803, the United States almost doubled its size when it bought the Louisiana Territory from France. This purchase included all the land from the Mississippi River west to the Rocky Mountains. No one knew for sure what that land was like. Native American peoples lived there. Fur trappers and hunters traveled parts of it. But there were no maps and, for the most part, the land was a mystery. President Jefferson asked an army captain, Meriwether Lewis, to lead an **expedition** of discovery. Lewis, along with his friend and co-captain William Clark, put together a crew of men. The Lewis and Clark expedition would keep journals and draw maps (like the one on page 167) of the land they explored.

expedition
(ek·spi·**dish**·uhn)—an organized trip

Meriwether Lewis

William Clark

interpreter
(in·**tur**·pri·tuhr)—person who restates something said in one language into another language

translate (**trans**·layt)—
to express in another language

Stop and Ask

If it doesn't make sense, what can I do? Go to the introduction and/or summary for help.

• • • • • • • • • • • •

I don't understand why Sacajawea is with Charbonneau. The introduction on pages 167–168 reminds me that Sacajawea was kidnapped by the Hidatsas. That's why she's with Charbonneau.

Sacajawea Joins the Expedition

The expedition got under way in the spring of 1804. By fall, the men had reached what is now North Dakota, where they found a friendly village of Mandan [**man**·dan] people. Lewis and Clark made their winter camp there. They named it Fort Mandan. Planning ahead for the journey, they hired an **interpreter**, a French trader named Charbonneau [**shar**·buh·noh]. Charbonneau would help **translate** the Native American languages into English. With him was a young Shoshoni woman. Her name—Sacajawea. Charbonneau may have bought her from the Hidatsas, or perhaps won her at gambling. In any case, he took Sacajawea to the Mandan village where he lived. Charbonneau called her his wife, but he treated her more like a servant. She cooked and worked for him as she had for the Hidatsas.

Strategy Alert!

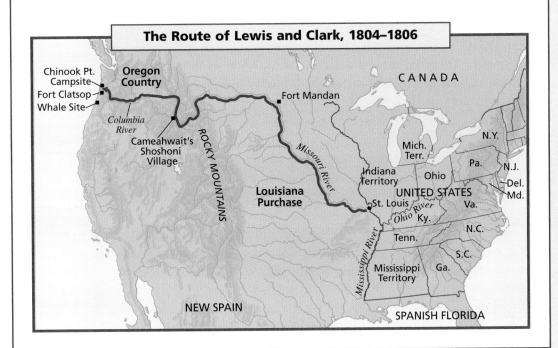

The Route of Lewis and Clark, 1804–1806

Captain Clark, Charbonneau, and Sacajawea with her baby

Charbonneau Makes a Deal

In his deal with Lewis and Clark, Charbonneau insisted on taking Sacajawea along on the expedition. The explorers were **reluctant**. When Lewis and Clark met her, Sacajawea was about 16 years old. She was expecting a baby. She would be the only female on the journey, alone among 35 men. On the other hand, she wanted to go, and she spoke Shoshoni, a language they would need. Finally they agreed to take her. *Strategy Alert!*

Sacajawea's baby boy was born before the expedition left Fort Mandan. His father named him Jean-Baptiste but Sacajawea called him Pomp, a Shoshoni word for "first born" or "leader." On April 7, 1805, the expedition left North Dakota with Sacajawea carrying Pomp on her back.

Sacajawea Pitches In

Almost immediately, Sacajawea made herself useful. She knew a lot of the wild plants and added them to the men's meals. Captain Clark, especially, grew fond of her and gave her the nickname "Janey."

As the men paddled the boats, heavy with supplies, upriver, Sacajawea often walked along the shore with Charbonneau and Captain Clark. Sometimes they traveled in the boats as well. These boats were pirogues [pi·**rohgz**], a kind of large canoe with a sail. One day when the captains were on shore, Charbonneau was steering a pirogue carrying Sacajawea. Suddenly, a wind came up and their pirogue began to tip. Charbonneau panicked and began to cry that he could not swim. He dropped the tiller (the part of the boat used to steer), making matters worse. The men grabbed kettles and began to bail the water out of the boat. Slowly, the boat **righted** itself. While all this was happening, Sacajawea sat at the back of the boat. Knowing that she could swim to shore, even with the baby on her back, she calmly began picking up the supplies that floated near her and putting them back in the boat. She probably saved such things as compasses and other instruments, books, and clothing. Captain Lewis later gave her credit for saving the entire expedition.

Overcoming Obstacles

Parts of the journey were very difficult. Sometimes the group had to face dangerous rapids. In other cases, however, shallow or rocky waters caused problems. Whenever the waterway became shallow or rocky, or at waterfalls, the boats had to be **portaged** over land. Other problems the crew endured included run-ins with grizzly bears, rattlesnakes, and mosquitoes. All these **obstacles** made the men exhausted. Many became sick. Captain Lewis was the expedition's "doctor." He had a bag full of medicines and a knowledge of many helpful plants. When Sacajawea grew ill, she became so weak that the captains were afraid she would die. Lewis and Clark took turns caring for the young woman. Finally, one of Lewis's remedies appeared to work, and Sacajawea recovered.

portaged (**por**·tijd)— carried boats and supplies over land between two waterways

obstacles (**ob**·stuh·kuhls)—things or people that stand in the way

A Summer Storm

The trip was slow, but there were moments of high excitement. One day, Clark, Charbonneau, and Sacajawea were walking along a little creek. Suddenly a storm blew up, and the group got under an overhanging rock to stay dry. With the baby in her arms, Sacajawea scrambled up the hill to safety with the others. In minutes, the place where they had been was filled with water. Sacajawea lost most of the baby's clothes, and Charbonneau lost his gun. But as always, she remained calm in a dangerous situation.

Sacajawea Comes Home

By late July, the expedition had reached Sacajawea's homeland. She showed the captains where her village had stood when the Hidatsas came, and pointed out the place where she had been captured. Soon, she said, they would come to the Shoshoni summer camp. The captains hoped to buy horses to cross the mountains in the winter. Lewis went ahead and, thanks to Sacajawea's **accurate** memory, found the Shoshoni. He persuaded the chief to go back with him to meet the others. The Shoshoni agreed, but they were afraid Lewis was trying to trick them. Dozens of warriors went, too.

Sacajawea, with her baby on her back, was traveling on foot with Captain Clark. They were walking through a valley near a river when the Shoshoni spotted the group. The warriors grew nervous and began to reach for their bows. Suddenly, among the crowd of white men, they spotted an Indian girl. As the Shoshoni warriors rode toward her, Sacajawea began to jump up and down with joy. *Strategy Alert!*

The party went back to the village. The women and girls crowded around Sacajawea. One young woman was a friend who had been captured with Sacajawea. She had escaped and returned to her people. The two chattered happily, each glad that the other was safe. Sacajawea had found her people!

Sacajawea with the expedition party

Stop and Ask ?

If it doesn't make sense, what can I do? Go to the introduction and/or summary for help.

I wonder why Sacajawea's so happy. The summary reminds me that Sacajawea was kidnapped from the Shoshoni tribe when she was a child. She hasn't seen her people, the Shoshoni, in years. That's why she's so happy to see them.

When the men were ready to meet, they sent for Sacajawea. She came into the tent and sat down to translate. When she looked at the Shoshoni chief, she could not believe her eyes. It was her own brother, Cameahwait [**ca·mee·**ah·wayt]! She jumped up and hugged him, tears running down her cheeks. The two spoke briefly, and Sacajawea learned that except for Cameahwait and one other brother, all of her family was dead. Her time of joy was also a time of sadness. Then, Sacajawea went back to the job of translating. She listened to the Shoshoni words and translated them into English. It was a slow process, but the meeting finally ended. The captains had bargained for horses, and Cameahwait drew them a map of the territory ahead. Sacajawea chose to go on with the expedition.

Sacajawea with Lewis and Clark

On to the Pacific

Crossing the mountains through deep snow was a challenge. Food became so scarce that they were forced to kill and eat some of the horses. Finally they came down into the Columbia River valley. There it rained almost constantly. But at least there was more game. They killed an elk, and Sacajawea showed the men how to boil the bones to get **tallow** for candles. She was helpful in other ways as well. The expedition sometimes met bands of hunters who might have attacked, but when they saw Sacajawea and her baby, they let the group pass.

tallow (**tal·**oh)—animal fat used to make candles

The expedition finally reached the Pacific Ocean in November of 1805. They built their winter camp, Fort Clatsop, near what is now Astoria, Oregon. Native Americans from neighboring tribes came to trade with them. One Chinook [shi·**nuk**] brought a beautiful otter robe that the captains wanted. In exchange for it, the robe's owner pointed to Sacajawea's blue beaded belt. She gave it to him. In return, the captains gave her a blue cloth coat.

Sacajawea met all the hardships that the men did, without complaining. But when she heard that a whale had washed ashore and a party of men was going to see it, she demanded to be taken along. She had, she said, traveled a long way to see the great waters. The men agreed and took her along.

The Road Home

In March 1806, the expedition left the Pacific and headed home. The trip back was no easier. The captains had come to depend on Sacajawea's advice about the best route. Many of the men were sick. Sacajawea's baby, Pomp, came down with a bad sore throat. The captains worried about him and gave him medicine. Soon he began to recover. The group went on.

As spring gave way to summer, the group suffered with sore feet, heat, and mosquito bites. Sacajawea continued to find food. She dug roots and gathered berries, welcome additions to their diet of elk. At last they reached Fort Mandan again. There the captains paid Charbonneau and said good-bye to Sacajawea and Pomp. Clark had become so fond of the little boy that he would have liked to adopt him. Of Sacajawea's contribution to the journey, Clark wrote that she "has been of great service to me as a pilot through this country." ⑦ *Strategy Alert!*

After the Expedition

No one knows much about Sacajawea's life after the expedition. The Shoshoni tell that she rejoined them and lived to an old age. However, other records suggest that Sacajawea probably died of a fever when she was in her early twenties. William Clark adopted Pomp and sent him to school. Sacajawea's son went to Europe. On his return, he went back to the West and lived out his life as a guide in his mother's tradition.

Summary

Sacajawea was born in a Shoshoni village and kidnapped as a child by the Hidatsas. She became the wife of a French trader when she was 12 or 13 years old. She was only about 16 when she set out for one of the great adventures in American history. With the Lewis and Clark expedition, she traveled—with her baby on her back—from Fort Mandan in North Dakota to the Pacific Ocean and back. She helped in countless ways—finding food, acting as an interpreter, and pointing out the best routes through the wilderness. Calm and uncomplaining, she endured all the hardships the men endured. Sacajawea probably died young. But she lives on in history as a courageous woman who joined the voyage of discovery through the American West.

Stop and Ask

If it doesn't make sense, what can I do? Go to the introduction and/or summary for help.

I'm not sure why Clark called Sacajawea a pilot. When I read the summary, I see that Sacajawea pointed out the best routes through the wilderness. That's why Clark called her a pilot.

Congratulations! You finished reading. Now read the habit and strategy for **After I Read**. Then read my notes below.

After I Read

Which **HABIT** will I learn?
Check to see what I remember.
If I develop this habit, I will check to see what I remember as soon as I finish reading. It helps me see if I really understood what I read and helps me remember it better, too.

Which **STRATEGY** will I use to learn this habit?
Use graphic aids, like maps and charts, to question myself.

My Notes

- Strategy says I should use graphic aids, like maps and charts, to question myself.

- This selection has a map I can use. Here are some questions this map can help me answer:

— Where did Lewis and Clark start their trip?

— Where did Lewis and Clark finish?

— How far along in their journey were they before they met Sacajawea?

— How far along were they when they met the Shoshoni?

Practice 3 of the 9 Habits

Now it's time to practice the three habits and strategies you learned when you read "Her Name Was Sacajawea." Start with **Before I Read**. Look at the box below. It should look familiar! Reread the habit you will practice. Reread the strategy you will use—then do it!

Before I Read

Which **HABIT** will I practice?
Decide what I need to know.
If I develop this habit, I will have a reason for reading. I will understand it better and remember more of what I read.

Which **STRATEGY** will I use to practice this habit?
Use the introduction and summary to ask purpose-setting questions.

 Use the **Before I Read Strategy Sheet** for "Survival on Ice" (page 36 in your *Strategy Practice Book*) to decide what you need to know.

Survival on Ice

Shackleton's Story

Sir Ernest Shackleton

Introduction

On October 27, 1915, Boss finally ordered his crew to abandon ship. For ten months the *Endurance* had been trapped in **pack ice**. Now the ice was crushing the vessel. Boss stood apart from his men, watching his dream die, listening to sounds of the ice killing his ship. Now he had just one job: to save his crew. He knew that this would be the greatest challenge of his life.

pack ice—large pieces of floating ice formed from smaller pieces frozen together

Reread the habit and strategy below. Look for the *Strategy Alerts!* as you read.

While I Read

Which **HABIT** will I practice?

Stop and ask, "If it doesn't make sense, what can I do?"
If I develop this habit, I will stop and figure out what to do so what I am reading makes sense. Then I can keep reading and not be lost.

Which **STRATEGY** will I use to practice this habit?
Go to the introduction and/or summary for help.

 Use the **While I Read Strategy Sheet** for "Survival on Ice" (page 37 in your *Strategy Practice Book*) as you read.

The Journey Begins

Boss's real name was Sir Ernest Shackleton. A British knight and adventurer, he had already been to Antarctica before he boarded the *Endurance*. In 1907, he had almost reached the South Pole. In 1908, he was planning to meet another challenge: to cross the frozen continent of Antarctica.

Planning the trip and raising huge sums of money to pay for a ship, supplies, and crew took years. Finally, everything was ready. On December 5, 1914, the *Endurance* left South Georgia with Boss and 27 crew members on board. (South Georgia is an island off the tip of South America in the **Southern Hemisphere**.) It was summer in this part of the world (December to March) and the crew hoped to reach the continent by the end of the month.

Southern Hemisphere (**suth**·uhrn **hem**·i·sfear)— the half of the earth that is south of the equator

Into the Weddell Sea

From South Georgia, the *Endurance* sailed for Antarctica. To the south was the Weddell Sea, where the ice was always **treacherous**. When the ship left, that ice was packed tight. Some seamen had warned the crew that their ship couldn't make it through.

The *Endurance* managed to push through ice, but progress was slow and frustrating. For a short time, they sailed effortlessly through clear water toward their goal. Soon, however, they hit ice again. This time they could not continue. The ice closed in on the *Endurance*. ⑦ *Strategy Alert!*

Trapped

Even in summer, Antarctic temperatures rarely get above freezing (32°F) on the coast. That summer, temperatures were colder than usual. By the end of the month, the *Endurance* was still tightly packed in ice. When cracks opened in the ice, the crew tried pushing the ship through to clear water. The men jumped on the ice to break it. They cut it with saws, picks, and other tools, but their efforts were in vain. Because of the **unseasonably** low temperatures, the ice froze over as quickly as the men could open it. After a while, Boss told his men to stop.

A month later, they were still stranded. Summer was winding down. Winter was approaching. The ice would surely not open again until spring. That meant that they would have to spend the winter on the ship. While the weather was still good, they hunted for seal meat and **blubber**—food for the men and fuel to cook it.

treacherous
(**trech**·uhr·uhs)—
dangerous

Stop and Ask ⑦

If it doesn't make sense, what can I do? Go to the introduction and/or summary for help.

unseasonably
(un·**see**·zuh·nuh·blee)—
not typical for the season

blubber (**blub**·uhr)—
the layer of fat beneath the skin of a sea animal

Average Antarctic Temperatures and Hours of Daylight				
	Average Winter Temperatures (June–September)	Average Summer Temperatures (December–March)	Hours of Daylight (Winter)	Hours of Daylight (Summer)
Inland	Low: -94°F High: -40°F	Low: -31°F High: 5°F	0 hours	Up to 20 hours
Coastal Areas	Low: -22°F High: -5°F	Low: 32°F High: 32°F	Daylight and darkness more balanced	Daylight and darkness more balanced

In May, as winter approached, the men saw the sun for the last time. The **polar night** fell. Boss and the crew settled in to a winter routine. They played games, talked, and sang together. They kept journals, read, and even performed shows. A stove kept them warm despite the cold temperatures, and there was enough to eat. As the days passed, the temperatures got colder and colder. Soon the ship was in the icy grip of a polar winter. The men dreamed of spring, when they believed the ship would break free.

Attack of the Ice

July brought huge winter storms. As winter moved into spring, the ice began to crack and the men waited for a breakup. They could see ice **floes** banging into each other, which meant that the ice was thawing. However, there was no open water near the ship. This worried them. What if the massive ice floes pushed into the ship? Could the *Endurance* withstand the pressure?

Weeks passed and now spring was really coming. The sun shone again, the air warmed up, and at last, the temperature climbed above zero. The ship had survived the test of winter, and the men were hopeful. Maybe the ship would push into open water! But ice kept closing in on the ship, and it didn't stop. The ice was **relentlessly** attacking, crushing, and splintering the ship. By the end of October, it began to leak dangerously. Their hopes were dashed. The men had no choice but to abandon the *Endurance* for good.

The *Endurance* trapped in ice

Ocean Camp

The men carried supplies off the ship, unloading food, clothing, cooking stoves, matches, and tools. They hauled three small boats off the ship as well; in time, they might need them to sail to safety. On a floe of ice one mile square, they pitched tents and constructed a lookout tower. They named this campsite "Ocean Camp."

Over time, the men returned to the *Endurance* for rope and more food. As the ship broke up, they used its wood to make fires. On November 21, their visit to the ship was different. They watched helplessly as the *Endurance* rose up in the ice and then began to sink. Within ten minutes she was gone, leaving the men more alone than ever. **(?)** *Strategy Alert!*

Shackleton and fellow explorer at campsite

Life at Ocean Camp was difficult, but at least chores kept the men occupied. Some men worked on the small boats, trying to make them more **seaworthy,** while others fixed tools. Most of the men hunted. At night they played cards, read, or talked; often their talk was about food!

The men feared they'd be stuck on this ice floe forever. They could not hike all the way to land; the ice between Ocean Camp and land was too broken to hold their boats and supplies. They could not sail back to land; the small boats could never stand up against the ice. But Boss had a plan. They would stay put for now and watch the way the ice drifted. In two months they would leave by boat or foot for Paulet Island, just off the tip of Antarctica.

Camp Patience

Finally, the men set off on foot with the boats and some supplies. Tramping across soft, broken ice proved slow and dangerous. Unable to continue, they set up a new camp which they called "Camp Patience." Life at the new camp was harder than ever. Now they were running out of food supplies. Their diet was seal and penguin, and the men were always hungry.

Stop and Ask **(?)**

If it doesn't make sense, what can I do? Go to the introduction and/or summary for help.

seaworthy
(**see**·wur·thee)—in good enough shape to be used on the sea

Because their lives depended on it, everyone kept track of the wind. Where would it carry the ice? Would it bring them closer to Paulet Island, or farther away? If they got closer, the small boats could carry them in. But the drift of wind and sea took them past Paulet Island. Now their hopes were set for two other islands, Elephant Island and Clarence Island, 100 miles to the north. Those islands were their last chance for survival.

Into the Boats

On April 10, 1916, the men launched the three boats although the two islands were still about 40 miles away. They must leave now—or never. The boats moved through the broken ice, entered clear water, then hit more ice. The wind lashed at the unprotected men, and the sea burst over the boats, soaking the men. Over the next few days, they fought for their lives as giant waves erupted and the boats took on more water.

Conditions were miserable. The men had no water, little food, and the temperatures were freezing. Their clothes were frozen solid, they all had frostbite, and **boils** popped out on their skin. When ice began to glaze the boats, the men had to beat the ice away. Everyone was tired and sick, but they could not give up. Surrender meant death. **(?)** *Strategy Alert!*

boils (boylz)—swollen sores; blisters

Stop and Ask **(?)**

If it doesn't make sense, what can I do? Go to the introduction and/or summary for help.

Broken ice off the coast of the Antarctic Peninsula

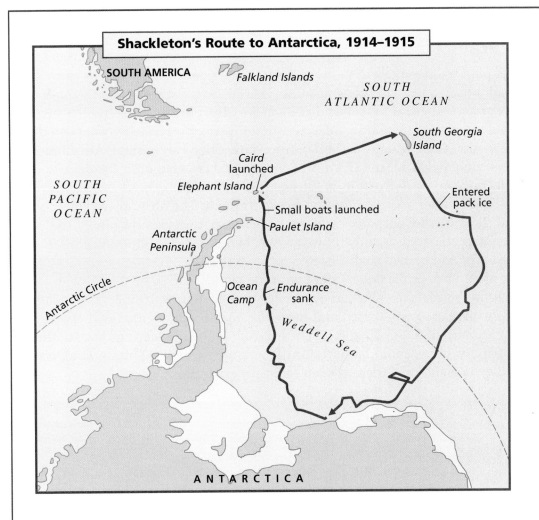

Shackleton's Route to Antarctica, 1914–1915

SOUTH AMERICA

Falkland Islands

SOUTH ATLANTIC OCEAN

South Georgia Island

Caird launched

Elephant Island

SOUTH PACIFIC OCEAN

Entered pack ice

Small boats launched

Paulet Island

Antarctic Peninsula

Antarctic Circle

Ocean Camp

Endurance sank

Weddell Sea

ANTARCTICA

Land at Last!

After seven days in the open boats, they neared their destination—
Elephant Island. That night, the wind roared as the sea **roiled** harder. It
was now 20 degrees below zero, and a snowstorm battered the boats. The
crew wondered whether they could survive the night. When dawn arrived,
they could see that the island was just ahead. At last they reached shore,
thankful that the entire crew was still alive.

The cook prepared a huge feast of seal meat, and the men ate all they
could. Then they unrolled their sleeping bags. The bags were soaked and
cold, but no one complained. Full of hope, the men slept soundly.

The next day brought more bad news—they would have to move again.
The area where they had landed was not safe from the sea. A search party
was sent out to look for a more protected spot. A new, safer area on
Elephant Island was found, and the entire crew departed at dawn the next
day. The trip was uneventful until the wind picked up and blew one of the
boats off course. Eventually all three boats returned safely to the island.
But help was still 800 miles away in South Georgia.  *Strategy Alert!*

roiled (royld)—churned;
stirred up

Stop and Ask ❓

If it doesn't make
sense, what can I do?
Go to the introduc-
tion and/or summary
for help.

A Brave Plan

The plan was for Boss to take five men in the *Caird*, the biggest of the small boats, and head for South Georgia. It was a risky journey through stormy, treacherous seas, but there was no **alternative**. Boss and his small crew set sail. As the *Caird* sailed through towering waves, spray soaked the crew. Always freezing, wet, and cramped, the men rarely slept. After four days, a cold **gale** hit the *Caird*. The weary men crawled onto the deck to chip ice away with frostbitten, blistered hands.

At last, after six days, the sun broke through. The air grew warmer, and the men saw porpoises and birds. Because it was sunny, one of the men was able to determine how far they had sailed. He announced that the *Caird* had made it halfway to South Georgia!

After 11 days, Boss saw a break in the clouds—or so he thought. In fact, the biggest wave he had ever seen was racing toward their tiny boat! As the gigantic wave tossed and flung the boat about, it filled with water. The exhausted men bailed for their lives, all the while fearing that another enormous wave would batter them. Thankfully, it didn't. Thirsty, cold, wet, and exhausted, they tried to keep their hopes alive.

Huge glaciers rise above the Weddell Sea in Antarctica.

Shackleton's camp with the British flag flying

The Final Adventure

Finally, Boss and his crew spotted the black cliffs of South Georgia on May 8. However, they needed to reach the other side of the island in order to get help. By sea, they were 140 miles from Leith Harbor; by land, they were 29 miles away. The overland route was through mountains and ice. No one had crossed it before, and Boss feared the route was impassable without skis or snowshoes.

But Boss said they must try. Boss would lead two men overland. They would walk day and night. They'd travel light, with each man carrying only food, rope, compasses, and a few tools. If help did not arrive soon, the other three men would try reaching the harbor by boat.

The first group set out at 2 A.M. on May 19. The route was dangerously rough. On and on they pushed. At one point, the path became so unsafe that they had to turn back to find another route. Progress was very slow. At dawn, they climbed a snowy slope and saw a harbor ahead. Their goal was just 12 miles away—12 difficult miles.

At 4 P.M., the men reached the harbor. Filthy, their hair overgrown, their beards dirty and matted, their clothes tattered, they struggled into the whaling station. Workmen in the harbor stopped to watch the three **disheveled** men. One worker took them to the manager of the whaling station. The manager came to the door of his home.

"Who are you?" he asked.

Boss replied, "My name is Shackleton."

The manager was shocked. Across the globe, people had assumed that the crew of the *Endurance* would never return. Boss and his men had been given up for dead. The world had **underestimated** Boss and his courageous crew. *Strategy Alert!*

Although it took three more months, a rescue party reached the men who remained on Elephant Island. All 27 men lived to tell a **miraculous** tale of survival.

disheveled
(di·**shev**·uhld)—messy; untidy

underestimated
(un·duhr·**es**·tuh·may·tid) —thought too little of

Stop and Ask

If it doesn't make sense, what can I do? Go to the introduction and/or summary for help.

miraculous
(mi·**rak**·yuh·luhs)— amazing

The crew that remained on Elephant Island waiting to be rescued

Summary

On December 5, 1914, Sir Ernest Shackleton and a crew of 27 men set out on an adventure. Their goal was to cross the frozen continent of Antarctica aboard the *Endurance*. After being stuck in pack ice for months, the group was forced to abandon the *Endurance*. They set up camp on a giant floe of ice. The men endured temperatures well below zero. Giant waves soaked their clothes and their gear. Food grew scarce. Yet these courageous men endured. First by foot, then by smaller boats they had hauled off the *Endurance* before it sank, the men tried to make their way back to civilization. Slowly, they made their way closer and closer to South Georgia. The entire crew could not get through. Chances were better for a small group. With a few others, and the expedition's only hope, Boss set out for South Georgia. Three months later, help arrived for those who had been left behind. Almost one and a half years after setting sail, Shackleton and every member of his crew were rescued.

Now that you've finished reading, review the **After I Read** habit below. Think about what you read in "Survival on Ice" as you practice the habit and strategy.

After I Read

Which **HABIT** will I practice?
Check to see what I remember.
If I develop this habit, I will check to see what I remember as soon as I finish reading. It helps me see if I really understood what I read and helps me remember it better, too.

Which **STRATEGY** will I use to practice this habit?
Use graphic aids, like maps and charts, to question myself.

Use the **After I Read Strategy Sheet** for "Survival on Ice" (page 38 in your *Strategy Practice Book*) to check what you remember.

Apply 3 of the 9 Habits

> Now read "The Incredible Voyage of the *Kon-Tiki*" and apply these habits and strategies.

Before I Read

Which **HABIT** will I apply?
Decide what I need to know.

Which **STRATEGY** will I use to apply this habit?
Use the introduction and summary to ask purpose-setting questions.

While I Read

Which **HABIT** will I apply?
Stop and ask, "If it doesn't make sense, what can I do?"

Which **STRATEGY** will I use to apply this habit?
Go to the introduction and/or summary for help.

After I Read

Which **HABIT** will I apply?
Check to see what I remember.

Which **STRATEGY** will I use to apply this habit?
Use graphic aids, like maps and charts, to question myself.

Use the **Self-Assessment Sheet** for "The Incredible Voyage of the *Kon-Tiki*" on pages 39–40 in your *Strategy Practice Book* as you read to see how well you can apply the habits and strategies.

The Incredible Voyage of the *Kon-Tiki*

Kon-Tiki

Thor Heyerdahl in 1952

Introduction

In 1947, Thor Heyerdahl [**hay**·uhr·dahl] believed something that no one else did. He believed that **ancient** people sailed 4,625 miles across the Pacific Ocean from South America to the islands of Polynesia. Proving that his **theory** was true would take much research and careful planning. It would also take a strong raft and confidence in himself and others. He knew it would be a dangerous journey. Even so, Heyerdahl and five other men set sail across the Pacific Ocean. They trusted their lives to each other and to a tiny wooden raft called the *Kon-Tiki*. It was to be an incredible journey.

ancient (**ayn**·shuhnt)— of times long past

theory (**thee**·uh·ree)— an idea, opinion, or guess

Solving a Mystery

anthropologist
(an·thruh·**pol**·uh·jist)—
scientist who studies the
origins and customs of
human beings

Thor Heyerdahl was a Norwegian adventurer and scholar. He was not a trained **anthropologist**. His life interest was learning about ancient people. On a research trip to Polynesia in 1937–1938, he saw some stone carvings on the Marquesas [mar·**kay**·zuhz] Islands. They were nearly the same as ones he had seen in Peru in South America. Heyerdahl began to wonder if the same people had made both sets of carvings.

Heyerdahl began to ask questions about legends of the islands. From an old man he heard a legend about a great chief and god named Tiki whose father was the sun. The legend explained that Tiki had led his people to these islands.

Inca (**ing**·kuh)—the
Indian people of ancient
Peru

Seven years later, while researching ancient people in Peru, Heyerdahl made a discovery. He learned that the **Inca** also worshipped a sun-god. That god's original name was Kon-Tiki. Was there a connection between Tiki and Kon-Tiki? Heyerdahl believed there was. Heyerdahl wanted to find out if ancient people from South America had sailed to the Pacific Islands of Polynesia. To test his idea, he wanted to make the same journey that he thought these people had made. At the time, experts thought that he was foolish to try such a risky thing. What made him undertake this dangerous journey into the past?

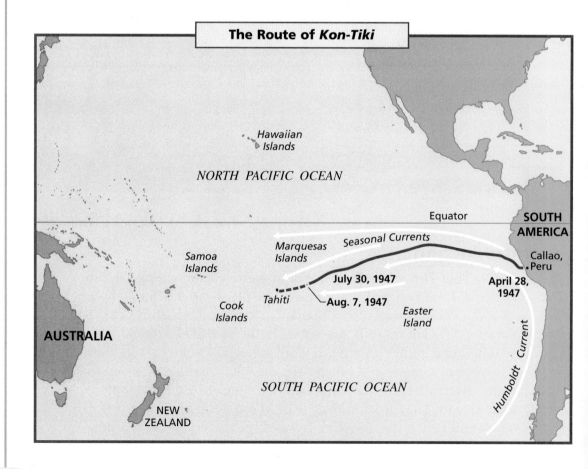

The Route of *Kon-Tiki*

Planning for the Journey

Every trip needs a plan. Heyerdahl needed to learn what kind of rafts the ancient people of Peru used. He needed to know what materials were used to build these rafts and how they were sailed. Also, he would need money to build and supply the raft. Last, he would need a crew to help him sail the raft and test his **hypothesis**. He hoped to prove that the islands of Polynesia were settled by Peruvians who sailed across the Pacific Ocean thousands of years ago.

hypothesis
(hie·**poth**·uh·sis)—an idea or opinion used to explain certain facts

Finding a Crew

Heyerdahl soon convinced five other men to join him on his journey. His crew included four Norwegians: Herman Watzinger, an engineer; Erik Hesselberg, a friend who had already sailed around the world; and Torstein Raaby and Knut Haugland, who knew how to operate radios. His sixth crewman was Bengt Danielsson from Sweden. Bengt spoke Spanish and could help with the work in Peru. Together, these six men completed the research and developed a plan for building the raft.

Deep in the Rain Forest

Heyerdahl learned that the ancient Peruvian rafts were made of balsa trees. These trees once grew along the coast of Peru. Now they grew in the rain forest of Ecuador. Balsa trees, if cut and not allowed to dry, stay full of sap. This allows the trees to absorb some water and still stay afloat. Heyerdahl and Watzinger went to Ecuador and traveled by jeep into the rain forest. Braving mud, raging rivers, deadly snakes, stinging ants, and scorpions, they found and cut 12 trees. This step accomplished, they started on their long journey to the sea.

First, a tractor dragged the trees to the river, where they were lashed together into two rafts. The men got on the rafts and guided them down the river to a port called Guayaquil [gwie·uh·**keel**]. When they reached Guayaquil, the logs were loaded on a boat and taken to Peru.

Thor Heyerdahl and crew building the bamboo shelter for the *Kon-Tiki*

Building the Raft

Heyerdahl and his crew built the raft at the naval dockyard in Peru. Imagine the strange looks of other shipyard workers! They were molding iron and steel into great ships as these men tied logs together with hemp ropes to make a raft! This raft was an exact **replica** of ancient rafts described in Heyerdahl's research. They used no nails or wire. Each of the nine logs was 30 to 45 feet long. The longest logs were used for the middle of the rafts. Gaps between the logs were filled with five pine boards that became the **centerboards** of the raft. On the raft the men built a simple bamboo shelter with a roof of banana leaves. Two trees were used to make a mast to carry the canvas sail. Hesselberg painted a picture of the sungod Kon Tiki on the sail; they named the raft *Kon-Tiki*. Finally, the raft was ready. Experts told the men that they doubted the raft would last long in the Pacific Ocean. Shipyard workers shook their heads in disbelief as the tiny raft was pulled away from the docks.

Setting Sail

The men stocked the raft with food, water, boxes for the equipment they would test, and a ship-to-shore radio. Of course, ancient people would not have had a radio, and Heyerdahl did not want to take one. He was finally convinced that the radio would allow interested people to follow *Kon-Tiki's* route. On April 27, 1947, the crew raised the Norwegian flag on the mast. Then they smashed a coconut across the logs to **christen** the raft. The next day, it was pulled out to sea, ready to begin an incredible journey.

replica (re·pli·kuh)— an exact copy

centerboards (sen·tuhr·bordz)—flat boards that can be lowered through the bottom of a sailboat to keep it from tipping

christen (kris·n)— to give a name to

With no modern equipment (except for the radio), the *Kon-Tiki* set sail. The crew had no electricity—only a lantern; no engines—only a sail; no **loran** to steer the raft by—only a **sextant** and compass. It took a few days to get used to the winds and the swell of the waves and to learn how to steer the little craft. The men found that the best way to steer was by raising and lowering the five centerboards. They took turns at the long wooden oar to keep the raft on course. Between the men and death in the vast, deep sea were only nine balsa logs. *Kon-Tiki* was a tiny speck in the world's largest ocean. Miraculously, after 45 days, the raft still sailed. The *Kon-Tiki* and the brave men aboard were halfway across the Pacific Ocean.

loran (lawr·an)— a navigating device that uses radio signals

sextant (seks·tuhnt)— instrument that finds a ship's position by measuring an angle between a star and the horizon

Life Onboard the *Kon-Tiki*

Long days at sea were a challenge for the men. They read, wrote in their diaries, sang, talked, and slept. They also carried out the experiments they had promised to do. Each day, one of the men had to swim under the raft to see if the hemp was still holding the raft together.

Many sea creatures swam by their little raft. Large turtles, squid, whales, dolphins, porpoises, flying fish, sharks, and many others kept them company as they sailed. Some of these creatures were caught to cook and eat. Others were saved for further study. For the first two months at sea, the days were mostly sunny and calm. As July approached, that was about to change.

Foul Weather at Sea

The month of July was full of angry storms that threatened to sink the tiny *Kon-Tiki*. At one point, the little raft was battered by wind, waves, and rain for more than two weeks. When the storms finally passed, Heyerdahl inspected the *Kon-Tiki*. He found a good deal of damage to the centerboards, the mast, and the shack. In spite of this damage, the nine logs remained lashed together—the raft was still seaworthy. How did the raft stay afloat? The answer was found in its ancient design. As the waves swept over the *Kon-Tiki*, water passed through the gaps and back into the sea. There was no chance for water to stay on the raft and sink it. The men made the necessary repairs, and the *Kon-Tiki* sailed on across the Pacific. Heyerdahl's dream lived on.

Most days on the *Kon-Tiki* were sunny and calm.

Land Ho!

By the end of July, the men spotted clouds on the horizon. They also saw more and more of certain types of birds. These sightings told them that they were getting closer and closer to land. After more than 90 days at sea, the crew saw land for the first time since they had set sail in Peru. The age-old shout of sailors arose from Watzinger. "Land ho!" he cried. Before long, the island of Puka-Puka came more clearly into view. The people on the island saw the tiny raft approach. They lit a fire to welcome the strangers, but the ocean currents were too strong. These currents kept the *Kon-Tiki* from entering the **lagoon**. Heyerdahl and his crew had no choice but to sail on.

The next day they tried to reach the nearby island of Angatau [**ahng·uh·tou**]. This time the islanders came out in their canoes to meet them. They were amazed to see that the little raft had no motor! They tried to pull the raft in, but the current was still too strong. Tired and disappointed, the crew of the *Kon-Tiki* had to move on.

A Crash-Landing

After three more days of drifting, it was time to end the journey. The men had been at sea for 102 days. When they saw an island ahead of them, they drifted toward it, but they knew there was a problem. Between the raft and the island was the Raroia [rah·ro·**ee**·uh] Coral Reef. The **reef** was made up of jagged rocks and sat in a patch of rough sea. Realizing there was no way to sail over the reef, the crew decided they would have to make a crash-landing.

Torstein used the radio to tell the world where the raft was landing. The men tied all their belongings onto the deck. They tossed what they could into waterproof bags. Then they lifted the centerboards, threw out the anchor, clung to the *Kon-Tiki*, and waited. As they hung on, a huge

lagoon (luh·**goon**)— shallow salt water that is protected from the sea by sand dunes

reef—a ridge of sand, coral, or rock just below the surface of the water

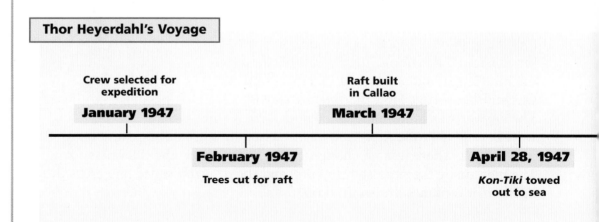

Thor Heyerdahl's Voyage

Crew selected for expedition		Raft built in Callao	
January 1947		**March 1947**	
	February 1947		**April 28, 1947**
	Trees cut for raft		*Kon-Tiki* towed out to sea

wave crashed into the raft. The wave threw them up and over the reef. The incredible journey was over. Heyerdahl and his crew reached land after sailing 4,625 miles across the Pacific Ocean!

Polynesia at Last

Sore but alive, the crew crawled onto the beach of an **uninhabited** island. Unbelievably, *Kon-Tiki's* logs were still lashed together as it washed up on shore. Slowly the men dried out their belongings, made a fire, rested, and ate fruits from the island trees. After a few days, they were able to get the radio working. With great joy, they told the world where they were—in the Polynesian Islands. A week later, people from a nearby island saw the fire and came to see them. The islanders were fascinated by the white men who knew of the god Tiki, and who had sailed across the ocean on a raft.

Summary

Heyerdahl and his crew proved that sailing across the vast ocean in a tiny, **primitive** raft was possible. Their modern adventure made people think about what ancient people could do. Heyerdahl didn't prove that the people who settled the Polynesian Islands came from Peru. In fact, anthropologists today think that the people who first settled Polynesia probably came from Asia, not from South America. Anthropologists also think that some islands in the Pacific were later visited by peoples from the Americas. Perhaps that is how the god Tiki became a part of the Polynesian legends, but no one knows for sure.

More than anything else, Thor Heyerdahl and his crew are remembered for their bravery and their spirit of adventure. They alone sailed in a tiny raft on a huge ocean. They ended up proving one thing for sure—that people who believe in themselves and their dreams can meet the challenges of a vast ocean and survive.

uninhabited (un·in·**hab**·it·ed)—having no one living there

primitive (**prim**·uh·tiv)—simple, like that of earliest times

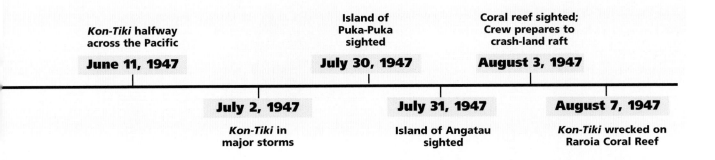

Kon-Tiki halfway across the Pacific
June 11, 1947

July 2, 1947
Kon-Tiki in major storms

Island of Puka-Puka sighted
July 30, 1947

July 31, 1947
Island of Angatau sighted

Coral reef sighted; Crew prepares to crash-land raft
August 3, 1947

August 7, 1947
Kon-Tiki wrecked on Raroia Coral Reef

Put Your Habits to Work in

Literature **Social Studies** **Science** **Math**

Before I Read Habit:
Decide what I need to know.

Remember to think about why you are reading **before** you read a chapter in a social studies textbook. If there is an introduction and/or summary, read that first and make up questions to guide your reading.

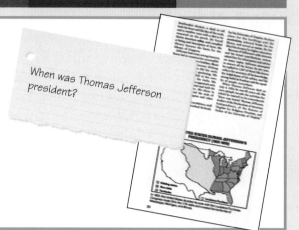

While I Read Habit:
Stop and ask, "If it doesn't make sense, what can I do?"

If something you are reading doesn't make sense, rereading the introduction or reading the summary might help.

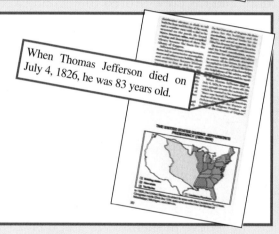

After I Read Habit:
Check to see what I remember.

When reading a social studies textbook, you're not finished until you see how much you remember about what you just read. You can do that by using graphic aids, like charts and maps, to question yourself.

You may wish to use the **Put Your Habits to Work Sheet** (page 41 in your *Strategy Practice Book*) to practice these habits in your other reading.

Unit 7
Understanding Me, Understanding Others
Theme: Myself

In this unit, you will develop these 3 habits for all readers.

Before I Read Habit:
Check it out!

While I Read Habit:
Stop and ask, "How does it connect to what I know?"

After I Read Habit:
React to what I've read.

In this unit, you will develop three habits—one for before you read, one for while you are reading, and one for after you finish reading. Start with **Before I Read**. Read the habit and strategy. Then read my notes below.

Before I Read

Which **HABIT** will I learn?
Check it out!
If I develop this habit, I can find out something about what I am going to read so that I know what to expect.

Which **STRATEGY** will I use to learn this habit?
Quickly skim the selection to see what it is about.

My Notes

- Strategy says to quickly skim—just kind of look it over—to see what the selection is about.

- The first sentence in the first paragraph tells me that the story is about two brothers, and it's summertime.

- When I skim a little more, I can tell the older boy wants a real job. Somehow he ends up in trouble with his neighbors.

First JOB

by Gary Soto

ON A HOT SUMMER DAY, Alex sat on the couch, sipping from a tall glass of homemade eggnog that he and his six-year-old brother, Jaime, had whipped up in the blender. They had followed a recipe from their mother's only cookbook. Alex had brought down a **canister** of sugar from the cupboard, and Jaime had carried the eggs and milk from the refrigerator. They'd washed their hands and begun to work. But immediately the sugar spilled.

"*Ay, menso,* look what you done!" Alex scolded. He scooped up a handful of sugar and tossed it back into the canister. He licked his palms for grains of sugar, one eye on Jaime.

Jaime followed suit. He ran his fingers over the spilled sugar and then licked them, from his little pinkie to his worm of a thumb.

"Come on, be careful," Alex said as he returned to work. He measured the sugar and milk, and cracked an egg on the edge of the counter.

canister (kan·i·stuhr)— a container used to hold sugar, flour, coffee, or other foods

menso (men·so)— Spanish word for "silly"

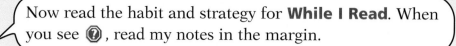

Now read the habit and strategy for **While I Read**. When you see , read my notes in the margin.

While I Read

Which **HABIT** will I learn?

Stop and ask, "How does it connect to what I know?"

If I develop this habit, I will think about how what I'm reading fits with what I know. This helps me understand the new material and remember it better.

Which **STRATEGY** will I use to learn this habit?

Decide whether I agree with the characters' actions.

They managed to make the eggnog and were in a good mood as they sat in front of the TV, their glasses of eggnog less than half gone, watching a game show. The prize was a trip to Hawaii and the second prize was a refrigerator packed with eight different kinds of meat. The third prize was a set of encyclopedias, bound in imitation leather but stamped with real gold-leaf letters.

"I want to go to Hawaii before I die," Alex said, trying to start up a conversation.

"Does it snow there?" Jaime asked. A mustache of foam was stuck to his upper lip.

"No, man, that's where they got the ocean."

"I like snow better. But sometimes I like the ocean better because it's got sand."

"You don't know what you like." Alex stopped talking and turned his attention to the game show. My brother is hopeless, he thought.

It was Alex's job to watch his little brother while his parents and his older brother and sister worked. For the most part Alex didn't mind taking care of Jaime, but now and then when he saw what his brother and sister bought with the money they earned, he grew jealous and upset.

Why can't I get a *real* job? he asked himself when he saw his brother slip into a new shirt. Why?

First Patricia had gotten a job. She worked two days a week for Mrs. McIntyre, a nurse on the night shift at St. Agnes Hospital. Patricia did mostly housecleaning. She washed dishes. She shoved a rag behind lamps where dust gathered. She swept the floor and **scoured** the bathroom. She changed burned-out light bulbs. But she also washed the car, careful to work slowly because Mrs. McIntyre loved her car more than anything in the world.

Then Alex's brother Bernardo, who was fourteen and only a year older than Alex, got a job with a gardener who cut lawns and hauled junk that was not really junk. They would turn around and sell this tossed stuff— lamps, chairs, racks of shoes, black-and-white TVs. Bernardo earned fifteen dollars a day, an eye-opening stash he kept in his sock drawer.

Today they were all at work. Alex was left alone with his little brother. His glass was now empty of eggnog, and he sighed from the heaviness of the midday drink. He touched his gut and burped.

"I'm bored," Alex said.

Jaime looked at his brother but didn't say anything. He was still loudly slurping his eggnog through a straw.

Alex went into the kitchen and saw the mess. The blender was sticky, the counter was sticky, and the eggshells were drooling idiotically.

"Aw, man," he said to himself. He tossed the eggshells into the trash and wiped the counter with a sponge. As he wiped the counter, he could hear the eggnog slosh in his stomach, moving back and forth like suds in a big washing machine. He burped again, the sweetness of eggnog filling his mouth. ② *Strategy Alert!*

Instead of returning to the living room to watch the rest of the game show, Alex went outside to the patio. Even though there was shade, the day was hot and flies flew lazy **halos** in the air. He picked up a tennis ball and began smacking it against the side of the house. He wanted to see if he could hit the ball thirteen times (his age and, for the time being, his lucky number) without missing. He did it once before he quit. It was too hot to play. Alex went out to the front yard and drank from the garden hose.

Chihuahua
(chi•**wah**•wah)—small dog with large ears

Muchacho, ven acá
(moo•**chah**•choh ven ah•**kah**)—Spanish for "Little boy, come here."

Stop and Ask

How does it connect to what I know? Decide whether I agree with the characters' actions.

• • • • • • • • • •

Alex isn't happy about having to go over to his neighbor's house. I think Alex feels like Mrs. Martinez once "told" on him and he's a little worried about what she wants now. I can understand that.

chiles (**chil**•eez)—spicy, hot peppers

Across the street his neighbor Mrs. Martinez was sweeping leaves into a cardboard box. She was a neighbor who constantly played the small yellow radio that sat in her window. She was the one who knit a red woolly coat for her shivering **Chihuahua** named Princesa and warmed up her car for half an hour before backing out with both hands on the steering wheel. She was the neighbor who told on Alex when he and his friend Jésus [**hay**•soos] tossed light bulbs in the alley.

*"**Muchacho, ven acá**,"* Mrs. Martinez yelled, waving at Alex. The flesh under her upper arm wiggled.

What does she want? Alex wondered, as he hiked up his pants and crossed the street. 🄰 *Strategy Alert!*

"You rake and burn the leaves," she said in Spanish. She handed him a rake with three teeth missing that was held together with black electrical tape. "I will pay you a dollar."

"A dollar?" Alex asked. He thought of Bernardo, how at the end of the day he came home with fifteen dollars in cash. But then he thought that it wouldn't take long to rake the leaves. He should do it. It would be the start of his working career, and Mrs. Martinez was a sure-bet job reference.

Alex followed Mrs. Martinez to her backyard, where two large roosters the color of smoke clucked and pecked at the ground. Chickens looked up when Alex opened the gate and he and Mrs. Martinez entered.

Her yard was mostly taken up by fruit trees and a scraggly patch of **chiles**, squash, and tomatoes. A bed sheet hung on the line. A doghouse stood empty, a rusty chain attached to its side. A bathtub leaned against the shed, along with an assortment of wood that was so old that the paint had peeled.

Mrs. Martinez pointed to the tree. Even though it was summer, the tree, a bottle brush, was shedding leaves. "Rake and burn over there," she commanded. She pointed to a pile of junk along the back fence, then handed him three wooden matches from her apron.

Mrs. Martinez went inside, leaving Alex eyeing the chickens that were eyeing him. He stomped his foot and they jumped, sending a few feathers seesawing in the air.

Alex began raking, the leaves quickly gathering in the old rake. He found a quarter, caked with earth. He spat on it and cleaned the mud from President Washington's face. He saw that the coin had been minted in 1959.

"Man, it could be worth something," he said. He pocketed the quarter and **resumed** raking. While he worked he thought of his brother Bernardo, who was probably out somewhere running a lawn mower. His sister was probably wiping down Mrs. McIntyre's car, the sunlight glinting off its perfect paint.

In no time Alex had raked the leaves and heaped them into a pyramid shape near the back fence. He wiped his sweaty face, then squatted down and struck a match against the wooden fence. The flame flared with a hiss and then calmed to a yellowish head of fire. He lowered the match into the leaves, which began to smoke and then caught fire. ⑦ *Strategy Alert!*

Alex stood back, waving the smoke away from his face. He coughed and stared at the fire. He turned and saw that the chickens were pacing nervously near the gate.

"You scaredy-cats," he shouted. He struck one of the other matches and threw it in their direction, the match falling harmlessly nearby. He clapped loudly and the chickens jumped, their claws splayed in midair.

Then Alex remembered his little brother.

"*Ay,*" he said, his eyes growing big with worry as he hurried toward the gate. He would come back to collect his money as soon as he had checked on Jaime. He hoped Mrs. Martinez would pay him with a crisp dollar, not bitter pennies and **grimy** nickels. As he started to leave he plucked a tomato from her vine and bit into it. The tomato squirted seeds into his mouth.

resumed (ri·**zoomd**)— went back to

Stop and Ask

How does it connect to what I know? Decide whether I agree with the characters' actions.

• • • • • • • • • • •

I would want to make some money, too, but I'm not sure I would have lit the fire there. Mrs. Martinez said to burn the leaves, but the chickens are kind of close, and there is other stuff that could catch fire. I think I disagree with what Alex did.

grimy (**grie**·mee)—dirty

Alex crossed the street and went inside his house. His brother was asleep on the couch, his empty glass of eggnog wedged between his legs. His upper lip was beaded with sweat, and his cheeks were pink. His curly hair looked soft. He looked like an angel, Alex had to admit. That's what their mother called Jaime—"angel" this, "angel" that. *Strategy Alert!*

"Wake up," Alex screamed. He turned off the television with a quick twist of his wrist. A man on the screen was selling used cars and laughing when his face collapsed into a shrinking gray dot and then vanished altogether.

"Come on, Jaime," Alex said. He shook his brother's shoulders and pinched his cheek. Jaime's wobbly body felt as loose and boneless as a Raggedy Andy doll.

Jaime woke slowly, rubbing his fists into his eyes. He looked down at his empty glass, then gazed up at Alex and asked, "Did you drink some of mine?"

"No, I was working." He held up the partially eaten tomato. "Mrs. Martinez gave me a tomato."

Jaime, still sleepy, looked at his brother, trying to shift his mind to wakefulness. "You were not," he said at last.

"I was. I was working for Mrs. Martinez. She's gonna pay me a dollar." He pointed in the direction of Mrs. Martinez's house.

Jaime got on his knees and looked outside. He didn't have to rub his eyes to see smoke coming from Mrs. Martinez's backyard.

"She's burning something," Jamie said. "Is she having a barbecue?"

"What?" Alex asked.

Alex looked out the front window and saw a wafer of smoke forming above Mrs. Martinez's roof. Her next-door neighbor was hurrying toward her backyard, barefoot and shirtless.

Stop and Ask ?

How does it connect to what I know? Decide whether I agree with the characters' actions.

• • • • • • • • • •

Alex came home to check on his brother. Jaime is too young to be left alone. I know how little kids can get in trouble! I agree with what Alex did, but he needs to be watching the fire, too.

"Don't tell Dad," Alex begged, wagging a grimy finger at his brother.

"Did you do something bad?" Jaime asked. "Dad said if you do something wrong we can't go on vacation."

Without answering, without listening, Alex was out the front door and flying across the street. Fear went up and down his back like a zipper. He could feel the lick of a belt across his legs, a fire that would die only when he held his legs under a cold, cold shower. He was in trouble, and he knew it.

"What have I done?" he muttered to himself. He threw the tomato into the gutter.

The neighbor stood, legs spread apart, squirting the small fire with a garden hose. The blaze had eaten the grass to a black stubble and had scared the chickens into the next yard. The smoky **stench** had pulled some kids from across the alley, and they had gathered to peek at the commotion.

"Turn on the water all the way," the neighbor said, motioning toward the faucet.

Alex did as he was told and stood motionless, paralyzed with fright.

 Strategy Alert!

When Alex realized the fire had climbed the fence and blackened some slats, he started to cry. His dime-sized tears fell to the ground. He coughed, and his nose began to run.

Stop and Ask ?

How does it connect to what I know? Decide whether I agree with the characters' actions.

• • • • • • • • • •

I know how it feels to be "paralyzed with fright" like Alex was. That happened to me when I was on stage in a play. He turned on the water—that was a good idea. I agree with that.

Ayúdame
(uh•**yoo**•duh•may)—
Spanish for "Help me!"

Stop and Ask

How does it connect to what I know? Decide whether I agree with the characters' actions.

. . . .

Alex begs Mrs. Martinez not to call the fire station. He wants to fix the problem himself. When I make a mistake, I know I like to fix it by myself, too. But I'm not sure how bad the fire is. The fire department may have to be called to put it out.

míra (**mee**•rhuh)—
Spanish for "look"

charred (chard)—
slightly burnt

Mrs. Martinez rushed out onto the porch. She was carrying a telephone book in one hand and her dog in the other. Princesa's red coat was buttoned all the way up to her jingling dog tags.

Mrs. Martinez shouted, "Alex, I'm looking for the fireman, *¡Ayúdame!*"

"Mrs. Martinez, don't call," Alex begged tearfully. "I'll pay you." He stuck one hand into his pocket and fingered the third and last match, snapping it in two because he was so angry with himself. He thrust the hand back into his pocket and brought out the quarter he had stashed along with a handful of sunflower seeds. "Mrs. Martinez, this is worth money." He held up the quarter, and President Washington's face seemed to wink in the sunlight. ❓ *Strategy Alert!*

The neighbor, his eyes stinging from the smoke, turned and said, "It's almost out. It'll be OK."

Mrs. Martinez put down the book. She yelled at Alex, "**Míra,** you ruined my rake." She pointed at the rake leaning against the fence. It was **charred,** and now all its teeth were gone. "And my chickens are in Mrs. Silva's yard."

Alex looked toward Mrs. Silva's house. He could see one of the chickens perched in a tree, looking down at the Silvas' mean, snaggle-toothed cat, Gavacho. He wondered if his dad had meant what he'd said about not taking them on vacation.

Princesa barked at Alex, who gazed at his shoes in misery. He could hear the chickens in the next yard, clucking and scratching the hard-packed earth. And he could hear the kids asking what had happened.

So ended Alex's first summer job. Alex had hoped to earn a dollar, but it hadn't worked out that way. Instead his dad had to shell out ten dollars to replace some wood, and Alex had to help Mrs. Martinez rebuild her fence while Princesa yapped at his heels.

Congratulations! You finished reading. Now read the habit and strategy for **After I Read**. Then read my notes below.

After I Read

Which **HABIT** will I learn?

React to what I've read.
If I develop this habit, I will take time to think about what I've just read. Deciding what I think and what I feel helps me remember it better.

Which **STRATEGY** will I use to learn this habit?
Decide whether the story would have ended differently in a different setting.

My Notes

- Strategy says to decide whether the story would end differently if the setting—where the story took place—were different.

- Mrs. Martinez's yard was part of the setting. She had a fence and chickens. That's where Alex started the leaves on fire.

- If her yard had been different (no fence) or if Alex had lived in a place where burning leaves is illegal, there might not have been a fire.

- Without the fire, the ending would have been different. Alex wouldn't have gotten in trouble.

Now it's time to practice the three habits and strategies you learned when you read "First Job." Start with **Before I Read**. Look at the box below. It should look familiar! Reread the habit you will practice. Reread the strategy you will use—then do it!

Before I Read

Which **HABIT** will I practice?
Check it out!
If I develop this habit, I can find out something about what I am going to read so that I know what to expect.

Which **STRATEGY** will I use to practice this habit?
Quickly skim the selection to see what it is about.

Use the **Before I Read Strategy Sheet** for "Family Resemblance" (page 42 in your *Strategy Practice Book*) to check it out.

Family Resemblance

By Holly Gems Timberline

Emma was furious. She slammed the photo album shut and banged her fist on top of it. Scowling out the window, she watched her cousins playing sharks and **minnows** in the swimming pool. Then the glass door slid open, and her four-year-old cousin, Jessie, peeked into the room.

"I want juice," Jessie said. "Please," she added hastily.

"Well, tell your mom to get it!" Emma snapped. "I'm busy."

"Are you mad?" Jessie looked up at Emma, the freckles on her nose wrinkling as she imitated Emma's frown.

"Yes, Jessie, I'm mad." Emma slammed her fist on the album again. "MAD, MAD, MAD!" She knew she was scaring Jessie, but she didn't care. Not now. She stood up, shoved her chair back into place, and stormed out of the room.

She ran upstairs, slowing down in the quiet hallway to look at the family **portraits**. There was her grandparents' wedding picture and a baby picture of Emma's mother, with her coppery bangs and straight-toothed smile. There were her uncle and aunt as babies, both with blond curls and rosy cheeks, then another photograph of the whole family. Unexpectedly, Emma caught sight of herself in the glass on the family portrait. Straight black hair, angled brown eyes, small pink mouth. How on earth had she landed here?

minnows (**min**·ohz)— any small fish

portraits (**por**·tritz)— drawings, paintings, or photographs of a person

Reread the habit and strategy below. Look for the *Strategy Alerts!* as you continue to read.

While I Read

Which **HABIT** will I practice?

Stop and ask, "How does it connect to what I know?"

If I develop this habit, I will think about how what I'm reading fits with what I know. This helps me understand the new material and remember it better.

Which **STRATEGY** will I use to practice this habit?

Decide whether I agree with the characters' actions.

Use the **While I Read Strategy Sheet** for "Family Resemblance" (page 43 in your *Strategy Practice Book*) as you read.

Stop and Ask

How does it connect to what I know? Decide whether I agree with the characters' actions.

---

genetic (juh·**net**·ik)— biologically passed from parent to child

"Em?" Oh no. Her mother was calling her. Emma slipped silently into the bathroom, closing the door behind her. "Emma? Are you up here?"

Emma rolled her eyes. "I'm in the bathroom, Mom."

Her mother called, "We have to go soon, so get your stuff together. O.K.?"

"O.K.," Emma answered. She leaned against the door, breathing in the fruity smell of the colored soaps on the sink. The beige rug was soft on her bare brown toes. She felt as if she belonged everywhere and nowhere at the same time. *Strategy Alert!*

Emma had always known she was adopted. But for the last year, whenever she looked at her family, all she could think was that they had nothing to do with who she was. She certainly didn't inherit her brown eyes from them, or her small hands. When her cousin Michael had learned that being able to roll one's tongue was **genetic,** they'd all tried it. Emma was the only one who couldn't do it.

She knew that her mother and grandmother had traveled to China to get her when she was a baby. Her mother had told her how all the Chinese ladies stopped them because of her mom's bright red hair and fair skin, and how some ladies said, "Lucky baby," while others spit on the ground in disgust to see one of their children with an American woman. Emma knew all this and more, yet she was certain there was something her mother was not telling her.

All summer she had been looking forward to the big Labor Day picnic at Grandma's. She'd planned to leaf through the photo album and find out for herself. Maybe there would be a picture of her real mother handing her over to the Americans, or an older brother or sister she'd never known.

But she hadn't seen anything different from the pictures in the album at home. There they all were at the hotel, right after Emma had been signed over. There they were on the plane, Emma's face frozen in a miserable wail and Mom and Grandma looking concerned. And there they were with the whole family, just minutes after landing in Philadelphia. And that was all.

Thinking about it now, while hiding from her mother in the bathroom, Emma felt a tear slide out of her eye. She caught it on her hand and looked at it. Water, she told herself. Nothing more. She wiped it away on a lace-edged towel. It was time to go home. She opened the bathroom door.

② *Strategy Alert!*

"Ready?" Emma looked up to see her mother standing in the hallway. She had been looking at the pictures, too. "Em? Are you O.K.?" Stupid tears, Emma thought. "Sweetie? What's wrong?" Emma shrugged, and Mom put an arm around her. Emma leaned her head on her shoulder. Mom was wearing the purple sweatshirt Emma had picked out for her birthday.

Stop and Ask **?**

How does it connect to what I know? Decide whether I agree with the characters' actions.

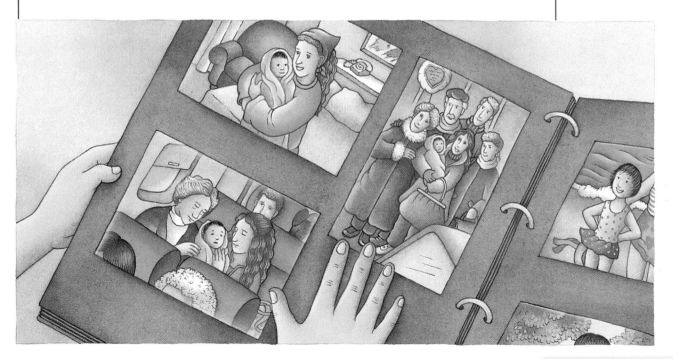

"Mom." Emma swallowed, then started in again. "Remember when you got me? In China?" Her mother nodded. "Well, why don't you have any pictures of the people who had me before? My . . . my real family."

Mom opened her mouth to say something, closed it again, and let her breath out with a sigh. "Emma, I didn't get to see your family. You know that."

Emma nodded, looking angrily away from her mother's concerned face. New tears were forming, starting down in her ribs and trying to sneak their way up into her eyes. Water. Just water, Emma thought. She shook her head, as if that would stop them, and looked down at the rug.

"Maybe I look like somebody," Emma went on, to the floor. "My mother or my aunt or somebody."

Mom squeezed Emma's shoulders. "To me, you look just like Emma."

"That's not what I mean, Mom! I'm sick and tired of hearing how Jessie is just like Aunt Molly when she was little, or how Michael looks exactly like Grandpa. It's not fair. Nobody says that about me!" Now Emma began to lose her fight against the tears, even as she crunched her fists against her eyes to stop them. Mom tried to hug her, but Emma broke away from her.

"Mom." Emma tried to sound calm, but her voice broke, and a sob slipped out. She sat on the stairway, covering her face with her hands. "Mom, just go away, please." ⑦ *Strategy Alert!*

"Emma," Mom said softly, "I know you must feel as if something's missing. As if you don't really know who you are." Emma shrugged, pressing her fingertips against her eyes. She could tell Mom didn't know what to say. "I wish I could tell you more. But there's no way to find out the things you want to know."

Mom put her hand on Emma's head. "Twelve years ago—even before that—I knew this day would come. But I thought I would have figured out

Stop and Ask ⑦

How does it connect to what I know? Decide whether I agree with the characters' actions.

what to say by now." Mom sat beside her. Emma peeked from between her fingers at her mother's white tennis shoes.

"Emma, the thing is, *nobody* knows who they are, not without a lot of work to figure it out. There aren't any simple answers. Even when we know who we came from." Emma finally took her hands from her face and put them on her knees, still staring at Mom's shoes. "You were all I wanted for so long, Em. And once you were here, you were better than I could ever have imagined." Mom chuckled softly, remembering. "I used to just sit around and stare at you. Grandma, too."

Emma suddenly felt so tired, she thought she could fall asleep right there. As if reading Emma's thoughts, Mom pulled her head into her lap, as she used to do when Emma was little. Emma curled up like a cat and closed her eyes gratefully.

"I don't know what else to say, Emma. I've told you everything I know. There's nobody in the world that means more to me than you do." Mom sat quietly, twirling a piece of Emma's braid around her finger.

Somewhere far away, in a country she didn't remember, was a family Emma had hoped to learn about today. Instead, she had learned only how impossible that would be. She could almost feel them slipping away from her now.

Mom brushed Emma's nose with the end of her braid. It felt like a paintbrush. "You O.K.?"

Maybe Mom was right. Maybe there were no easy answers, for her or anybody. Maybe Emma would have to live with things just the way they were. She knew her mom was looking at her. She shrugged. "Yeah, I guess." Eyes still closed, she tried to smile, but it turned into a yawn. "It's freezing in here." ❷ *Strategy Alert!*

"Well, let's go home and get warmed up," said Mom. "All right?" She stood up slowly, wincing as she rubbed the small of her back.

Stop and Ask ❓

How does it connect to what I know? Decide whether I agree with the characters' actions.

unveiled (un·**vayld**)—
revealed

"Gettin' old, Mom," Emma teased. Mom just smiled and shook her head.

Following her mother downstairs, Emma felt a strange sense of peace. Earlier today, she'd been sure a huge part of her past would be **unveiled** for her. It hadn't been. Not only that, but Emma had no idea where else to look. Still, she felt O.K., at least for now.

Michael flashed by the bottom of the stairway and was gone, then Jessie slid into view, giggling and shrieking. "Gimme my shoe, Michael!" She chased him awkwardly in her socks, slipping and bumping into walls and furniture. Emma bounded down the last four steps to catch Michael, then tickled him until he released Jessie's small blue sneaker. Jessie put it on and grabbed Emma's hand. "I got my shoe-oo, I got my shoe-oo," she teased Michael, pressing close to Emma for safety. Emma looked at her mom, who was leaning over the banister watching them. Mom winked at her, and Emma winked back.

> Now that you've finished reading, review the **After I Read** habit below. Think about what you read in "Family Resemblance" as you practice the strategy.

After I Read

Which **HABIT** will I practice?
React to what I've read.
If I develop this habit, I will take time to think about what I've just read. Deciding what I think and what I feel helps me remember it better.

Which **STRATEGY** will I use to practice this habit?
Decide whether the story would have ended differently in a different setting.

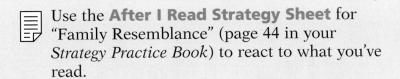 Use the **After I Read Strategy Sheet** for "Family Resemblance" (page 44 in your *Strategy Practice Book*) to react to what you've read.

Apply 3 of the 9 Habits

Now read "Thank You, M'am" and apply these three habits and strategies.

Before I Read

Which **HABIT** will I apply?
Check it out!

Which **STRATEGY** will I use to apply this habit?
Quickly skim the selection to see what it is about.

While I Read

Which **HABIT** will I apply?
Stop and ask, "How does it connect to what I know?"

Which **STRATEGY** will I use to apply this habit?
Decide whether I agree with the characters' actions.

After I Read

Which **HABIT** will I apply?
React to what I've read.

Which **STRATEGY** will I use to apply this habit?
Decide whether the story would have ended differently in a different setting.

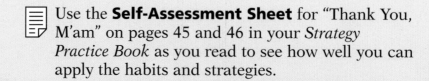 Use the **Self-Assessment Sheet** for "Thank You, M'am" on pages 45 and 46 in your *Strategy Practice Book* as you read to see how well you can apply the habits and strategies.

Thank You, M'am

BY LANGSTON HUGHES

She was a large woman with a large purse that had everything in it but hammer and nails. It had a long strap and she carried it slung across her shoulder. It was about eleven o'clock at night, and she was walking alone, when a boy ran up behind her and tried to snatch her purse. The strap broke with the single tug the boy gave it from behind. But the boy's weight and the weight of the purse combined caused him to lose his balance, so instead of taking off full blast as he had hoped, the boy fell on his back on the sidewalk, and his legs flew up. The large woman simply turned around and kicked him right square in his blue-jeaned sitter. Then she reached down, picked the boy up by his shirt front, and shook him until his teeth rattled.

pocketbook
(**pok**·it·buk)— a bag
used to carry money and
other small items; purse

permit (puhr·**mit**)—to
allow

frail (frayl)—thin; weak

After that the woman said, "Pick up my **pocketbook,** boy, and give it here."

She still held him. But she bent down enough to **permit** him to stoop and pick up her purse. Then she said, "Now ain't you ashamed of yourself?"

Firmly gripped by his shirt front, the boy said, "Yes'm."

The woman said, "What did you want to do it for?"

The boy said, "I didn't aim to."

She said, "You a lie!"

By that time two or three people passed, stopped, turned to look, and some stood watching.

"If I turn you loose, will you run?" asked the woman.

"Yes'm," said the boy.

"Then I won't turn you loose," said the woman. She did not release him.

"I'm very sorry, lady, I'm sorry," whispered the boy.

"Um-hum! And your face is dirty. I got a great mind to wash your face for you. Ain't you got nobody home to tell you to wash your face?"

"No'm," said the boy.

"Then it will get washed this evening," said the large woman starting up the street, dragging the frightened boy behind her.

He looked as if he were fourteen or fifteen, **frail** and willow-wild, in tennis shoes and blue jeans.

The woman said, "You ought to be my son. I would teach you right from wrong. Least I can do right now is to wash your face. Are you hungry?"

"No'm," said the being-dragged boy. "I just want you to turn me loose."

"Was I bothering *you* when I turned that corner?" asked the woman.

"No'm."

"But you put yourself in contact with *me*," said the woman. "If you think that that contact is not going to last awhile, you got another thought coming. When I get through with you, sir, you are going to remember Mrs. Luella Bates Washington Jones."

Sweat popped out on the boy's face and he began to struggle. Mrs. Jones stopped, jerked him around in front of her, put a **half nelson** about his neck, and continued to drag him up the street. When she got to her door, she dragged the boy inside, down the hall, and into a large kitchenette-furnished room at the rear of the house. She switched on the light and left the door open. The boy could hear other **roomers** laughing and talking in the large house. Some of their doors were open, too, so he knew he and the woman were not alone. The woman still had him by the neck in the middle of her room.

She said, "What is your name?"

"Roger," answered the boy.

"Then, Roger, you go to that sink and wash your face," said the woman, whereupon she turned him loose—at last. Roger looked at the door—looked at the woman—looked at the door—and went to the sink.

"Let the water run until it gets warm," she said. "Here's a clean towel."

"You gonna take me to jail?" asked the boy, bending over the sink.

"Not with that face, I would not take you nowhere," said the woman. "Here I am trying to get home to cook me a bite to eat and you snatch my pocketbook! Maybe you ain't been to your supper either, late as it be. Have you?"

"There's nobody home at my house," said the boy.

"Then we'll eat," said the woman. "I believe you're hungry—or been hungry—to try to snatch my pocketbook!"

"I wanted a pair of blue **suede** shoes," said the boy.

"Well, you didn't have to snatch *my* pocketbook to get some suede shoes," said Mrs. Luella Bates Washington Jones. "You could of asked me."

"M'am?"

half nelson
(haf **nel**·suhn)—
a wrestling hold

roomers (**roo**·muhrz)—
people who rent rooms
to live in

suede (swayd)—a soft
leather that feels velvety

The water dripping from his face, the boy looked at her. There was a long pause. A very long pause. After he had dried his face and not knowing what else to do dried it again, the boy turned around, wondering what next. The door was open. He could make a dash for it down the hall. He could run, run, run, run, *run*!

The woman was sitting on the **day-bed**. After awhile she said, "I were young once and I wanted things I could not get."

There was another long pause. The boy's mouth opened. Then he frowned, but not knowing he frowned.

The woman said, "Um-hum! You thought I was going to say *but*, didn't you? You thought I was going to say, *but I didn't snatch people's pocketbooks.* Well, I wasn't going to say that." Pause. Silence. "I have done things, too, which I would not tell you, son—neither tell God, if he didn't already know. So you set down while I fix us something to eat. You might run that comb through your hair so you will look presentable."

In another corner of the room behind a screen was a **gas plate** and an **icebox**. Mrs. Jones got up and went behind the screen. The woman did not watch the boy to see if he was going to run now, nor did she watch her purse which she left behind her on the day-bed. But the boy took care to sit on the far side of the room where he thought she could easily see him out of the corner of her eye, if she wanted to. He did not trust the woman *not* to trust him. And he did not want to be mistrusted now.

day-bed (**day**·bed)—
a couch that can be changed into a bed

gas plate (gas playt)—
a single burner for cooking

icebox (**ies**·boks)—
a refrigerator

"Do you need somebody to go to the store," asked the boy, "maybe to get some milk or something?"

"Don't believe I do," said the woman, "unless you just want sweet milk yourself. I was going to make cocoa out of this canned milk I got here."

"That will be fine," said the boy.

She heated some lima beans and ham she had in the icebox, made the cocoa, and set the table. The woman did not ask the boy anything about where he lived, or his folks, or anything else that would embarrass him. Instead, as they ate, she told him about her job in a hotel beauty-shop that stayed open late, what the work was like, and how all kinds of women came in and out, blondes, red-heads, and Spanish. Then she cut him a half of her ten-cent cake.

"Eat some more, son," she said.

When they were finished eating she got up and said, "Now, here, take this ten dollars and buy yourself some blue suede shoes. And next time, do not make the mistake of latching onto *my* pocketbook *nor nobody else's*—because shoes come by devilish like that will burn your feet. I got to get my rest now. But I wish you would behave yourself, son, from here on in."

She led him down the hall to the front door and opened it. "Goodnight! Behave yourself, boy!" she said, looking out into the street.

The boy wanted to say something else other than, "Thank you, m'am," to Mrs. Luella Bates Washington Jones, but he couldn't do so as he turned at the **barren** stoop and looked back at the large woman in the door. He barely managed to say, "Thank you," before she shut the door. And he never saw her again.

barren (bar·uhn)— empty; bare

Put Your Habits to Work in

Literature   Social Studies   Science   Math

Before I Read Habit:
Check it out!

Remember to quickly skim before you read a chapter in any piece of literature. This will give you an idea about what you will be reading about.

It seems to be about mysterious events at a school.

While I Read Habit:
Stop and ask, "How does it connect to what I know?"

Don't read the whole story all at once! Stop and ask yourself how what you've read connects to what you know. One way to find out is to decide whether you agree with the characters' actions.

I think she should have ...

After I Read Habit:
React to what I've read.

Remember, no matter what you're reading, you're not finished until you react to what you've read. You can do that by deciding whether the story would have ended differently in a different setting.

What if it happened at our school?

You may wish to use the **Put Your Habits to Work Sheet** (page 47 in the *Strategy Practice Book*) to practice these habits in your other reading.

Unit 8
Imaginary Animals of Literature
Theme: Animals

In this unit, you will develop these 3 habits for all readers.

Before I Read Habit:
Decide what I need to know.

While I Read Habit:
Stop and ask, "Does it make sense?"

After I Read Habit:
React to what I've read.

Learn 3 of the 9 Habits

In this unit, you will develop three habits—one for before you read, one for while you are reading, and one for after you finish reading. Start with **Before I Read**. Read the habit and strategy. Then read my notes below.

Before I Read

Which **HABIT** will I learn?
Decide what I need to know.
If I develop this habit, I will have a reason for reading. I will understand it better and remember more of what I read.

Which **STRATEGY** will I use to learn this habit?
Read to identify the problem in the story.

My Notes

- Strategy says to read to identify the problem in the story.

- I read the introduction and the first paragraph of the chapter. I think the problem in this first chapter is how the rats and mice were caught and where they were taken.

Mrs. Frisby (a widowed mouse) and her four children are losing their home. They must move. Desperate, Mrs. Frisby meets with the rat leader Nicodemus and asks for help. At that meeting, she learns that Mr. Frisby (her dead husband) and other rats and mice had been captured by scientists years ago. How they were captured and where they were taken is the subject of this chapter from Mrs. Frisby and the Rats of NIMH.

In the Cage

From *Mrs. Frisby and the Rats of NIMH*
by Robert C. O'Brien

Mrs. Frisby said: "But why did they want to catch you? And how did you ever get away again?"

"At first," said Nicodemus, "I thought it must be because they didn't like our stealing the food. And yet you could hardly even call it stealing—it was waste food, and all they did with it was haul it away to the city **incinerator**. So what harm if we ate some of it? Of course, there are people who just dislike rats, whether they're doing any harm or not."

"And mice, too," said Mrs. Frisby.

"True," said Nicodemus. "Though not so much as rats, I think. Anyway, that wasn't the reason at all; but what the real reason was, I didn't find out for a while. As to getting away—that, too, didn't happen until much later."

No, I was firmly and **inextricably** caught, snared in the net and helpless (Nicodemus continued). When the man who held it saw that he had four rats, he pulled a draw string that closed it up. He put the net down and picked up another, an empty one. He moved on into the square, leaving us to lie there. I tried **gnawing** my way out, but the strands were made of some kind of plastic, as hard as wire.

incinerator
(in·**sin**·uh·ray·tuhr)—a furnace for burning waste

inextricably
(in·**ek**·stri·kuh·blee)—without being able to get free

gnawing (**naw**·ing)—biting

Now read the habit and strategy for **While I Read**. When you see ❓, read my notes in the margin.

While I Read

Which **HABIT** will I learn?

Stop and ask, "Does it make sense?"

If I develop this habit, I will stop now and then to make sure I understand what I'm reading.

Which **STRATEGY** will I use to learn this habit?

Decide whether what I am reading helps me understand the problem.

The noise and movement began to die down eventually; I supposed the rats in the square had all either been caught or had escaped. I heard one man call to another: "I guess that's the lot." Someone else was turning a light this way and that, searching the rest of the market area.

"Not a one to be seen."

"We could hide and wait for another wave."

"There won't be another wave. Not tonight. Probably not for four or five nights."

"Word gets around."

"You mean they communicate?" A third voice.

"You bet they communicate. And the next time they do come, you can be sure they'll case the place carefully. We were lucky. These rats hadn't been bothered for years. They'd grown careless."

"How many did the lab order?" Someone was turning out the lights one at a time.

"Five dozen. How many have we got?"

"About that. Maybe more."

"Let's load the truck."

In a minute or so I felt myself being lifted up; and swinging back and forth in the net, I was carried with my three companions to the white truck I had seen earlier. Its back doors were open, and it was lighted

inside. I could see that its whole interior was a large wire cage. Into this our net was thrust; the man then opened the draw string and we were dumped onto the floor, which was covered with sawdust. The other nets were emptied one at a time the same way; and in a few minutes there was a good-sized crowd of us on the floor, all more or less dazed and all (if I was typical) terrified. The cage was locked, the doors clanged shut, and the lights went out. I heard the truck motor start; a second later the floor lurched beneath me. We were moving. Where were they taking us? For what purpose? *Strategy Alert!*

Then, in the dark, I heard a voice beside me.

"Nicodemus?" It was Jenner. You can imagine how glad I was to hear him. But I was sorry, too.

"Jenner. I thought maybe you got away."

"I was in the last net. I thought I saw you across the floor."

"Where are we going?"

"I don't know."

"What's a lab?"

"A laboratory."

"Yes, but what is it?"

"I don't know. I've just heard the word somewhere."

"Well, I think that's where we're going. Whatever it is."

Stop and Ask ❓

Does it make sense? Decide whether what I am reading helps me understand the problem.

• • • • • • • • • • •

I know that Nicodemus and the other rats were captured. That's the problem. So far, I've learned about how Nicodemus was caught and how he doesn't know where he's going, or why.

Does it make sense?
Decide whether
what I am reading
helps me understand
the problem.

• • • • • • • • • •

I'm still finding out
about the capture
of the rats. They
have been taken in a
truck to a building.
That helps me
make sense of the
situation. But I
don't know what
kind of building or
why they were
captured.

The truck rumbled along through the dark, over bumpy streets at first, then, at a higher speed, over a smooth highway. There were no windows in the back, so it was impossible to see where we were going—not that I would have known anyway, never before having been more than half a dozen blocks from home. I think we drove for about two hours, but it might have been less, before the truck slowed, and turned, and finally came to a stop.

The back doors were opened again, and through the wire wall of the cage I saw that we had come to a building, very modern, of white cement and glass. It was square and big, about ten stories tall. Night had fallen, and most of its windows were dark, but the platform to which our truck drove us was lighted, and there were people waiting for us.

A door opened, and three men came out. One of them pushed a cart, a hand truck piled with small wire cages. The man beside him was dressed in a heavy coat, boots, and thick leather gloves. The third man wore heavy horn-rimmed glasses and a white coat. He was obviously the leader.

The men from the truck, the ones who had caught us, now joined the men from the building. ❓ *Strategy Alert!*

"How many did you get?" asked the man in the white coat.

"Hard to count—they keep moving around. But I make it between sixty and seventy."

"Good. Any trouble?"

"No. It was easy. They acted almost tame."

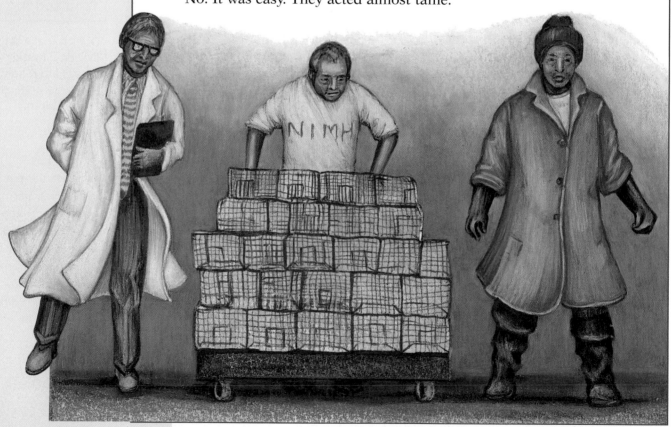

"I hope not. I've got enough tame ones."

"Oh, they're lively enough. And they look healthy."

"Let's get them out."

The man with the gloves and the boots then donned a wire face-mask as well, and climbed in among us. He opened a small sliding trapdoor at the back of our cage; a man outside held one of the small cages up to the opening, and one at a time we were pushed out into our individual little prisons. A few of the rats snarled and tried to bite; I did not, and neither did Jenner; it was too obviously futile. When it was finished, the man in the white coat said, "Sixty-three—good work." A man from the truck said, "Thanks, Dr. Schultz." And we were racked on the hand truck and wheeled into the building.

Dr. Schultz. I did not know it then, but I was to be his prisoner (and his pupil) for the next three years.

We spent the rest of that night in a long white room. It was, in fact, a laboratory, with a lot of equipment at one end that I didn't understand at all then—bottles and shiny metal things and black boxes with wires trailing from them. But our end held only rows of cages on shelves, each cage with a tag on it, and each separated from its neighbors by wooden **partitions** on both sides. Someone came around with a stack of small jars and fastened one to my cage; a little pipe led through the bars like a sipping straw—drinking water. Then the lights were dimmed and we were left alone.

partitions
(pahr·**tish**·uhns)—partial walls that divide an area

Stop and Ask

Does it make sense?
Decide whether
what I am reading
helps me understand
the problem.

. . . .

*Now I know where
the rats were
taken. The rats are
prisoners. They're
locked in cages in
a laboratory and
they're scared! That
all makes sense.
What doesn't make
sense is why they're
there. Why would
people want rats?*

compiled
(kuhm·**pield**)—put
together

That cage was my home for a long time. It was not uncomfortable; it had a floor of some kind of plastic, medium soft and warm to the touch; with wire walls and ceiling, it was airy enough. Yet just the fact that it was a cage made it horrible. I, who had always run where I wanted, could go three hops forward, three hops back again, and that was all. But worse was the dreadful feeling—I know we all had it—that we were completely at the mercy of someone we knew not at all, for some purpose we could not guess. What were their plans for us? (?) *Strategy Alert!*

As it turned out, the uncertainty itself was the worst suffering we had to undergo. We were treated well enough, except for some very small, very quick flashes of pain, which were part of our training. And we were always well fed, though the food, scientifically **compiled** pellets, was not what you'd call delicious.

But of course we didn't know that when we arrived, and I doubt that any of us got much sleep that first night. I know I didn't. So, in a way, it was a relief when early the next morning the lights snapped on and Dr. Schultz entered. There were two other people with him, a young man and a young woman. Like him, they were dressed in white laboratory coats. He was talking to them as they entered the room and walked toward our cages.

". . . three groups. Twenty for training on injection series A, twenty on series B. That will leave twenty-three for the control group. They get no injections at all—except, to keep the test exactly even, we will prick them with a plain needle. Let's call the groups A, B, and C for control; tag them and number them A-1 through A-20, B-1 through B-20, and so on. Number the cages the same way, and keep each rat in the same cage throughout. Diet will be the same for all."

"When do we start the injections?"

"As soon as we're through with the tagging. We'll do that now. George, you number the tags and the cages. Julie, you tie them on. I'll hold."

So the young woman's name was Julie; the young man was George. They all put gloves on, long, tough plastic ones that came to their elbows. One by one we were taken from our cages, held gently but firmly by Dr. Schultz while Julie fastened around each of our necks a narrow ribbon of yellow plastic bearing a number. I learned eventually that mine was number A-10. *Strategy Alert!*

They were kind, especially Julie. I remember that when one rat was being tagged, she looked at it and said, "Poor little thing, he's frightened. Look how he's trembling."

"What kind of biologist are you?" said Dr. Schultz. "The 'poor little thing' is a she, not a he."

When my turn came, the door of my cage slid open just enough for Dr. Schultz to put his gloved hand through. I **cowered** to the back of the cage, which was just what he expected me to do; one hand pressed me flat against the wire wall; then his fingers gripped my shoulders. The other hand held my head just behind the ears, and I was powerless. I was lifted from the cage and felt the plastic collar clipped around my neck. I was back inside with the door closed in less than a minute. The collar was not tight, but by no amount of tugging, twisting or shaking was I ever able to get it off.

Stop and Ask ?

Does it make sense? Decide whether what I am reading helps me understand the problem.

. . . .

The rats were brought to the laboratory to be part of an experiment. That explains why they were caught. But now there's a new problem—the injections.

cowered (**cow**·uhrd)— shrunk away in fear

Stop and Ask

Does it make sense? Decide whether what I am reading helps me understand the problem.

• • • • • • • • • •

This really doesn't help me understand the problem. They're still captured, and I don't know how the injections changed their lives. Maybe I'll read the rest of the book!

I watched through the wire front of my cage as the others were caught and tagged. About six cages down from me, on the same shelf, I saw them put a collar on Jenner; but once he was back in his cage, I could see him no longer.

A little later in the morning they came around again, this time pushing a table on wheels. It was loaded with a bottle of some clear liquid, a long rack of sharp needles, and a plunger. Once more I was lifted from the cage. This time George did the holding while Dr. Schultz fastened one of the needles to the plunger. I felt a sharp pain in my hip; then it was over. We all got used to that, for from then on we got injections at least twice a week. What they were injecting and why, I did not know. Yet for twenty of us those injections were to change our whole lives. ⑦ *Strategy Alert!*

If you want to know what happens next, read the rest of Mrs. Frisby and the Rats of NIMH.

Congratulations! You finished reading. Now read the habit and strategy for **After I Read**. Then read my notes below.

After I Read

Which **HABIT** will I learn?
React to what I've read.
If I develop this habit,
I will take time to think
about what I've just read.
Deciding what I think and what
I feel helps me remember it better.

Which **STRATEGY** will I use to learn this habit?
Consider all the characters' points of view and explain their similarities and differences.

My Notes

- Strategy says to consider the characters' points of view. Nicodemus is telling the story, so the story is told from his point of view.

- Nicodemus was one of the rats, so the story is told from the point of view of a trapped rat. He's scared!

- The scientists trapped the rats. If a scientist were telling the story, it would be a lot different. I can see a little of the scientists' point of view on page 230. The scientists are talking about the experiment. They're mostly thinking about science, not how the trapped rats feel. After all, most people don't like rats!

Now it's time to practice the three habits and strategies you learned when you read "In the Cage." Start with **Before I Read**. Look at the box below. It should look familiar! Reread the habit you will practice. Reread the strategy you will use—then do it!

Before I Read

Which **HABIT** will I practice?
Decide what I need to know.
If I develop this habit, I will have a reason for reading. I will understand it better and remember more of what I read.

Which **STRATEGY** will I use to practice this habit?
Read to identify the problem in the story.

 Use the **Before I Read Strategy Sheet** for "The Mermaid Summer" (page 48 in your *Strategy Practice Book*) to decide what you need to know.

Do you believe in mermaids? Fisherman Eric Anderson, a character in the novel The Mermaid Summer, *didn't—until a mermaid smashed his boat against the sharp rocks called* The Drongs. *After that, no one would sail with him. Eric had to leave his village in Scotland and go to sea. He left behind his wife Sarah, their grown son Robert, Robert's wife Kristine, and their children Jon and Anna. Everyone missed him. Sarah was so unhappy that she became sick. Fortunately, a visit from the Howdy (a wise woman) seemed to cure her. Read the following selection to find out how the mermaid continues to be a problem for the family.*

From

The Mermaid Summer

by Mollie Hunter

Now whether or not it was the Howdy's healing stone that cured Sarah of her ailments, it was certainly true that her health never once looked back after that visit.

Eric was as good as his word, too, in sending money to her; and so she was further cheered by the letters that eventually began to arrive along with the money. Then, at the end of the summer when Jon was eleven and Anna was ten—which was about nine months after Eric's departure—he did better than write. He sent a present to each member of the family.

The presents came in a box that had a large number of brightly colored foreign postal stamps on it, and the first present they opened was for Robert. It was a compass—"So that you'll never again have to depend on the mother wave to guide you in a fog," wrote Eric in the letter that came with the presents.

Reread the habit and strategy below. Look for the *Strategy Alerts!* as you continue to read.

While I Read

Which **HABIT** will I practice?

Stop and ask, "Does it make sense?"

If I develop this habit, I will stop now and then to make sure I understand what I am reading.

Which **STRATEGY** will I use to practice this habit?

Decide whether what I am reading helps me understand the problem.

Use the **While I Read Strategy Sheet** for "The Mermaid Summer" (page 49 in your *Strategy Practice Book*) as you read.

brooch (brohch)—a large fancy pin

whelk (hwelk)—a large snail with a pointed, tower-shaped shell

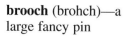

Stop and Ask ❓

Does it make sense? Decide whether what I am reading helps me understand the problem.

Kristine's present was a **brooch** made of silver inset with a single large and gleaming white pearl. Anna's present was a necklace of pale-pink coral. For Jon, there was a shell, a great big shell shaped like that of a **whelk**. The outside of it was rough and pinkish-brown in color. Inside, it was a smooth and glowing pink.

"They call this kind of shell a 'conch [konk],'" said Eric's letter. "And if you blow into one end of it like the natives hereabouts do, it will give out a sound like the sound of a trumpet."

The very last present to be opened was for Sarah, and it was a lace shawl of purest white, very cunningly woven with a pattern of flowers; and of this shawl Eric wrote:

"I'd never before seen a shawl that could pass the test of the ones you knit—not until I saw this one! Try it and see."

Sarah laughed at this and pulled off her wedding ring because—like all fisher wives, of course—she could knit lacy-patterned shawls in very fine wool; and her test of success in this was to finish up with a shawl so delicate in texture that she could draw the whole of it through her wedding ring. *Strategy Alert!*

Everyone gathered round to see her put the white lace shawl to this test, but the threads of it were so cobweb fine that there wasn't the slightest doubt of her being able to draw it easily through the ring; and it was while the rest of the family were laughing at this and admiring once more the beauty of the shawl, that Jon slipped out of doors with *his* present.

"The sound of a trumpet"—that's what his Granda Eric had said he could get from the conch shell. And he was desperate to find out if that was true!

Down to the harbor he ran, carefully hiding the conch from view by thrusting it up inside his gansey—the dark-blue woolen sweater that was the common dress of boys and men alike in fisher villages. By keeping it secret like that, he reckoned, he could give his schoolmates all the more of a surprise when it finally came to showing off the sound he hoped to get from the conch; and it was with this in mind, too, that he went on past the harbor till he reached the rocky **foreshore** on its northward side.

Right out to the edge of the rocks he went, right to the point where deep water lapped against them. Carefully then, he looked around to make sure he was quite alone. There was no one else on the rocks; no one between himself and the village. He looked seaward, out over water that was as blue as the blue summer sky above it.

Nothing moved on the sea either, nothing except gold sparkles of sun on the broken water around The Drongs. Jon took the conch shell out from underneath his gansey, raised it to his lips, and blew into one end of it. ⑦ *Strategy Alert!*

foreshore (**for**·shor)— the part of a shore covered at high tide

Stop and Ask ⑦

Does it make sense? Decide whether what I am reading helps me understand the problem.

Nothing came out of the shell except a sound that was between puffing and wheezing. Jon tried again, changing the position of his lips around the end of the shell; and this time he got a sort of moaning sound from it. He was beginning to get the hang of the proper way to blow, he thought, and tried again, but still got only the moaning sound. A fourth time he tried, then a fifth, and this last time the conch gave out a sound that startled him.

It was deep, and it was **mournful**—a sound like that of a captive bull sadly bellowing; but it was also a loud and weirdly powerful sound, and Jon was delighted with it. Once again he sent out the same call, and then again, before he lowered the conch and stood trying to get his breath back.

"I'll show them!" he told himself, thinking **exultantly** of the envy of his schoolmates when they heard him blowing the conch. "I'll show them!"

He raised the conch to his lips for one last blow before he went racing homewards with it; and just as he did so, there was a flash of silver in the broken water among The Drongs. The flash was followed by a tremendous burst of spray rising from the sea between The Drongs and the place where he stood on the rocks; and greatly puzzled by all this, Jon lowered the conch to stand staring at the place where the spray had arisen.

It had to be a mighty big fish, thought he, to make a splash like that! But what kind of a fish? A basking shark, maybe? It was true that basking sharks were sometimes seen off that coast, and they certainly were big fish; big enough, in fact, to overturn a fishing boat if one of them decided to charge it—which, indeed, Jon knew, was something that had happened more than once to various of the boats from the village. And he had never seen a basking shark before, so maybe now was his chance!

 Strategy Alert!

mournful (**morn**·fuhl)— expressing grief

exultantly (ig·**zul**·tuhnt·lee)— joyfully

Stop and Ask

Does it make sense? Decide whether what I am reading helps me understand the problem.

For long minutes after this thought had occurred to him, Jon stood waiting in the hope that the basking shark or whatever it was would swim close enough to the rocks for him to get a sight of it. Nothing happened. The gold-tipped swirl of water around The Drongs danced as before. The rest of the sea remained calm, with a shine on its unbroken surface like the shine of blue glass.

Jon began to wonder if he should take time for another blow at his conch shell, or whether he should race home there and then to boast about it to Anna. His gaze, traveling inwards from scanning the sea, came to rest on the water that lapped the rock on which he stood. The lapping water swirled into sudden movement. "The fish!" Jon thought. "I'm going to see the fish, after all!" But the creature that surfaced from that swirl of water, was the mermaid.

Her head came first, then her hands came up to grip the edge of the rock. The hands had nails of the same pale pink as Anna's coral necklace. The hair streaming down on either side of her face was the dark-gold color of wet sand. This was all that Jon was able to realize in the shock of that first moment of seeing her. And so close to him, too! Hurriedly he backed a step, then would have turned and ran except that he was too fascinated by her to do so.

Her face, he noticed then, was the color of the pearl in his mother's new brooch—white, yet with a lustrous glow to its **pallor**. Her eyes were green; but how could you describe such a green—so deep, so dark, so full of some terrible inner fire! And those same eyes, so beautiful yet so frightening, were staring at him, staring in a way that made his insides quiver with fear. Yet still, it seemed, he could not call up the will to turn and run from her.  *Strategy Alert!*

pallor (**pal**·uhr)—
extreme paleness

Stop and Ask ?

Does it make sense?
Decide whether
what I am reading
helps me understand
the problem.

He thought of his grandfather's boat being wrecked on The Drongs, and his fear grew even greater. Questions leapt into his mind. Would she sing to him? And would her song be the same deathly one she had sung to Granda Eric? The mermaid opened her coral-pink lips; but to his great wonder then, instead of singing she spoke to him, and to his even greater wonder, what she said was:

"Well, what d'you want? Why did you summon me?"

Summon her? Jon gaped, his thoughts in a whirl, and finally managed to stammer, "I—I—didn't. I mean, how could I summon *you*!"

The strange green of the mermaid's eyes sparked angrily. "But you did. You know you did."

"I don't know anything of the kind," Jon protested fearfully. "All I did was blow this thing here—the conch shell."

"Three times," the mermaid reminded him. "Three times you blew the conch. And so you *did* summon me, because the three-times sound of a conch shell is the call that all mermaids must answer."

"I didn't know that," Jon confessed. "I—I'm sorry. I just didn't know."

The mermaid stared at him, the fire in her eyes beginning to die down until it was replaced by a look of **contempt**. "Land creatures!" she said **scathingly**. "They're all like you—stupid. They don't know anything."

"I won't do it again."

Jon could still feel his insides quivering with fear of this strange sea creature, and so he said this very **humbly**; but the mermaid, it seemed, was not entirely satisfied with this assurance.

"If you do," she warned, "and if it turns out that your call was without cause, you had better stick to the land, because never again will you be safe at sea." ❓ *Strategy Alert!*

On the word "sea," her hands released their grip on the rock. She slid downwards, her hair swirling for a moment on the water's surface before her head disappeared from Jon's view.

The next moment, however, he saw the whole length of her tail flicking upwards out of the water in a sparkle of scales that flashed in the sun like a firework display of blue and green and silver. The glittering tail gave a last flash as it speared cleanly downwards in the dive that took her finally back into the depths of the sea. And it was only then, with the knowledge that she was really gone, that Jon found he was able to turn and run.

Panting, scrambling, leaping from rock to rock, and finally racing madly over the stretch of shingle between rock and harbor, he made his way homewards; but he was still only halfway there when a sudden

contempt
(kuhn·**tempt**)—bitter scorn

scathingly
(**skay**·thing·lee)—harshly

humbly (**hum**·blee)—meekly

Stop and Ask

Does it make sense? Decide whether what I am reading helps me understand the problem.

thought slowed him to a halt. Supposing he told the rest of the family what had happened—as he had certainly meant to do, up till that moment. What would they say?

It was true he hadn't intended to summon the mermaid. But maybe they wouldn't take that as an excuse. Maybe they would still blame him for causing her to appear again. Maybe they would fear that would bring bad luck to the new boat his father had finally managed to buy to replace the old one Jimsie Jamieson had loaned him. And maybe that was exactly what *would* happen!

Jon felt his inward quivering begin again as he stood and considered all these questions; and when he remembered the angry green of the mermaid's eyes, he quivered even more. But a decision still had to be made before he reached home again; and, as it happened, the decision he finally came to was that he would say nothing at all about having summoned the mermaid. And that way, he reckoned, he would not be blamed for anything that might happen as a result of having done so.

It was not a brave decision to make, of course—quite the opposite in fact; but Jon, it has to be remembered, was only just eleven years old at this time, and it can be very difficult at that age to make brave decisions. Also as it happened, he did not reach home that day until he had met unexpectedly with the Howdy; so unexpectedly, in fact, that he had no chance to run from her as he would otherwise have done.

There was no chance either of hiding the conch shell from her, because her eyes went immediately to the bulge it made under his gansey, and nothing would satisfy her but to be given a sight of it. Very unwillingly, then, Jon showed her the shell.

"It's a present from my Granda," he explained. "He sent presents to all of us."

"Indeed," the Howdy exclaimed. "Did he so! And what, pray, were those other presents?"

"A shawl," Jon told her, "a compass, a silver brooch, and a coral necklace."

"Oh, aye?" the Howdy said thoughtfully. "The shawl for your Granny, eh? The compass for your father, the brooch for your mother, and the necklace for your wee sister—is that right?" Jon nodded, wondering what was coming next, and was not long left in doubt.

"Well now," the Howdy told him. "Heed me, boy. Of all these presents it is only the shell that is important to you and yours. And so take care of it. Take very good care!" *Strategy Alert!*

On she went, then, with her fat little figure in its black dress looking, all of a sudden, mysteriously dark against the brightness of the day. Jon stared after her, wondering what on earth she had meant about the shell being the only thing that was important to him and his family; and the more he wondered about this, the more nervous it made him.

When he got home, he vowed to himself, he would not only hide from his family the fact that he had summoned the mermaid. He would put the conch shell itself away in some hiding place and never take it out again. Or not until he had some reason for doing so, anyway—and considering what had happened with his Granda and the mermaid, that reason would certainly have to be a very good one!

Three years later, Jon meets the mermaid again. Read The Mermaid Summer *to find out what happens!*

Stop and Ask (?)

Does it make sense? Decide whether what I am reading helps me understand the problem.

Now that you've finished reading, review the **After I Read** habit below. Think about what you read in "The Mermaid Summer" as you practice the strategy.

After I Read

Which **HABIT** will I practice?
React to what I've read.
If I develop this habit, I will take time to think about what I've just read. Deciding what I think and what I feel helps me remember it better.

Which **STRATEGY** will I use to practice this habit?
Consider all the characters' points of view and explain their similarities and differences.

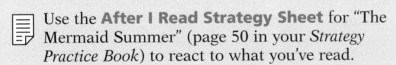 Use the **After I Read Strategy Sheet** for "The Mermaid Summer" (page 50 in your *Strategy Practice Book*) to react to what you've read.

Now read "Stinker From Space" and apply these three habits and strategies.

Before I Read

Which **HABIT** will I apply?
Decide what I need to know.

Which **STRATEGY** will I use to apply this habit?
Read to identify the problem in the story.

While I Read

Which **HABIT** will I apply?
Stop and ask, "Does it make sense?"

Which **STRATEGY** will I use to apply this habit?
Decide whether what I am reading helps me understand the problem.

After I Read

Which **HABIT** will I apply?
React to what I've read.

Which **STRATEGY** will I use to apply this habit?
Consider all the characters' points of view and explain their similarities and differences.

 Use the **Self-Assessment Sheet** for "Stinker From Space" (pages 51–52 in your *Strategy Practice Book*) as you read to see how well you can apply the habits and strategies.

A wild and scary chase through space finds Tsynq Yr crash landing on Earth. His spaceship is destroyed—and he quickly needs to find a new body. Will problems on Earth be more scary than the Delta Arm of the Confederacy? Read more about this alien's problems in these first two chapters from the novel Stinker From Space.

From Stinker From Space
by Pamela F. Service

1

Fugitive

Again the deadly blue light **engulfed** him. Flinching from the brilliance, Tsynq Yr struggled with the controls. Abruptly his scout ship veered away, and the cool glow faded.

He knew he was a crack space pilot, one of the best in the Sylon Confederacy, but that Zarnk cruiser was closing on him fast. He was hopelessly outgunned and outpowered in this cheap scout ship he'd had to steal to escape the orbital fort. What he wouldn't give now for his own trim little Sylon fighter.

Blue radiance flared again, and Tsynq Yr abruptly changed the ship's course. He could not let them get him now. Three years of miserable **skulking** and spying, and finally he'd pieced it all together. He'd found out the Zarnk plan for attacking the Delta Arm of the **Confederacy**. He must get that information back to Sylon High Command, and he wasn't about to let a blundering Zarnk cruiser stop him.

The cramped cabin burst into blue glare. On Tsynq Yr's right, the control panel fizzed and crackled.

engulfed (en·**gulfd**)— surrounded

skulking (**skulk**·ing)— moving about secretively

confederacy (kuhn·**fed**·uhr·uh·see)— a union of persons, parties, or states

maneuver
(muh·**noo**·vuhr)—a skillful or tactical movement

He surveyed the damage. Now that's done it! The stabilizers were out.
There was only one choice left, he realized, and he didn't like it. The
maneuver was difficult and dangerous at the best of times. In this piece
of flying space scrap. . . .

Before the Zarnk could fire again, Tsynq Yr slid the drive control to the
top of the scale, well beyond the safety limit. The little ship shuddered and
shot off through space. With the rising speed, the blackness around him
began to waver and vibrate as he neared the fringes of hyperspace. This
ship was not equipped to make the jump into that dimension, but with
skillful piloting and split-second timing, it skipped along the dimensional
boundaries like a stone skips over water.

obliterate
(uh·**blit**·uh·rayt)—to do
away with

Tensely Tsynq Yr played the controls. If he didn't **obliterate** himself,
this little trick should throw off pursuit for a time, enough time perhaps
for him to repair the ship or find some Sylon reinforcements.

As space pulsed and shivered around the speeding ship, an alarming
hum rose from the controls. That last Zarnk hit must have done more
damage than he'd thought. Suddenly the hum turned into a scream and
the ship abruptly lost speed, spinning off through black, star-spotted
space.

havoc (**hav**·uhk)—
disorder

When, with much cursing, he'd brought the spinning under control,
Tsynq Yr looked out at those stars. Where was he? Skipping along the
edges of hyperspace played **havoc** with physical location, and he had no
idea where he'd been dropped off. Of course, his pursuers wouldn't either,
but that would be no help if he'd been plunked somewhere in the Zarnk
Dominion.

But no, the stars showed he was in neither Zarnk nor Sylon territory. Terrific! Exploring uncharted regions was all very well, but not when he had top secret information to pass on.

A quick glance at the smoking control panel showed that here he was and here he was likely to remain, at least until he could work some repairs. He trained his scanners on the nearest star system. Planets, yes, mostly useless. One **marginal,** one fully habitable. He homed in on the latter.

If the Zarnk ever managed to trace his wild route here, this planet would be an all too obvious **refuge,** but he had no choice. His little ship was making new alarming sounds.

He sped toward the target, a globe swirling with greens and blues and whites. Pleasant-looking, all right, but too much water. With half the ship's systems out, this landing was going to be rough enough. Tsynq Yr hoped it would at least be on land.

Plummeting down toward the planet's night side, he knifed into the atmosphere. Too steep. He tried to pull up but failed. Worse, he seemed to be heading into a local storm system.

Dark clouds closed in. Everywhere the atmosphere discharged in long forked bolts. Suddenly the ground, splotched with vegetation, was hurtling toward him. Too fast. Much too fast.

When Tsynq Yr awoke, he realized two things. First, his ship was nearly destroyed. Second, he was dying.

This body had served him well. At first, he'd taken it on merely as a convenience to his spy mission. Like most active Sylons, he'd lost track of how many bodies he'd used since the one he'd had at birth. But this body had worked well, was attractive in its own way—and he'd grown attached to it.

marginal (**mahr**·juh·nuhl)— barely acceptable

refuge (**ref**·yooj)— a place providing shelter

And he would die in it, too, if he didn't find a suitable **host**—soon. His mind cast about, seeking life forms. Vegetation was plentiful, but all seemed rooted and subintelligent. He sensed other creatures that did move, but he probed and found they weren't much more intelligent than the plants. Tiny flying creatures seemed interested only in finding out if his own dying body was good to eat.

Desperate now, he probed elsewhere. Here was something larger. It wriggled through soil, but its brain was **negligible**. He doubted his intelligence could even fit into it. And besides, it had no **appendages**. He could never repair a ship in that body.

Suddenly the thing he probed at was snatched up and eaten by another creature. This new one would have to do. He hadn't the strength to look further. Yes, there was a brain, not a big one, but he'd worked with worse. And there were even hands of sorts.

With his last shred of strength, Tsynq Yr shot his being into the alien creature. The native's intelligence registered brief surprise before it was pushed to the back of the mind and the Sylon took over.

Beady black eyes blinked as he gazed at the alien world around him. Vegetation everywhere, tall and short, orange, brown, and green. Moisture blew from a clouded night sky. His eyes, it seemed, were designed for seeing in the near dark.

Curiously Tsynq Yr examined his new body. There was a head and a tail, and four short legs supporting a body that was low to the ground. Mammalian, apparently; the whole body was covered with hair.

That hair was clearly the most impressive feature. It was long, soft, and marked in a striking pattern. The background was glossy black. White capped the head, and two bold white stripes swept down the back and out onto the bushy plume of a tail. Quite handsome, really.

2 Meeting in the Woods

Dark Destroyer dropped in beside the Princess of Light. One by one the other action figures followed before Karen slammed down the lid.

Swinging the old battered lunch box in one hand, she clattered down the stairs and into the kitchen. Her mother looked up, her face **taut** with the unfamiliar strain of sewing curtains.

"Going out to play?"

"Yes," Karen replied as she scooped several peanut butter cookies into her pocket.

Mrs. Blake's frustration over the curtains **ricocheted** against her daughter. "Karen, honestly! Why don't you ever play *with* anyone?"

"Oh, Mother! There's no one here I want to play with."

"We've been here two whole months now, Karen. Surely you've made some friends by now."

Karen swayed by the doorway, hand itching to grab the knob. "Oh sure, some of the girls at school are okay, but they aren't like. . . . They don't play my sort of games." She'd barely avoided saying "like Rachel." Her mother had threatened to scream if she whined any more about leaving her best friend behind in their own hometown.

taut (tawt)—tense

ricocheted (**rik**·uh·shayd)—bounced back after hitting a sur-face

sidled (**sied**·ld)—moved
sideways

indignantly
(in·**dig**·nuhnt·lee)—with
anger over something
unjust

interstellar
(in·tuhr·**stel**·uhr)—
between or among the
stars

Karen **sidled** toward the door. "These girls just want to dress up, put on makeup, and play with dolls."

"And those things in the lunch box aren't dolls, I suppose?"

Karen sputtered **indignantly**. "These are action figures! They aren't silly dolls that wet and poop on demand. They're characters in great **interstellar** dramas, adventures bounded only by imagination!"

She placed her hand on the doorknob and threw out a line that was sure to divert her mother's train of thought. "Besides, all the other girls live in town."

"Yes, your father *would* choose a picturesque 'handyman's delight' way out in the sticks." Mrs. Blake sighed and gave the curtain an angry stab with her needle. "But still, it's not completely isolated out here. Why don't you play with that kid who lives up the road?"

"But he's a boy!"

"Well, I can't help that. Besides, if you're so nuts about space, you two should be made for each other. I understand he's wacky over space, too."

"Mother, it's not the same at all. When Jonathan Waldron looks at stars, all he sees is numbers and facts—not the drama, the romance!"

Sewing calmly again, her mother seemed to ignore this comment. "I was talking with his mother the other day, and she said Jonathan's room is full of space posters and models, and he knows the names of every astronaut, Soviet or American, since the year dot."

"There weren't any astronauts in the year dot."

"Talk about being too factual! Oh, go on out and play."

Quickly Karen slipped out the door. Last night's storm had polished the sky to a bright blue. Against it, the autumn colors of the woods ahead rose like a jeweled crown.

Freed from parental plans, she skipped toward those trees, heading for the hidden clearing she had already made her special place. But as she hopped over the rain puddles, she found herself still thinking about Jonathan Waldron.

He might be interested in space, but he was a real nerd nonetheless. All numbers and no soul. It was bad enough having to ride the bus with him. But be friends with him? In school Jonathan was a whiz at math and science, but hopeless in English. His poems stank. Of course, she thought with a giggle, boys stink generally. Still, she wouldn't mind seeing his room and all those models and posters.

Reaching the clearing, Karen dropped all unpleasant thoughts. It was breathtakingly beautiful here. In the brilliant sunlight, the flaming red maple leaves glowed like stained glass. Settling down among the maple's gnarled roots, she leaned back and looked up at the gleaming leaves. She was a medieval princess taking refuge in an ancient cathedral. The stark white branches of the sycamore across the clearing were the soaring marble pillars. Or maybe she was a princess on another planet, taking refuge in the heart of the giant Sacred Jewel to escape the soldiers of the Dark Empire.

adaptable
(uh·**dap**·tuh·buhl)—able
to adjust

olfactory
(ohl·**fak**·tuh·ree)—
relating to the sense of
smell

Opening the lunch box, she spilled the action figures over the grass. Birds chirped busily in the leafy recesses of the woods. From a distance, the crisp air carried the tang of burning leaves. It mingled with the rich moldy odor of damp earth and fleeting whiffs of woodsy animals.

Although Tsynq Yr's first hours on this planet had been trying ones, he was fairly pleased with his new body. The creature's native intelligence was not high, but the brain was **adaptable,** and Sylon intelligence was very compact. And besides looking elegant, the little beast had some very interesting senses. Hearing and eyesight were keen, and there was another sense, the **olfactory** one, that he'd seldom had before. Life was suddenly full of interesting odors, not the least of which was his own.

The state of his ship, however, was far less satisfactory. It had smashed into the boggy earth, and the outside structure had all but disintegrated. Already the remains were sinking from sight. Somehow, he'd have to construct or borrow another vehicle.

That meant finding out something about the level of native civilization. During his fateful descent, the little ship's scanners had shown signs of civilization on this planet, but he had no idea how advanced it was.

He had set out to discover this about the time dawn came to this world, with its medium-size sun appearing in the east. His host's body was suddenly telling him it was time to sleep. He put aside the message easily enough, but messages from the empty stomach were harder to ignore.

industriously
(in·**dus**·tree·uhs·lee)—in
a hard-working way

His rations were gone with the ship, so he let his body's instincts take him to food. Soon he was **industriously** turning over dead logs and snapping up the bugs and fat white grubs underneath. He didn't dare let his own instincts rise to the surface, for fear he'd be instantly sick. Even so, the rotten raw bird's egg he ate was almost too much.

It was the smell of food enticing to both his selves that brought him to the clearing. Under a red-leafed tree, a **bipedal** creature was sitting, eating a round flat piece of food.

His mind as well as his sense of smell reached out, and instantly he realized that here was a species of considerable intelligence. Perhaps one of this planet's civilized beings. Artificial garments, large brain capacity. He probed into the thoughts.

There was a running account of soldiers of a vast interstellar empire pursuing the female **monarch** of a rival power. So these beings had achieved space travel. He was in luck!

He decided to make himself known—mentally. His new body clearly didn't have much speech ability. How should he start—ask what sort of space drive they used? Maybe he should inquire if they had any knowledge of the Sylon Confederacy or the Zarnk Dominion. Or maybe, part of him urged, he should just ask what the creature was eating.

"I am dreadfully hungry," he thought. "Would you share some of that?"

The girl looked startled, then muttered, "Karen, you dope, don't have Dark Destroyer ask for a peanut butter cookie."

"He wasn't asking, I was," came the thought as Tsynq Yr stepped into the clearing.

Karen's look of surprise changed to alarm. Slowly she stood up and began backing away.

The Sylon stopped advancing and studied her. She was clearly frightened—of him. Puzzled, he probed her mind. It had something to do with the olfactory sense. A word jumped to the front of her thoughts, a word with very negative associations. Skunk.

bipedal (bie·**ped**·l)— two-footed

monarch (**mon**·uhrk)—a ruler, such as a king or queen

Put Your Habits to Work in

Before I Read Habit:
Decide what I need to know.

Remember to read to identify the problem in the story.

The problem is that . . .

While I Read Habit:
Stop and ask, "Does it make sense?"

Don't finish the whole story! Stop and ask yourself if it makes sense. One way to do this is to decide whether what you are reading helps you understand the problem.

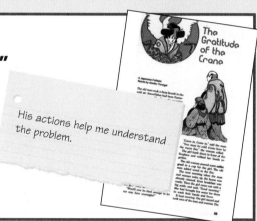

His actions help me understand the problem.

After I Read Habit:
React to what I've read.

You're not finished reading the story until you react to what you've read. You can do that by thinking about the characters' points of view and explaining how they are alike and how they are different.

Are these characters alike?

You may wish to use the **Put Your Habits to Work Sheet** (page 53 in your *Strategy Practice Book*) to practice these habits in your other reading.

Unit 9
Great Sports Stars, Great People
Theme: Sports

In this unit, you will develop these 3 habits for all readers.

Before I Read Habit:
Think about what I know about the subject.

While I Read Habit:
Stop and ask, "If it doesn't make sense, what can I do?"

After I Read Habit:
Use what I've read.

In this unit, you will develop three habits—one for before you read, one for while you are reading, and one for after you finish reading. Start with **Before I Read**. Read the habit and strategy. Then read my notes below.

Before I Read

Which **HABIT** will I learn?

Think about what I know about the subject.
If I develop this habit, I will bring to mind what I already know about the subject. This gets me ready to connect what I read to what I know so I will understand it better.

Which **STRATEGY** will I use to learn this habit?
Look at graphic aids and decide what I know about what they show.

My Notes

- Strategy says to look at graphic aids and decide what I know about what they show.

- I found a time line on pages 258–259. It gives information about Roberto Clemente's life. In 1973, he entered the Baseball Hall of Fame. I've heard of that.

Roberto Clemente

Pride of Pittsburgh, Glory of Puerto Rico

On March 20, 1973, Roberto Clemente [roh·**bair**·toh kluh·**men**·tay] was **inducted** into the Baseball Hall of Fame. This was only three months after his death. Originally, players could not receive this honor unless they were out of the game for five years. The fact that the sportswriters of America voted to **suspend** this rule says something about Clemente. It says that he must have been talented. In fact, he was. He led the Pittsburgh Pirates to victory in the World Series twice. But Clemente was more than talented. He was a special human being. He overcame huge obstacles to succeed in his career, and he used his success to help people from his home, Puerto Rico.

inducted (in·**duk**·tid)— accepted as a member of a club

suspend (suh·**spend**)— to overlook or ignore

Growing Up in Puerto Rico

Roberto Clemente was born in Puerto Rico in 1934. When he was growing up in the 1940s, young people in Puerto Rico, like those in the United States, played baseball. But Roberto and his friends didn't always play with the proper equipment. Roberto's bat was a stick carved from a guava [**gwah**·vuh] tree. His glove was made from an old coffee sack. When Roberto was 14, he was chosen for a top **amateur team**. What impressed the scout most was how far Roberto could hit tomato cans with a stick!

For the next five years, Roberto played baseball for teams in Puerto Rico. After years of practicing with sticks and cans and wads of rags, Roberto could hit anything. He could also catch anything, run forever, and throw with great accuracy. In February 1954, Al Campanis, a scout for the Brooklyn Dodgers, gave Clemente a contract. The Dodgers sent him to play for the Montreal [mahn·tree·**awl**] Royals, their top minor league club.

amateur team (**am**·uh·chur teem)— a team whose players do not get a salary

Now read the habit and strategy for **While I Read**. When you see , read my notes in the margin.

While I Read

Which **HABIT** will I learn?

Stop and ask, "If it doesn't make sense, what can I do?"

If I develop this habit, I will stop and figure out what to do so what I'm reading makes sense. Then I can keep reading and not be lost.

Which **STRATEGY** will I use to learn this habit?

Use graphic aids to help me understand.

awkward
(**awk**•wuhrd)—
not clear or smooth

Stop and Ask

If it doesn't make sense, what can I do? Use graphic aids to help me understand.

· · · · · · · · · · ·

I didn't understand why Roberto's English wasn't very good. The time line shows he was born in Puerto Rico where they speak Spanish.

From Minors to Majors

Before Montreal, Roberto had never lived with English speakers. He had studied English in high school, but he never had to speak it all the time. Now, everyone he met spoke English, and they expected him to speak it, too. This was hard for Roberto. He didn't always understand what people said to him. Once a player from another team cursed him. Because he did not understand what had been said, Roberto thanked him for the curse! His English was **awkward,** at best. Sportswriters and even his own managers sometimes made fun of the way he spoke. Throughout his career, Roberto would often feel that people didn't give him enough credit.

 Strategy Alert!

After two seasons in Montreal, the Dodgers still hadn't promoted Roberto to their major league team. In the fall of 1955, under the "bonus rule," Roberto could be drafted by another team. The Pittsburgh Pirates had finished last that year. So, they had first pick of the minor league players. The Pirates drafted the Dodgers' young outfielder.

Roberto Clemente

Recruited by top amateur team in Puerto Rico — **1949**

Drafted by Pittsburgh Pirates; Hit by car — **1955**

1934 — Born in Carolina, Puerto Rico

1954 — Signed with Brooklyn Dodgers; Played for Montreal Royals

1960 — Defeated N.Y. Yankees to win World Series

Clemente sliding into home plate, 1955

Accident and Injury

In 1955, Clemente became a player for the Pittsburgh Pirates. But before he even got a chance to play his first major league game, a terrible thing happened. He had an accident that would affect him for the rest of his life. A drunk driver skidded into his car, and Clemente's back was injured. As a result, he had **chronic** back problems. During every game, he had to keep stretching and exercising his back. Each time he stepped up to the plate, he went through a **ritual** of twisting, turning, and stretching. He had to do this because of his bad back. His critics, however, didn't understand. They thought he was doing it so people would feel sorry for him.

Clemente did not want anyone to feel sorry for him, and he did not feel sorry for himself. Instead, he found a way to put his injuries to good use. He spent so much time with doctors that he became an expert on back problems. He used his knowledge to help others. During the off-season, he ran a free **chiropractic** clinic in Puerto Rico. People with severe back pain would come to his house, and he'd help them. They would lie on the pool table in his basement, and he'd use massage to ease their pain. Roberto's "patients" swore that he had magic in his hands.

chronic (kron·ik)— constant; all the time

ritual (rich·oo·uhl)— a routine

chiropractic (kie·ruh·prak·tik)— using pressure to treat pain or injury to the spine or joints

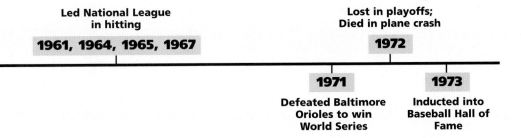

Led National League in hitting

1961, 1964, 1965, 1967

Lost in playoffs; Died in plane crash

1972

1971

Defeated Baltimore Orioles to win World Series

1973

Inducted into Baseball Hall of Fame

Stop and Ask

If it doesn't make sense, what can I do? Use graphic aids to help me understand.

I didn't remember how long it took the Pirates to get better after Clemente came. The time line shows that Roberto played for five seasons with the Pirates before they won the World Series in 1960.

Stop and Ask

If it doesn't make sense, what can I do? Use graphic aids to help me understand.

I didn't understand why the Pirates were so bad. Did Clemente play worse? The table showed he played well. I don't think it was his fault.

KEY
BA Batting Average **2B** Doubles
AB At Bats **3B** Triples
H Hits **HR** Home Runs
Boldface means "National League champion."

Turning the Pirates Into Winners

Clemente worked magic with the Pittsburgh Pirates, too. He showed his teammates how to be winners. Before long, the Pirates started improving. In 1960, the Pirates were known as the worst team in the league. Unbelievably, they beat the New York Yankees that year and won the World Series! It was one of the most exciting contests in history. The final score in Game Seven was Pirates 10, Yankees 9. Ten of the 19 runs were scored in the last two innings. *Strategy Alert!*

The Pirates' World Series win surprised everyone except Clemente. He always knew the team could be a winner. In the series, he led his team in hitting. But he wasn't happy with his playing. He wanted to be better. That winter he promised his parents he would become the best hitter in the league. The next season, he lived up to his promise.

An Unrecognized Hero

In 1961, Clemente had a batting average of .351. This means that out of 100 turns at bat, Clemente made 35 hits. That made him the National League's best hitter. He repeated that achievement in 1964, 1965, and 1967. For 10 of the next 11 years, he had an average of .300 or better. During this period, he scored a record 3,000 hits. Even so, the Pirates did not make it back to the World Series until 1971. *Strategy Alert!*

Clemente's Statistics 1955-1972

	GAMES	BA	AB	H	2B	3B	HR
1955	124	.255	474	121	23	11	5
1956	147	.311	543	169	30	7	7
1957	111	.253	451	114	17	7	4
1958	140	.289	519	150	24	10	6
1959	105	.296	432	128	17	7	4
1960	144	.314	570	179	22	6	16
1961	146	**.351**	572	201	30	10	23
1962	144	.312	538	168	28	9	10
1963	152	.320	600	192	23	8	17
1964	155	**.339**	622	**211**	40	7	12
1965	152	**.329**	589	194	21	14	10
1966	154	.317	638	202	31	11	29
1967	147	**.357**	585	**209**	26	10	23
1968	132	.291	502	146	18	12	18
1969	138	.345	507	175	20	**12**	19
1970	108	.352	412	145	22	10	14
1971	132	.341	522	178	29	8	13
1972	102	.312	378	118	19	7	10

Third in from the left, Clemente poses with other Pittsburgh Pirates at Forbes Field.

Despite a record-making performance, Clemente didn't think he was getting enough **recognition**. He thought that sportswriters were ignoring him and other **Latin** players.

Clemente may not have been appreciated enough in Pittsburgh, but in Puerto Rico he was a hero. He spent the off-season working there on projects that helped his people. One of these projects was Sports City. Clemente wanted the Puerto Rican government to build a children's sports center. There, poor children could come to learn baseball and other sports. He envisioned playing fields, coaches, and proper sports equipment. He wanted the children to have all the things that he didn't have when he was learning to play ball.

Playing to Win

In 1970, the Pirates made it to the National League playoffs but lost three games in a row to the Cincinnati Reds. The next year, the Pirates beat the San Francisco Giants in the playoffs and went to the World Series. That series, against the Baltimore Orioles, started badly for the Pirates. They lost the first two games. After Game Two, which the Orioles won 11 to 3, the press said that the Orioles would win the Series. But Clemente, who always felt the press ignored him, urged his teammates to ignore the press. He told them, "Do not read the newspapers and you will see. We will win."

In Game Three, Clemente showed what playing to win was all about. Late in the game, they had only a one-run lead. Clemente hit a ground ball back to the **mound**. It should have been an easy out. Clemente ran so hard to first base that he confused the Oriole pitcher. The pitcher made a bad throw and Clemente was safe on first base. Clemente's spirit inspired the Pirates to win the game.

recognition (rek·uhg·nish·uhn)— attention; notice

Latin (la·tin)—people from Mexico, Puerto Rico, and other Latin American countries

mound (mownd)—the raised ground where a pitcher stands

If it doesn't make sense, what can I do? Use graphic aids to help me understand.

● ● ● ● ● ● nor ● i ● ● ● ● ●

Did Roberto mean what he said about playing well? I think he meant it because the table shows his batting average stayed good throughout his career.

Clemente connects for a home run in Game 6 of the 1971 World Series.

The Pirates won two more games and the Orioles won one. The Series went on to Game Seven. When it was over, the Pirates had won the World Series! That year, Clemente was named Most Valuable Player. His batting average for the season had been .341. In the playoffs he hit .333. In the World Series he hit an amazing .414. He knocked in four runs and hit a triple, two doubles, and two home runs. He told sportswriter Roger Angell, "I want everybody in the world to know that this is the way I play all the time. All season, every season, I give everything I have to this game." ❼ *Strategy Alert!*

A Tragic End

In a 1971 TV interview, Clemente asked his parents' blessing in Spanish. Then he said, "I love the poor people, the workers, the **minority** people, the ones who suffer. They have a different outlook on life."

The events of 1972 would show Clemente's love for the ones who suffer. It was not a great year for him as a ball player. His batting average fell to .312—not good enough for a player who wanted to be the best. That year the Pirates lost to the Cincinnati Reds in the playoffs, three games to two. Clemente told his friends that he would play one more season. Then he planned to retire.

minority
(muh·**nor**·i·tee)—
a smaller group of people different from the main group

That winter, on December 23, a terrible earthquake struck Nicaragua [nik·uh·**rah**·gwuh], a country in Central America. It killed 6,000 people and injured 20,000 more. Another 3,000 people were left homeless. Clemente had many friends in Nicaragua. He had been there a month earlier for the World Series of Amateur Baseball. Clemente was manager of Puerto Rico's team. The Nicaraguans were his *compañeros* [kuhm·pah·**nyair**·ohs]—his brothers. He wanted to help them survive the disaster. He collected food, clothing, and medical supplies for the victims. He went on radio and TV to ask the public for help. Soon shipments of **relief** supplies were on their way from San Juan [san **hwahn**] to Managua [mah·**nah**·gwuh], the capital of Nicaragua.

relief (ri·**leef**)—giving help in time of tragedy

The shipments didn't reach the people who needed them fast enough. There were rumors that the people in charge were keeping the supplies for themselves. These reports upset Clemente and he made a decision. He would travel with the next shipment to see what happened when it reached Managua.

Earthquake in Nicaragua, 1972

If it doesn't make sense, what can I do? Use graphic aids to help me understand.

• • • • • • • • • • •

I didn't know how old Roberto was when he died. This is what I found out from the time line: He was only 38 years old at the time of his death.

mourned (mornd)— showed sadness

On the night of December 31, 1972, Clemente boarded a cargo plane. It was loaded with baby formula and hospital supplies for the people of Nicaragua. The plane was 20 years old and not in the best shape. There was trouble with the engines. The flight was delayed several times while a mechanic tried to fix the problem. Finally, the plane rumbled down the runway and took off. Minutes later, one of the engines started shaking. Then the other engine caught fire. The pilot tried to turn around and return to the airport but failed. At 9:30 that New Year's Eve, the plane vanished from the radar screen and crashed into the sea. Clemente and the pilot were both killed. Sadly, Clemente's body was never found.

 Strategy Alert!

Mourning the Loss of a Hero

On New Year's Day, 1973, all of Puerto Rico **mourned** the loss of a hero. The day was gray and rainy. One newspaper writer wrote, "even the sky was in mourning." The governor of Puerto Rico said, "Our people have lost one of their glories." In the United States, the Pittsburgh Pirates, and all of baseball mourned the loss of a man who had won their respect. Clemente's tragic death moved many people.

On March 20, 1973, Roberto Clemente became the first Latin American inducted into the Baseball Hall of Fame. But Clemente was more than a great baseball player. He was a generous and caring human being.

Roberto Clemente's statue was shown to the public for the first time at an unveiling ceremony on July 8,1998.

Congratulations! You finished reading. Now read the habit and strategy for **After I Read**. Then read my notes below.

After I Read

Which **HABIT** will I learn?
Use what I've read.
If I develop this habit, I will think about how I can apply what I read to my schoolwork and my life. This makes reading really useful.

Which **STRATEGY** will I use to learn this habit?
Decide what the author didn't tell me that I would like to know.

My Notes

- Strategy says to decide what else I would like to know.

- I learned that Roberto Clemente was the first Latin American ball player inducted into the Baseball Hall of Fame.

- I wonder if any other Latin American ball players have been inducted into the Hall of Fame.

- Have other baseball players tried to help others like Clemente did?

Now it's time to practice the three habits and strategies you learned when you read "Roberto Clemente." Start with **Before I Read**. Look at the box below. It should look familiar! Reread the habit you will practice. Reread the strategy you will use—then do it!

Before I Read

Which **HABIT** will I practice?
Think about what I know about the subject.
If I practice this habit, I will bring to mind what I already know about the subject. This gets me ready to connect what I read to what I know so I will understand it better.

Which **STRATEGY** will I use to practice this habit?
Look at graphic aids and decide what I know about what they show.

 Use the **Before I Read Strategy Sheet** for "Babe Didrikson Zaharias" (page 54 in your *Strategy Practice Book*) to think about what you already know.

Babe Didrikson Zaharias

Natural-Born Athlete

Babe Didrikson pitching

Who was the greatest woman athlete of the last century? In the past 50 years, many women have excelled in sports. Women athletes star in track, swimming, tennis, and golf. **Professional** women's basketball teams draw big crowds. But one athlete stands out above all the rest. Her name was Mildred Didrikson Zaharias. Everyone called her "Babe."

professional (pruh•**fesh**•uhn•l)—team on which the players earn their living

"The Babe" Is Born

Mildred Didrikson was born in Texas in 1914. From an early age, she loved sports and she played them all. She competed in swimming, diving, tennis, golf, and volley-ball. She wanted to be the best at every sport she tried. If there were not enough girls to play, she joined the boys' teams. They didn't mind. She could kick a football farther than the boys could. She could throw a base-ball farther, too. And she could hit! In one baseball game, playing against boys, she slugged five home runs. From then on she was called "Babe"— after the great Babe Ruth.

Reread the habit and strategy below. Look for the *Strategy Alerts!* as you continue to read.

While I Read

Which **HABIT** will I practice?

Stop and ask, "If it doesn't make sense, what can I do?"

If I practice this habit, I will stop and figure out what to do so what I'm reading makes sense. Then I can keep reading and not be lost.

Which **STRATEGY** will I use to practice this habit?

Use graphic aids to help me understand.

 Use the **While I Read Strategy Sheet** for "Babe Didrikson Zaharias" (page 55 in your *Strategy Practice Book*) as you read.

A Basketball Star

She was just as skilled on the basketball court as she was on the baseball diamond. In high school, Babe was the star forward. She averaged 40 points a game. In one basketball game she scored 104 points!

In those days, there were no professional women's sports teams. There were no college teams for women, either. In fact, women had few chances to play sports at all. There was one way, however. They could play on teams sponsored by local companies. These teams were part of the Amateur Athletic Union (AAU). By playing for these teams, women players could compete for national titles. ⓘ *Strategy Alert!*

Melvin McCombs, the coach of the women's basketball team for an insurance company, saw Babe play. He asked her to go to work for his company. Babe agreed. She put in a full day's work in the office, but this wasn't her main job. Her main job was to play basketball for the company's team, the Golden Cyclones. Babe was barely 16 years old, but she scored more than 32 points a game. She led the Cyclones to a national basketball title.

Stop and Ask ❓

If it doesn't make sense, what can I do? Use graphic aids to help me understand.

Track and Field

McCombs recognized Babe's amazing skill. He felt she could do more than play basketball. He got her to try her hand at track and field. In 1932, the company sent her to a national meet. Winners of this event would qualify for the Olympics. Babe entered eight of the ten events. She won five of them. Her javelin throw set a new American record. So did her baseball throw.

Babe also won the **shot put,** long jump, and 80-**meter hurdles**. She tied for first in the high jump and finished fourth in the discus throw. She broke four world records. She earned points for each event—a total of 30 points for the meet. The entire second-place team scored eight points less than Babe scored all alone! *Strategy Alert!*

Babe was breaking records in every sport she played. People couldn't help noticing her. Besides, Babe was never shy. She was a lively character who loved being famous. Sportswriters loved writing about her and people loved reading about her. Just by being herself, she put women's sports in the spotlight. People started to notice women's sports as they never had before. And it was all because of Babe Didrikson.

Babe throwing the javelin

shot put—a contest in which athletes throw a heavy metal ball to see who can throw it the farthest

meter (mee·tuhr)—a distance equal to a little less than 40 inches

hurdles (hur·dlz)— small fences that runners jump over

Stop and Ask ?

If it doesn't make sense, what can I do? Use graphic aids to help me understand.

Olympic Silver and Gold

Next Didrikson went to the 1932 Olympics. There the rules limited her to three events. She won the 80-meter hurdles. Then she won the javelin throw, breaking the world record by more than 11 feet. Her third event was the high jump. She and a teammate both set world records. But the judges said that her head had gone over the bar before the rest of her body. So Didrikson won the silver medal, and her teammate got the gold. Babe didn't believe she had broken a rule. And nobody had **objected** to her style earlier. Even so, she accepted the ruling with good grace. Everyone guessed that the judges just didn't want to give all the gold medals to the same woman. *Strategy Alert!*

With her Olympic wins, Babe was truly famous. She was named Woman Athlete of the Year. A car company asked her to let them use her picture in ads. She agreed and enjoyed the fame. Unfortunately, the AAU ruled that these ads would cost Babe her amateur **status**. They barred her from further amateur competition.

Babe Didrikson's Sports Records, 1930-1954	
basketball	All-American 1930, 1931, 1932
80-meter hurdles	AAU Champion, 1932
	World Record, 1932
	Olympic Gold Medal, 1932
shot put	AAU Champion, 1932
javelin throw	AAU Champion, 1932
	World Record, 1932
	Olympic Gold Medal, 1932
baseball throw	AAU Champion, 1932
	World Record, 1932
high jump	AAU Champion, 1932
	World Record, 1932
	Olympic Silver Medal, 1932
long jump	AAU Champion, 1932
track	U.S. Women's National Champion, 1932
golf	U.S. Women's Amateur Champion, 1946
	British Amateur Golf Champion, 1947
	U.S. Women's Open Champion 1948, 1950, 1954

objected (ob·**jek**·tid)— gave a reason for not liking something

 Stop and Ask

If it doesn't make sense, what can I do? Use graphic aids to help me understand.

status (**stay**·tuhs)— position or rank

Turning Pro

Didrikson was no longer allowed to play as an amateur. But she wanted to keep playing sports. She had no choice but to turn professional. In those days it was almost impossible for a woman to make a living as a professional athlete. If anyone could do it, though, Babe could. She toured the country, displaying her skills. She put together her own basketball team—Babe Didrikson's All Americans. With them, she gave **exhibition** games. She also toured with a baseball team.

Didrikson enjoyed showing off her skills for the crowds. There was no challenge she wouldn't accept. She wore a football uniform to show how far she could kick a football— more than 75 feet! She put on a baseball uniform to pitch for the St. Louis Cardinals. She **sparred** with a professional boxer and split his lip. She played **billiards** matches. She even showed off her typing skills! She could type 86 words a minute on an old standard typewriter. She wanted to give the people who came to see her good value for their money, and they got it.

Daring to be Different

People had admired Babe when she was winning medals and prizes. Now they pointed to her as an oddity. She had never done the usual things that girls did. She cut her hair short. She refused to wear makeup. She went around in pants instead of skirts. Today, these things are common. In the 1930s, however, people judged Babe harshly and often cruelly. They used her as an example of what would happen to girls who played sports. One writer said that Didrikson would be better off if she put on a dress, stayed home, and waited for the phone to ring. She didn't let such comments bother her. She even made a joke of them. Once when a writer asked if there was anything she didn't play, she snapped back, "Dolls!"

exhibition (ek·suh·**bish**·uhn)—in sports, a game that does not count in a team's standing

sparred (spahrd)—boxed for practice

billiards (**bil**·yuhrdz)— a game played with balls and a stick on a felt-covered table

A Return to the Top

When she was 19, Babe took up golf. (This was one sport that people thought was all right for women.) She took lessons for just six months. As with everything else she did, Didrikson put everything she had into learning the game. She practiced for hours and hours. Sometimes she hit as many as 1,000 golf balls a day! She played until her hands were raw and blistered. The practice paid off, though. She could hit the ball an average of 240 yards off the tee. This was farther than many men hit. ❓ *Strategy Alert!*

After only one year of playing, she won the Texas Women's Amateur Championship. But the Golfing Association was reminded of her professional status in other sports. They ruled that it made her a professional in golf, too. So she was barred from playing amateur golf. She announced that she would play as a professional. For a time, she toured with Gene Sarazen, a well-known male golfer. But she couldn't compete officially since there was no professional golf organization for women. Nevertheless, she stayed in the public eye. Babe was still the best-known woman athlete of her time.

In 1937, she met her future husband, a professional wrestler named George Zaharias. A year later, the two were married. She was now Babe Didrikson Zaharias. She continued to work as a professional golfer. She also sold the use of her name to advertise golf products. However, she missed playing in tournaments. She applied to the Golfing Association to have her amateur status **restored**. In 1943, the Association declared her an amateur again. Two years later, she was named Woman Athlete of the Year for the second time. The first time—after the 1932 Olympics—had been for track and field. This time the award was for golf.

The Glory Years

Starting in the summer of 1946, Zaharias won 17 straight golf tournaments. She liked playing in tournaments. However, she made much more

Stop and Ask ❓

If it doesn't make sense, what can I do? Use graphic aids to help me understand.

restored (ri•**stord**)— given back

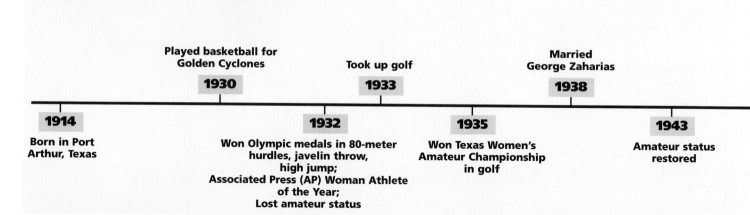

Mildred "Babe" Didrikson Zaharias

| 1914 | 1930 | 1932 | 1933 | 1935 | 1938 | 1943 |

- **1914** Born in Port Arthur, Texas
- **1930** Played basketball for Golden Cyclones
- **1932** Won Olympic medals in 80-meter hurdles, javelin throw, high jump; Associated Press (AP) Woman Athlete of the Year; Lost amateur status
- **1933** Took up golf
- **1935** Won Texas Women's Amateur Championship in golf
- **1938** Married George Zaharias
- **1943** Amateur status restored

money doing exhibitions. Men made money playing professional golf. Why shouldn't women do the same? Zaharias spoke to Patty Berg, another woman golfer. Together, they started the Ladies' Professional Golfing Association. The LPGA gave women's golf new status. It drew enthusiastic audiences. People enjoyed watching these first-rate golfers. The games were hard-fought and tough. With Zaharias leading the way, women's golf was no longer a "nice little game." It was a game of power and skill for real athletes. And the fans loved it.

Babe Didrikson Zaharias on the 18th green in the Women's All-American Golf Tournament, August 4, 1950

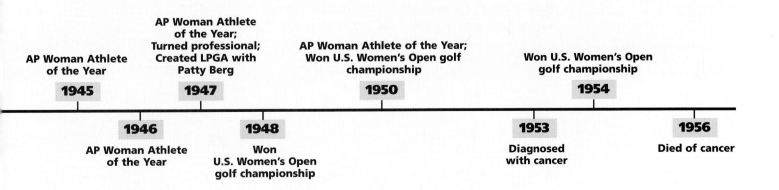

AP Woman Athlete of the Year
1945

AP Woman Athlete of the Year
1946

AP Woman Athlete of the Year; Turned professional; Created LPGA with Patty Berg
1947

Won U.S. Women's Open golf championship
1948

AP Woman Athlete of the Year; Won U.S. Women's Open golf championship
1950

Diagnosed with cancer
1953

Won U.S. Women's Open golf championship
1954

Died of cancer
1956

The next six years were glory years for "the Babe." She won the U.S. Women's Open golfing championship in 1948 and again in 1950. The LPGA was a success. She was doing what she had always wanted to do. In 1950, she was named the greatest woman athlete of the first half of the twentieth century. *Strategy Alert!*

Then, in 1953, she learned she had cancer. She would need major surgery. Doctors told her that she would never play golf again. But the doctors did not know Babe Zaharias. In just 14 weeks, she was back on the golf course. In her next tournament she finished third. By the end of the year, she was the sixth highest earner among women golfers. Her courage won her the Comeback of the Year award. In 1954, she went on to win five tournaments. One of these was the U.S. Open, which she won by 12 strokes. It was the third time she had taken that title. She was once again on top of her sport. In 1955, Babe once again began to have serious health problems. The cancer had returned. This time it could not be stopped. Zaharias died on September 27, 1956.

The Greatest Athlete That Ever Lived

Babe Didrikson Zaharias was never shy or modest. "My goal," she wrote, "was to be the greatest athlete that ever lived." She said "the greatest athlete," not "the greatest woman athlete." In 1960, four years after her death, there was an international vote to name history's greatest athlete. She came in seventeenth. This put her ahead of many famous men. Few athletes of either **gender,** however, have been so good at so many sports. She won five track and field events in a single AAU meet. She won two gold medals and a silver medal in the Olympics. She also set three world records. As a golfer, she won a total of 82 tournaments. Women's sports in America are forever different because of "the Babe." At the end of the twentieth century, she was listed among the top ten athletes of the century. Sportswriter Grantland Rice summed up her career in a few words: "She is without any question the athletic **phenomenon** of all time, man or woman." *Strategy Alert!*

Babe displays one of her many trophies.

Stop and Ask ?

If it doesn't make sense, what can I do? Use graphic aids to help me understand.

gender (**jen**·duhr)—male or female

phenomenon (fuh·**nom**·uh·non)— an unusual or amazing person or thing

Stop and Ask ?

If it doesn't make sense, what can I do? Use graphic aids to help me understand.

Now that you've finished reading, review the **After I Read** habit below. Think about what you read in "Babe Didrikson Zaharias" as you practice the habit and strategy.

After I Read

Which **HABIT** will I practice?
Use what I've read.
If I practice this habit, I will think about how I can apply what I read to my schoolwork and my life. This makes reading really useful.

Which **STRATEGY** will I use to practice this habit?
Decide what the author didn't tell me that I would like to know.

Use the **After I Read Strategy Sheet** for "Babe Didrikson Zaharias" (page 56 in your *Strategy Practice Book*) to use what you've read.

Apply 3 of the 9 Habits

Now read "Arthur Ashe—A Class Act" and apply these habits and strategies.

Before I Read

Which **HABIT** will I apply?
Think about what I know about the subject.

Which **STRATEGY** will I use to apply this habit?
Look at graphic aids and decide what I know about what they show.

While I Read

Which **HABIT** will I apply?
Stop and ask, "If it doesn't make sense, what can I do?"

Which **STRATEGY** will I use to apply this habit?
Use graphic aids to help me understand.

After I Read

Which **HABIT** will I apply?
Use what I've read.

Which **STRATEGY** will I use to apply this habit?
Decide what the author didn't tell me that I would like to know.

 Use the **Self-Assessment Sheet** for "Arthur Ashe—A Class Act" on pages 57 and 58 in your *Strategy Practice Book* as you read to see how well you can apply the habits and strategies.

Arthur Ashe— A Class Act

On a cold morning in 1993, more than 5,000 people stood outside the **Executive Mansion** in Richmond, Virginia. All these people had come to pay their final respects to hometown hero and tennis great, Arthur Ashe. Displays such as these are often seen for war heroes, movie stars, or heads of state. But to the thousands of **mourners** in Richmond on this day, no one deserved such a tribute more than Ashe. He had been admired not only for his skills as an athlete but also for the traits he showed off the court.

Executive Mansion (ig·**zek**·yuh·tiv **man**·shun)— governor's home

mourners (**mor**·nurz)— people who show sadness over a death

Early Signs of Talent

Arthur Robert Ashe, Jr., was born in Richmond, Virginia, on July 10, 1943. At the time, Richmond was segregated, as were most southern towns and cities. This meant that black people and white people had their own schools, hospitals, churches, restaurants, and parks. Arthur's father worked as a special police officer in a black people's park. The Ashes lived in a house on the park grounds. Young Arthur loved playing in all parts of the park. He especially liked the four tennis courts. Because he was sick as a baby, Arthur was a weak and thin child. Tennis was one of the only sports he could play well. He started to swing tennis rackets when he was six. He soon became known for his skill at the game.

Young Arthur Ashe in front of a "Members Only" tennis club in the South

The Growth of a Star

When he was seven, Arthur met Ronald Charity, one of America's top black tennis players. Ronald began teaching Arthur the game of tennis. Arthur would practice by himself for hours each day. Soon, he was competing with much older boys. Before long, he began playing tennis against adults! It was clear that he had talent. Charity knew that Arthur needed a better coach to keep growing as a player.

Charity introduced Arthur to Dr. Robert Johnson. A doctor and a great tennis player, Dr. Johnson wanted to teach black children to play tennis. He invited promising black tennis players to his home each summer. There he taught them tennis skills, good manners, and **sportsmanship**. Arthur went to Dr. Johnson's tennis camp every year until he was 18. Arthur learned well and won many **tournaments**.

Arthur Leaves Richmond

Arthur played and won many games around the country. But sadly, he could not escape the racism of Richmond. Arthur was not allowed to compete in his hometown because he was black. Also, no blacks could play in "Members Only" indoor tennis courts in Richmond. Without the use of indoor courts, Arthur could not practice tennis in the winter. His father thought that his son could not improve his skills at home. He decided to send Arthur to high school up north in St. Louis, Missouri. There he could practice tennis indoors and play against great athletes. Arthur excelled in tennis and in his classes. In 1961, he graduated from Summer High School with the highest grades in the school.

College Years

The University of California, Los Angeles (UCLA), gave Arthur an athletic **scholarship**. At college, he had the chance to play against some of the country's best tennis players. Even so, Arthur still faced prejudice. When a private club held a tournament, he was not asked to play because he was

sportsmanship
(**sports**·muhn·ship)—fair play, especially in sports

tournaments
(**tor**·nuh·mintz)—a series of games or matches involving many players

scholarship
(**skol**·uhr·ship)—a gift of money to help a student continue his or her education

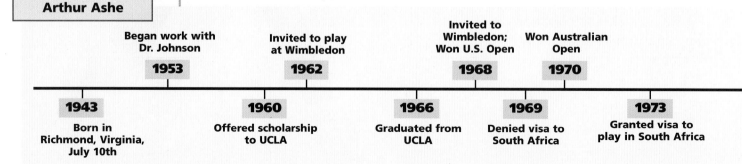

Arthur Ashe					
	Began work with Dr. Johnson	Invited to play at Wimbledon	Invited to Wimbledon; Won U.S. Open	Won Australian Open	
	1953	**1962**	**1968**	**1970**	
1943		**1960**	**1966**	**1969**	**1973**
Born in Richmond, Virginia, July 10th		Offered scholarship to UCLA	Graduated from UCLA	Denied visa to South Africa	Granted visa to play in South Africa

black. One teammate offered to stay out of the games in support of his friend. The coach thought that the whole team should sit out in protest. Arthur was proud that his coach and teammates supported him, but he didn't want to cause any trouble. He quietly sat out while his team played. Later, when Arthur became a tennis star, that same club asked him to play there every year. Thinking about how he had been treated in the past, he always turned the club down.

In his second year at UCLA, Arthur won a major college tournament. He was asked to play at Wimbledon, England. Tennis has been played at Wimbledon for more than 100 years. An invitation to Wimbledon would be an honor for any player. It was a special honor for a black student in the 1960s. Arthur did not win the Wimbledon title that year, but he won enough games to rank as the sixth best tennis player in the United States.

Ashe makes a return during a match at Wimbledon in 1963.

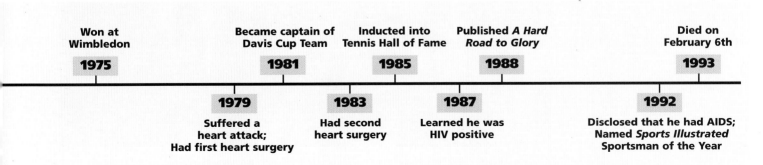

Won at Wimbledon		**Became captain of Davis Cup Team**	**Inducted into Tennis Hall of Fame**	**Published *A Hard Road to Glory***		**Died on February 6th**
1975		**1981**	**1985**	**1988**		**1993**
	1979	**1983**	**1987**		**1992**	
	Suffered a heart attack; Had first heart surgery	**Had second heart surgery**	**Learned he was HIV positive**		**Disclosed that he had AIDS; Named *Sports Illustrated* Sportsman of the Year**	

In 1966, Arthur graduated from college. Now proud of its hometown hero, Richmond declared Arthur Ashe Day and held a special celebration. To Arthur, this was a good sign. It showed that Richmond was taking steps in the fight against racism.

Making a Difference

While Richmond was showing signs of progress, Arthur Ashe grew concerned about events far away. He worried about issues in South Africa. South Africa had a strict set of laws called *apartheid* [uh·**par**·tied]. Under apartheid, black people had different laws than white people did. The laws for black people were much harsher. In 1969, Ashe wanted to go to South Africa for a tennis tournament. His request for a **visa** was turned down because he was black. He was upset by this decision, but he was more upset by the treatment of black people in South Africa. To draw attention to these injustices, he had South Africa's tennis teams banned from playing in America's Davis Cup. He was one of the first people to bring worldwide attention to apartheid. Although it would be years before policies were changed, Ashe helped to begin the long fight. In 1973, South Africa finally allowed Ashe to play in a tournament. He became the first black person to compete in South Africa's Open. He lost the singles title but won the doubles title. He said at the time, "In a way, this might have been the most important doubles match I ever won, for now a black's name rests on the list of South African champions. **Etched**. Forever."

visa (**vee**·zuh)— official form permitting entry into a country

etched (echt)—carved; recorded

Ashe talking with Charles C. Diggs, chairman of the House Foreign Affairs subcommittee on Africa, after being denied a visa by South Africa in 1969

After an exhausting match at Wimbledon in 1975, Ashe beat reigning champ Jimmy Connors.

A New Chapter in Life

Ashe went on to win at Wimbledon in 1975. Four years later, he woke up with chest pains. When he got to the hospital, he learned that he had had a heart attack. Ashe needed open-heart surgery. He had the operation, but his body never fully recovered. He could not get back his full strength. In April of 1980, Ashe retired from playing tennis. He set to work writing his life story and sports articles. When Davis Cup team officials needed a captain, they asked Ashe. He was grateful for the chance to lead the team. Even if he could no longer play, he would still be a part of a tennis team.

Once he became the captain, Ashe faced new problems. Most of the trouble came from two talented players—John McEnroe and Jimmy Connors. While they were great athletes, they could be ill-mannered. Remembering the lessons that Dr. Johnson had taught him, Captain Ashe asked for good sportsmanship and good manners. McEnroe and Connors would not cooperate. Loud and rude, they yelled at the refs, other players, and the fans. Ashe did not want to work with them and gave up his job as captain.

These troubles did not help his health. Ashe soon had to have a second heart surgery. When he got well, he began work as a **commentator** for tennis matches on TV. He also continued to fight apartheid. In 1985, Ashe went to a protest in Washington, D.C. He and others were arrested for taking part. He bravely said, "It is the least we can do in the name of freedom."

commentator (kom·uhn·tay·tuhr)— a person who talks about sports events on TV or radio

That same year, Ashe had much to celebrate. He was named to the Tennis Hall of Fame. In his whole tennis career, he had 818 wins and only 260 losses. At the awards ceremony, he was honored for his tennis success. He was also praised for his success off the court. Many said that he was a true sportsman. One writer wrote, "Sure there have been better players than Ashe, but no one played with more class."

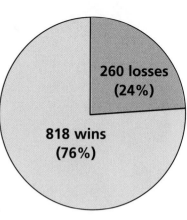

260 losses
(24%)

818 wins
(76%)

A Tragic Turn of Events

The year 1987 began with a joyful event. Arthur and his wife Jeanne brought a baby girl into the world. They named the baby Camera because the couple had met when Jeanne came to take Arthur's picture. But life soon took a tragic turn. Ashe had more and more health problems. At first, doctors didn't know what was wrong with him. But finally the news came—Ashe was HIV positive. That meant that his blood had the AIDS virus. Doctors realized that Ashe must have gotten the disease from blood he received during his second operation. Those two pints of blood must have had the AIDS virus. Today, all donated blood is tested for the AIDS virus, but that rule was not in effect at the time. The Ashes were crushed by the news. They decided to keep Arthur's illness a secret. They decided this, in part, to protect their daughter.

Although infected with the virus, Ashe lived an almost normal life. In 1983, he had taught a course on the black athlete in modern America. Finding that there were few books on the subject, he began writing one. In 1988, he finished his three-volume book *A Hard Road to Glory*. The book was about the history of African Americans in sports.

In 1991, Ashe visited South Africa with other black leaders. He noted that there was still much work to do, but he was happy to see improved conditions for black South Africans.

Arthur and his wife, Jeanne, at Jeanne's photography exhibition in France, 1979

Sharing His Secret

Little by little, Ashe grew sicker and weaker. In 1992, a reporter asked Ashe about his illness. Ashe felt that the time had come to tell his secret to the public. Then he began working to teach people about AIDS. Many people thought that getting AIDS was somehow the patient's fault. Ashe showed that this was not true. He also helped raise money to find a cure for the disease.

Even in the middle of his problems, Ashe did not forget about others. He learned that the United States was not letting people from Haiti into the country. (There was fear these people might carry HIV.) When Ashe publicly protested this policy, he was again arrested. Soon after, his health grew worse, and he had another heart attack. His doctors and his family warned him to slow down. AIDS had made his body very weak. When Ashe got pneumonia, he went into the hospital in New York. On February 6, 1993, he died.

The news of Ashe's death saddened people all over the world. President Bill Clinton paid him a special **tribute**. He said, "Arthur Ashe never rested with his fame. He used the strength of his voice and the power of his example to open the doors for other African Americans, fighting **discrimination** in America and around the world."

Arthur Ashe continues to be honored after his death. Many programs and places bear his name. Both Richmond, Virginia, and Chicago, Illinois, have schools named after him. The Arthur Ashe Tennis Academy was built in Soweto [soh·**way**·toh], South Africa. In 1997, the United States Tennis Association (USTA) named its new stadium after Arthur Ashe. The president of the USTA said, "We are naming our new stadium in his honor because he was the finest human being the sport of tennis has ever known. Arthur was—and through the example he set, still is—a **role model** to people throughout the world." Arthur Ashe was a tennis great in a class of his own.

tribute (**trib**·yoot)— something to show thanks or respect

discrimination (dis·**krim**·in·ay·shun)— the practice of treating some people differently because of prejudice

role model (rohl **mah**·duhl)— a person to look up to and try to be like

A statue in Richmond, Virginia, honors the city's hometown hero—Arthur Ashe.

Put Your Habits to Work in

Literature | **Social Studies** | **Science** | **Math**

Before I Read Habit:
Think about what I know about the subject.

Remember to look at graphic aids **before** you read a chapter in your math textbook. Then decide what you already know about what they show.

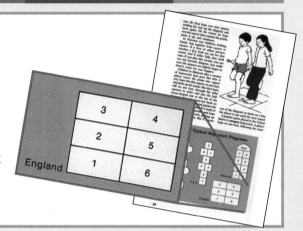

While I Read Habit:
Stop and ask, "If it doesn't make sense, what can I do?"

When you read your math book, don't forget to stop and ask yourself if what you're reading makes sense. One way to find out if it makes sense is to use tables, graphs, and charts to help you understand.

I see a pattern.

After I Read Habit:
Use what I've read.

When you're reading a math book, you're not finished until you use what you've read. You can do that by deciding what the chapter didn't tell you that you would like to know.

I still want to know about . . .

You may wish to use the **Put Your Habits to Work Sheet** (page 59 in your *Strategy Practice Book*) to practice these habits in your other reading.

Habits and Strategies

Use this chart to review the nine good habits and the strategies you have been using. If you want, review the strategies by looking back at the unit.

Before I Read

1. Check it out!
- Identify features to preview the selection and decide which are the most useful. (Unit 1)
- Decide what the internal organization of the selection is. (Unit 5)
- Quickly skim the selection to see what it is about. (Unit 7)

2. Think about what I know about the subject.
- Read the questions, introduction, and/or summary to decide what I know about this. (Unit 3)
- Identify the genre and decide what I know about this genre. (Unit 4)
- Look at graphic aids and decide what I know about what they show. (Unit 9)

3. Decide what I need to know.
- Use the graphic aids and pictures to decide what the author wants me to understand. (Unit 2)
- Use the introduction and summary to ask purpose-setting questions. (Unit 6)
- Read to identify the problem in the story. (Unit 8)

While I Read

4. Stop and ask, "How does it connect to what I know?"
- Picture specific details. (Unit 2)
- Decide whether I agree with the characters' actions. (Unit 7)
- Identify things the author is comparing and contrasting. (Unit 5)

5. Stop and ask, "Does it make sense?"
- Decide how the examples help explain a main point. (Unit 1)
- See if I can explain important words. (Unit 3)
- Decide whether what I am reading helps me understand the problem. (Unit 8)

6. Stop and ask, "If it doesn't make sense, what can I do?"
- Use context clues to help me understand words. (Unit 4)
- Go to the introduction and/or summary for help. (Unit 6)
- Use graphic aids to help me understand. (Unit 9)

After I Read

7. React to what I've read.
- Weigh the evidence to draw conclusions. (Unit 5)
- Decide whether the story would have ended differently in a different setting. (Unit 7)
- Consider all the characters' points of view and explain their similarities and differences. (Unit 8)

8. Check to see what I remember.
- Decide why the story ended the way it did. (Unit 4)
- Decide why certain events happened and whether they had to happen that way. (Unit 2)
- Use graphic aids, like maps and charts, to question myself. (Unit 6)

9. Use what I've read.
- Recap the main points (or big ideas) in the selection. (Unit 1)
- Describe ways the selection could have been made better. (Unit 3)
- Decide what the author didn't tell me that I would like to know. (Unit 9)